Second G
Phonics & F

Teacher's Manual *(Part 1)*
Lessons 1 to 80

Visit **McRuffy.com** for helpful resources to teach this curriculum!

Teacher's Manual *(Part 1)*
ISBN 9781592693146

Part of the **McRuffy Press Second Grade Phonics & Reading Curriculum** 978159269-2057

Written and illustrated by
Brian Davis M. A. Ed.

Graphic Design by
Sherylynn Davis

McRuffy Press, LLC
P.O. Box 212
Raymore, MO 64083

816-331-7831

sales@mcruffy.com

www.McRuffy.com

Puppy Place Game

Play games and rescue puppies on the back of the Language and Reading (LAR) workbook!

All games: Use the reading book for the week to create questions for the games. Players answer a question or complete a task before earning a roll. Players will get a point for each correct answer or completed task. If a player lands on a puppy space, rescue the puppy and take it home (move to the center of the board). On the next turn, the player will roll and move from the start space.

Players earn a point for each task completed successfully. Players earn an extra point for each puppy they rescue. Players also earn a point for completing the path when they cross the start space (not from the doghouse). Players may keep track of points using small objects such as counters, beans, or coins. Points can also be kept on paper as a scorecard. The first player to score 10 points wins.

Use a die, spinner, or draw numbers to move on the board with game pieces (small objects or game pawns).

Games (tasks to complete before moving)

Word List Reading Game: Read a word from the list. You may limit it to words that are also a part of the week's phonics theme.

Word List Meaning Game: This game would most likely require an adult to create questions or clues. Direct questions to a player on their turn to find a word on the word list according to the meaning. It does not need to be a formal clue. Find a word that means ___. or What is something that ___?

Word List Rhyme Game: Find a word on the list that rhymes with ____.

Word List Sentence Game: Use the word ______ in a sentence.

Find A Word Story Game: Find the word ______ on page ____.

Read A Sentence Game: Read the (first, second, third...) sentence on page _____.

Answer Sentence Game: Find a sentence on this page that tells _________.

Finish the Sentence Game: One player or the teacher reads part of a sentence. The player taking the turn finishes the sentence. You may tell the player the page the sentence is on or a choice of two pages.

Answer a Question Game: Make up questions to ask about the story that a player must answer before moving on the board.

Skate Spelling

Play a game on the back of the Spelling and Phonics workbook!

Move to spaces to collect the letters needed to spell words from the weekly spelling lists. Players can use a die, spinner, or draw numbers from a container to move around the board. Players can move in any direction on the board and even change directions in a turn, but players cannot move diagonally. They can only move along the lines behind the spaces. Use game pawns or small objects for playing pieces.

If a player's playing piece is on a space, another player cannot move to the same space. The player must choose another direction to move. If the same letter is used more than once in a spelling word or spelling word list, the player must visit that letter space once for each time it is used.

Players can start on any penguin space in the corners of the board. On other turns, players can move to a penguin space and jump to any other penguin space and keep moving. For example, if a player is two spaces away from the penguin on the bottom left and rolls a five, the player can move to that penguin space and jump to the top right penguin and then move three more spaces.

Players will write the letters they capture to spell the words on a piece of paper or students can write the words first leaving space between letters so they may be circled as they are captured on the board.

Games: *Choose the rules for playing the game.*

Choose one:

Same Words Rule: All players race to spell the same spelling word.

Different Words Rule: Players choose different words from the spelling list. If a player chooses a word that has more letters than another player's word, the player with the longer word may automatically fill in enough letters so that both players are moving to get the same number of letters.

Choose one:

Letter Order Rule: Letters must by moved to in the order they are used in the words.

Letter Scramble Rule: Letters can be moved to in any order.

Choose the number of words: You may play a shorter game and only spell one word or a longer game and spell more words, such as a list of three words. You may write the words before the game with spaces between letters and then circle the letters as you move to them and land on them.

Second Grade SE Phonics & Reading Introduction

This curriculum has been designed to teach children the basics of reading. Its main emphases are decoding (phonics), reading (giving meaning to printed material), language (applying communication skills), and handwriting. The goal of the program is to give parents and teachers a complete and easy method to follow. Successful learning begins with successful teaching.

The SE edition features a new spelling book and many new language activities. Two new workbooks are organized by subjects: Spelling and Phonics workbook and the Language and Reading workbook. Although the workbooks are organized by subject, the McRuffy approach still integrates all aspects of language instruction.

The new workbooks greatly expand the spelling activities. Additional writing instruction, poems, and story elements are expanded in the new Language and Reading workbook. The aesthetics of the workbooks have also greatly improved. Workbooks are printed in color with many more illustrations and photographs.

We hope that you and your child or students enjoy using this curriculum. More importantly, we hope it is a fruitful learning experience. Your questions and comments are appreciated.

Optional Handwriting Books

McRuffy SE Handwriting Books

The handwriting books provide additional practice, letter tracing, and guidance arrows that support the lessons in the SE curriculum. They are not included in the curriculum package.

Books are available in three handwriting styles:

Traditional Modern Cursive

The second grade level also include two additional choices that begin with either the traditional or modern printing style and transitions to the cursive style.

Reference Section

Program Contents

1. Teacher's manual
2. Language and Reading workbook (LAR)
3. Spelling and Phonics workbook (SAP)
4. Reading books (28)
5. Resource Pack
6. Handwriting Book (optional)

Organization of the Teacher's Manual

The teacher's manual consists of:

1. Introduction
2. Word Lists
3. Lesson plans

Lesson Plan Key

- Lesson objectives briefly state the concepts that are covered in the lesson. They answer the question: "What should the child be learning?" The objectives are numbered. The numbers correspond to the numbers in the teaching section. The letter at the end of each objective indicates what category the activity falls into, although some activities could be classified in many ways.

  P = phonics, S = spelling, R = reading, L = language,
  CW = creative writing, W=writing skills, H = handwriting

- The materials section lists any materials needed as well as any advance preparation needed to teach the lesson.

- The teaching section explains how to teach the lesson. Again, the numbers correspond with the numbers under lesson objectives. Some lessons are scripted. They have words in bold print that can be read directly to the students. It does not have to be followed exactly. Modify it if you would feel the child would understand better if things were said in a different way. You may have to elaborate more and check for understanding more.

Lesson Plans are organized into groups of five. Although this is to correspond to a school week, teachers should not hesitate to extend a lesson an extra day if that best fits the needs of the students. A school year consists of roughly 180 days. There are 160 numbered days of lessons in this program. An additional ten lessons have been added between lessons 80 and 81 to update to current standards. The total of 170 lessons will allow some flexibility for review, additional testing time, missed classes, etc.

Since each week introduces a new concept (except testing weeks) the program should be completed before moving on to the next program. For this reason, the program was designed to be slightly shorter than a school year.

Spelling assignments are based on the phonics word list. Most of the time, the words that were chosen were the ones most likely to be in the child's speaking vocabulary. Occasionally a word was chosen to highlight a particular spelling. Most spelling lists are relatively short. This allows the teacher the option to add more words or review words.

Handwriting assignments incorporated spelling words and correspond to the phonics concepts. The handwriting program not only reinforces handwriting skills, but also increases learning of phonics concepts.

The general rules for the optional handwriting book are as follows: Trace the letters. Write a full line of the given words or parts of words. Copy the sentences at least once (two lines are given).

At times the line sizes change to accommodate longer sentences. This also provides the students an opportunity to adjust the size of their printed to the space provided.

There are no handwriting assignments for lessons 39 and 40. These are the first quarterly testing days.

Language assignments also incorporate phonics concepts. Most weeks have at least three language assignments. Refer to the Language Scope and Sequence for an overview of language concepts covered.

Reading books are assigned for all weeks except testing weeks. Each book emphasizes the weekly phonics concept. Students will read the book more than once during the week. The books were intended to be entertaining as well as educational. The books have real plots. Students are asked questions about the books to help increase comprehension. Some books use words that may not be in the child's reading vocabulary or may use words with concepts that haven't been taught yet. These words are referred to as additional vocabulary words. Suggestions for introducing the words are given.

The backs of each book contain a word list. Most lists have omitted common words. The list emphasizes key words, words related to the current and recent phonics concepts, and additional vocabulary words. The reading section of fourth lesson in each week emphasizes questions over the word list. The questions focus on word meanings as well as phonics concepts.

Phonics readers (as opposed to whole language readers) actually try to increase the number of different words used. This emphasizes decoding concepts instead of memorizing word lists. That is also why there is much less repetition of sentences. This also makes the stories much more interesting and appealing to the students. The teacher's manual includes the texts from the reading books, so you can follow as the students read.

Two Writing assignments are given weekly. The creative writing assignments are tied to the reading book in some way. The assignments are given on the fourth lesson of the week. Students are asked to write stories. They may even make books like the reading books. Students are asked to read their books in the following lesson. Teachers may want to alter the format presented in the lesson. You may want to assign a story on the fourth day of the week, but not have the students read them until the fifth day of the following week.

Students may then have time to go through the writing process: brainstorming, writing, rewriting, producing and illustrating the book. Since this can be rather involved, you may not want to do the creative writing exercise every week. If students come up with ideas beyond what is presented in the teacher's manual, encourage them to develop those ideas. The creative writing starters are meant as suggestions, not rigid guidelines or assignments.

Additional weekly writing assignment are given in this reference section of the teacher's manual. These writing assignments emphasize opinion pieces, informative and explanatory texts, and narratives. These can be assigned at anytime during the week and can take the place of the creative writing assignments.

Resource Pack

Tests and Assessments: The four tests may be copied. Tests are given about every forty lessons. Assessments are given every five lessons. A test and assessment refill pack is also available.

Coloring Sheets: Each book has a coloring sheet showing a scene or characters from the story. At the bottom of each sheet is a set of lines. Students may write a caption for the picture, copy a sentence from the story, or leave it blank. This is an optional activity and is not referenced in the lesson plans.

Puppet Cut-outs: Students may interact with the reading books in a very creative way. Once a week, (every five lessons) students are given the opportunity to act out the book. This can be done as a skit or a puppet theater. The puppet cut-outs may be used in this activity. They may be colored and glued to craft sticks. The puppets are surrounded by a dashed cut-out line. The purpose is to allow students to be creative and demonstrate an understanding of the story. This is an optional activity and is not referenced in the lesson plans.

Fable Cards: Each 8.5" x 11"card features one or two fables for ten special lessons presented between Lessons 80 and 81.

Copy masters: Sheets can be copied or used as is.

Posters: Five 8.5" x 11" posters highlight various concepts such as collective nouns, irregular nouns and verbs, reflexive pronouns, and question words.

Dog Pound Compound Word Game

Phonics Scope and Sequence

Week	Lessons	
1	1 - 5	First Grade Review
2	6 10	First Grade Review
3	11 - 15	Review, suffixes er, and est
4	16 - 20	air, -ear, -are
5	21 - 25	wh, review e sounds
6	26 - 30	nce, -nse
7	31 - 35	dropping y adding ie, -ies, ied
8	36 - 40	Review & Test 1
9	41 - 45	ue, ui, oe as in shoe and canoe
10	46 - 50	Long a sounds spellings: -eigh, ei, ey, ea
11	51 - 55	dge
12	56 - 60	Two-syllable compound words
13	61 - 65	Silent letters - review and new
14	66- 70	review long o (oa & ow) add 2 syllable ow
15	71 - 75	ief, ield
16	76 - 80	Review & Test 2
17	81 - 85	ew, ou
18	86 - 90	ie-
19	91 - 95	wa (short 0 sound)
20	96 - 100	ough, augh, au
21	101 - 105	prefix un-
22	106 - 110	ph, school, gh=f
23	111 - 115	ea- as in bread
24	116 - 120	Review & Test 3
25	121 - 125	o = short u
26	126 - 130	tion
27	131 - 135	ly
28	136 - 140	re-
29	141 - 145	-ent
30	146 - 150	More two-syllable compound words,
31	151 - 155	Three-syllable compound words and silent u
32	156 - 160	Review & Test 4

Language Scope and Sequence

Lesson

2 Review –ed
3 Review contractions
4 Review prefixes a, be
7 Choosing the correct suffix
8 Contractions
9 Picture clues
12 Suffixes er and est
13 Opposites
16 Homophones
17 Proofreading
18 Reading non-fiction
19 Choosing the correct suffix
20 Poetry
21 Vocabulary development
22 Opposites in sentences
22 Questions (W words)
23 Reading non-fiction
24 Unscrambling sentences
25 Graphic organizer - story details
26 Vocabulary development
27 Synonyms
29 Nouns
30 Nouns and verbs
31 Word arrangement in sentences
31 Singular and plural nouns
32 Past and present tense
32 Categorization
33 Nouns
34 Comprehension skills
35 Graphic organizer - story sequence
36 Suffixes er and est
37 Categorization
38 Nouns
41 Suffixes
42 True and False
42 Contractions
42 Synonyms
43 Comprehension skills
44 Sequence of a story
46 Vocabulary development
46 Days of the week
47 Homophones
47 Nouns and verbs
48 Writing a letter
49 Story sequence
50 Non-fiction reading comprehension
51 Vocabulary development
52 Proofreading and nouns
54 Story sequence
56 Compound words
57 Verbs
58 Verbs
59 Story sequence
60 Poetry reading
61 Proofreading
62 Vocabulary
63 Combining sentences
63 Nouns and verbs
64 Story sequence
65 Cloze story (fill in missing words)
66 Vocabulary development
67 Syllables
67 Noun and verb agreement
68 Using prepositions
69 Story sequence
70 Non-fiction reading comprehension
71 Vocabulary development
72 Suffixes dropping y
73 Suffixes
73 Nouns and verbs
74 Story sequence
75 Book report writing
81 Vocabulary development
82 Homophones

Language Scope and Sequence

Lesson

83 Nouns and verbs
83 Past tense
84 Recipe writing
85 Story sequence
86 Vocabulary development
87 Combining sentences
87 Complete and incomplete sentences
88 Homophones
88 Past and present tense
89 Graphic organizer - story details
90 Story sequence
91 Vocabulary development
92 Quotation marks
92 Nouns and verbs
93 Non-fiction reading comprehension
94 Background information for writing
95 Story sequence
96 Vocabulary development
97 Comprehension skills
98 Using tenses
98 Quotation marks
99 Graphic organizer - cause and effect
100 Story sequence
101 Opposites (adding un)
102 Adjectives
103 Combining sentences
103 Complete and incomplete sentences
104 Poem
105 Story sequence
106 Root word meanings
107 Adjective, nouns, verbs
108 Comprehension skills
109 Graphic Organizer - character map
110 Story sequence
111 Vocabulary development
112 Categories
113 Comprehension
114 Combining sentences
114 Complete and incomplete sentences
115 Story sequence
116 Using the correct tense
118 Adjectives
121 Vocabulary development
122 Opposites
123 Finding all nouns in sentences
123 Adding adjectives to sentences
124 Graphic organizer - story elements
125 Story sequence
126 Vocabulary development
127 Meanings of root words
128 Verbs
128 Combining sentences
129 Main idea
130 Rhyming sentences
131 Adverbs
132 Adjectives
133 Adverbs
133 Opposites
134 Graphic organizer - story details
135 Story sequence
136 Pronouns
137 Pronouns and matching nouns
138 Parts of speech
138 Complete and incomplete sentences
139 Main idea
140 Writing answers to questions
141 Vocabulary development
142 Compound sentences (and)
143 Compound sentences (but, or)
143 Parts of speech
144 Main idea
145 Writing answers to questions
146 Writing definitions based on context
147 Review parts of speech

Language Scope and Sequence

148 Parts of speech
148 Complete and incomplete sentences
149 Writing dialogue
150 Writing answers to questions
151 Vocabulary development
152 Parts of speech
153 Main idea
154 Graphic organizer - story elements
155 Writing answers to questions
156 Review
157 Review
158 Review

Fables and Folktales Special Unit (After lesson 80 and before lesson 81):

A Collective nouns, reflexive pronouns
B Collective nouns, reflexive pronouns
C Collective nouns, reflexive pronouns
D Collective nouns, reflexive pronouns
E Collective nouns
F Proper nouns, irregular nouns
G Irregular nouns, irregular verbs
H Irregular nouns, irregular verbs
I Irregular nouns, irregular verbs
J Collective nouns, reflexive pronouns

Spelling Lists

Lesson 1: snow, spider, clay, glove, plant, blink, flavor, sleeve, brain, treat, crash, drawer, frost, prince

Lesson 6: skill, scout, swift, smell, after, held, self, salt, loud, poodle, cool, pillow, bottom, twinkle

Lesson 11: poison, loyal, happy, beetle, shook, cookie, floor, night, knife, limb, write, tower, jaw, scream, shrink

Lesson 16: there, pear, bear, hair, rare, very, airplane, pair, chair, marry, fair, square, carry, cherry

Lesson 21: whale, wheat, wheel, where, which, while, whimper, whip, whisker, white, whoa, why, whirl, what

Lesson 26: bounce, pounce, dance, sense, wince, balance, glance, ounce, fence, rinse, once, princess, cleanse, immense

Lessons 31: jellies, babies, puppies, families, bunnies, hobbies, pennies, thirties, hurried, copied, worried, fried, tried, cried

Lesson 36: *Review List:* bear, hair, square, very, whale, where, which, whisker, bounce, dance, rinse, princess, puppies, tried, hurried, pennies

Lesson 41: due, canoe, clue, bruise, blue, glue, juice, true, fuel, cruise, cruel, fruit, shoe, pursue, nuisance

Lesson 46: Sunday, Monday, Tuesday, Wednesday, Thursday, Friday, Saturday, reindeer, weigh, eight, obey, great, feign, neighbor

Lesson 51: ledge, badger, fudge, hinge, smudge, change, plunge, stingy, wedge, sponge, edge, danger, angel, gadget

Lesson 56: toothbrush, mushroom, cupcake, goldfish, mailbox, fireplace, shoestring, flashlight, sailboat, bobcat, haircut, drumstick, butterfly, bathtub

Lesson 61: fasten, gnash, hatch, gnaw, honest, hour, catch, ditch, stitch, sign, soften, listen, whistle, kitchen

Lesson 66: sparrow, follow, doe, below, window, hoe, goes, shadow, borrow, rowboat, owner, toenail, mower, poem

Lesson 71: thief, piece, chief, fiesta, shield, field, brief, grief, niece, yield, siege, fierce

Lesson 76: *Review List:* glue, fruit, great, neighbor, change, stingy, toothbrush, flashlight, gnaw, catch, whistle, sparrow, tomorrow, piece, field

Lesson 81: grew, blew, threw, chew, soup, youth, flew, knew, screw, stew, group, drew, jewel, view

Lesson 86: why, dryer, spied, fry, cried, eye, buy, spy, tied, fried, flies, pie, diet, goodbye, try

Spelling Lists

Lesson 91: what, walnut, wander, watch, washtub, waffle, warn, wallaby, warm, wallet, waltz, walrus, want, water

Lesson 96: auto, thought, cause, launch, author, autumn, sausage, laundry, haul, brought, pause, sauce, applause, fault

Lesson 101: unsnap, understand, unknown, unplug, unwrap, unkind, unload, until, undershirt, unzip, unselfish, untwist, underline, unhappy

Lesson 106: rough, photograph, alphabet, tough, orphan, cough, phrase, gopher, elephant, laugh, enough, telephone, dolphin, pamphlet

Lesson 111: ready, feather, bread, healthy, spread, weather, measure, head, treasure, pleasant, heavy, pheasant, sweat, thread

Lesson 116: *Review List:* grew, soup, walrus, warm, taught, bought, understand, unwrap, elephant, laugh, rough, feather, pheasant, eye, pie,

Lesson 121: welcome, cover, company, above, month, another, shovel, falcon, color, nothing, confuse, onion, love, mother

Lesson 126: station, nation, question, fraction, action, information, celebration, mention, vacation, direction, condition, commotion, solution, location

Lesson 131: completely, terribly, happily, unlikely, sweetly, lovely, slowly, suddenly, rarely, quickly, carefully, secretly, softly, noisily

Lesson 136: rely, repair, refill, relax, reward, recount, remember, replace, require, remove, remain, relief, recess, return

Lesson 141: silent, apartment, compliment, present, different, parent, agreement, basement, garment, moment, excitement, instrument, enjoyment, payment

Lesson 146: bedtime, raindrops, keyboard, earthworm, lighthouse, without, horseshoe, playground, yourself, friendship, sidewalk, bullfrog, skateboard, footstool

Lesson 151: guess, business, guitar, penguin, league, fatigue, built, guardrail, anguish, building, tongue, guilty, disguise, guarantee

Lesson 156: *Review List:* welcome, another, question, direction, unlikely, sweetly, remember, replace, agreement, basement, friendship, sidewalk, waterfall, building, guitar

Word Lists

Lesson 16: air, aircraft, airport, airplane, affair, bare, barrel, bear, berry, Blair, blare, care, careful, careless, carrot, carry, chair, cherry, Clair, dare, downstairs, fair, fare, flare, flair, ferret, glare, hair, hare, Harry, Kerry, lair, mare, merry, pair, parrot, pear, prepare, rare, repair, scare, share, snare, spare, square, stair, stare, swear, tear, Terry, their, there, upstairs, very, ware, wear, where

Lesson 21: whack, whale, wham, whap, what, wheat, wheel, wheeze, when, where, whether, which, whiff, while, whim, whimper, whip, whir, whirl, whisk, whisker, whisper, white, whither, whittle, whiz, whoa, whoosh, whop, why

Lesson 26: bounce, dance, lance, chance, France, Francis, glance, ounce, pounce, prance, stance, trance, fence, since, sense, mince, rinse, dunce, dense, hence, once, wince, prince, princess

Lesson 31: armies, bellies, berries, bodies, buggies, bunnies, candies, carries, cities, copies, daddies, families, fifties, forties, grannies, hobbies, hurries, jellies, kitties, mommies, nineties, parties, pennies, puppies, sixties, stories, thirties

carried, hurried, copied

Lesson 41: due, hue, Sue, blue, clue, flue, glue, true, fuel, duel, fruit, juice, bruise, cruise

Lesson 46: vein, feign, veil, rein, reign, skein, reindeer, eight, weigh, weight, neigh, neighbor, freight, sleigh, whey, they, hey, prey, survey, obey, grey, steak, break, great, Shea, yea

Days of the week: Sunday, Monday, Tuesday, Wednesday, Thursday, Friday, Saturday

Lesson 51: hedge, ledge, wedge, dredge, pledge, sledge, edge, badge, badger, ridge, fudge, budge, lodge, Madge, hodgepodge, bridge, pudgy, judge, nudge, dodge, sludge, trudge, smudge

plunge, change, hinge, binge, flange, singe, stingy, lunge

Lesson 56: airplane, backpack, baseball, bathtub, bobcat, bookcase, campsite, cardboard, chipmunk, cowboy, cupcake, daydream, daytime, doorbell, dugout, eyebrow, eyelash, fireman, fireplace, fireworks, flashlight, football, goldfish, grapefruit, groundhog, haircut, iceberg, icebox, jigsaw, jukebox, knapsack, lifeboat, mailbox, milkman, mushroom, muskrat, network, nightfall, noontime, oatmeal, pickup, popcorn, pushup, rainbow, sailboat, sandbox, sawmill, scarecrow, scoreboard, seacoast, seesaw, shoelace, shoestring, shortstop, snowflake, spaceship, stagecoach, steamboat, steamship, stickup, strongbox, subway, sundown, sunrise, sunset, sunshine, teaspoon, teenage, thumbnail, toothbrush, toothpaste, towboat, tugboat, woodchuck

Lesson 61: gnarl, gnash, gnat, gnaw, gnu, heir, honor, honest, hour, batch, botch, catch, ditch, Dutch, etch, fetch, hatch, hitch, hutch, itch, latch, match, Mitch, notch, patch, pitch, retch, snatch, snitch, stitch, thatch, castle, hasten, listen, moisten, nestle, thistle, witch, bustle, hustle, rustle, whistle, wrestle

Lesson 66: bellow, below, borrow, fellow, follow, hollow, mellow, narrow, pillow, shadow, sorrow, sparrow, tomorrow, wallow, willow, window, yellow
doe, foe, goes, hoe, Joe, toe, woe

Word Lists

Lesson 71: brief, chief, Connie, Debbie, field, fierce, grief, Jackie, niece, piece, pier, pierce, shield, siege, thief, tier, Vinnie, yield

Lesson 81: dew, few, hew, Jew, knew, new, pew, blew, brew, chew, crew, flew, grew, screw, skew, stew, threw, you, youth, group, soup, mousse

Lesson 86: buy, by, cry, dye, dry, eye, fly, fry, guy, lye, my, ply, pry, rye, shy, sky, sly, spy, spry, sty, thy, try, why, brier, crier, die, dried, drier, flier, flies, fries, fried, lie, pie, spied, tie, vie

Lesson 91: wad, waddle, waffle, wahoo, walk, wall, wallaby, wallet, wallop, wallow, walnut, walrus, Walter, waltz, wand, Wanda, wander, want, war, warble, ward, warden, wardrobe, warfare, warm, warmth, warn, warning, warp, warpath, warrant, warship, wart, warthog, was, wash, washtub, washy, wasp, watch, water, watt, what

Lesson 96: because, caught, cause, daughter, daunt, fault, flaunt, fraud, fraught, gaunt, gauze, haul, haunt, jaunt, launch, Maud, maul, naught, naughty, Paul, paunch, pause, Saul, slaughter, staunch, taught, vault, bought, brought, fought, ought, sought, thought

Lesson 101: unaware, unbolt, unbutton, unbuckle, unchain, unclean, uncoil, uncover, uncut, underfoot, undergo, underground, underline, undermine, undershirt, understand, understood, undertake, undo, undress, unfair, unfold, unforgiving, unfriendly, unglued, unhappy, unhitch, unjust, unkind, unknown, unlatch, unless, unlike, unload, unlock, unpack, unplug, unquiet, unreal, unrest, unroll, unscrew, unselfish, unskilled, unsnap, unsound, unstop, unstring, unstuck, untidy, untie, until, unto, untold, untrue, untwist, unwilling, unwind, unwise, unwrap, unzip

Lesson 106: cough, enough, laugh, rough, tough, trough
Alphabet, elephant, dolphin, gopher, graph, orphan, pamphlet, phantom, phase, Phillip, phone, phonics, phonograph, photograph, phrase, physical, physics, telegraph, telephone

Lesson 111: ahead, bread, breakfast, breast, breath, cleanse, dead, deaf, death, dread, feather, head, headache, health, heavy, instead, lead, meadow, measure, peasant, pheasant, pleasant, pleasure, read, ready, realm, spread, stead, steady, stealth, sweat, thread, threat, threaten, tread, treasure, unhealthy, unpleasant, unread, unsteady, wealth, wealthy, weapon, weather

Lesson 121: above, another, become, beloved, blood, collide, color, come, comfort, comfortable, commend, community, company, compass, compare, compete, complain, complete, computer, conclude, confuse, connect, consider, control, cover, done, dove, falcon, from, front, glove, love, lovely, mammoth, month, mother, none, nothing, of, onion, other, oven, shove, shovel, some, somewhat, somewhere, someone, sometime, something, son, ton, undone, welcome

Lesson 126: action, affection, attention, auction, carnation, caution, celebration, commotion, condition, decoration, direction, emotion, formation, fraction, hesitation, information, instruction, irritation, lotion, mention, motion, nation, notion, occupation, portion, position, proportion, question, relation, relaxation, sensation, station, vacation

Word Lists

Lesson 131: angrily, boldly, bravely, bubbly, carefully, carelessly, certainly, closely, coldly, completely, constantly, happily, harshly, jointly, joyfully, kindly, lately, lightly, likely, loosely, lovely, meanly, merrily, mildly, monthly, noisily, oddly, pleasantly, powerfully, proudly, quickly, quietly, rarely, really, sadly, scraggly, secretly, selfishly, Shelly, shortly, shyly, simply, sleepily, slightly, slowly, softly, strangely, suddenly, sweetly, swiftly, terribly, tightly, unkindly, unlikely, unselfishly, weakly, wobbly, yearly

Lesson 136: react, recall, recess, reclaim, recline, record, recount, recover, recruit, redecorate, redeem, redouble, reduce, reduction, refill, refinish, reflect, reflex, refresh, refrigerate, refund, refuse, regain, regret, rehearse, rejoice, rejoin, relate, relax, relay, release, relief, relieve, relive, rely, remain, remake, remark, remember, remote, remove, renew, renumber, repair, repay, repeat, repent, rephrase, replace, replant, replay, reply, report, reprint, request, require, resign, respect, respond, result, resume, retell, retire, retrace, retreat, return, reveal, revenge, reverse, review, revue, reward, rewind

Lesson 141: Agent, agreement, announcement, apartment, basement, cement, comment, compliment, content, department, different, element, enjoyment, excitement, experiment, garment, instrument, lament, moment, monument, movement, ornament, parent, payment, present, prevent, repent, silent, statement, treatment

Lesson 146: Barnyard, hoedown, sidewalk, sidekick, skateboard, homework, schoolwork, grown-up, handcuffs, himself, herself, keyboard, playground, quicksand, someday, sixteen, somewhere, themselves, therefore, without, bagpipe, bedroom, blackboard, footstool, footstep, know-how, punchbowl, haystack, bedtime, nighttime, hayloft, pitchfork, washtub, horseshoe, hushpuppies, cornbread, hayride, applesauce, background, backwoods, blacksmith, blackbird, campfire, catfish, crawfish, doorway, earthworm, homestead, friendship, greyhound, hardship, homework, lighthouse, livestock, pinecone, playground, raindrops, withdraw, yourself, buckshot, bug-eyed, bullfrog, bull's-eye, icehouse

Lesson 151: Anything, anyway, anywhere, applesauce, arrowhead, automobile, basketball, blackberry, blueberry, bumblebee, buttercup, butterfly, buttermilk, cowpuncher, everyone, everything, everywhere, eyeglasses, fingernail, fingerprint, firecracker, freshwater, gingerbread, gooseberry, granddaughter, grandfather, grandmother, grasshopper, lumberjack, handkerchief, hamburger, headquarters, honeysuckle, housekeeper, however, huckleberry, hushpuppies, jellybean, jellyfish, microphone, microscope, marshmallow, mulberry, neighborhood, nevertheless, newspaper, nonetheless, peppermint, petticoat, pineapple, policeman, rattlesnake, screwdriver, seventeen, shoemaker, skyrocket, somebody, strawberry, tablecloth, tablespoon, troublemaker, typewriter, understand, undertaking, waterfall, watermelon, woodpecker

build, builder, building, built, disguise, guarantee, guard, guardrail, guess, guesswork, guest, guide, guidebook, guideline, guidepost, guilt, guiltless, guilty, guinea hen, guinea pig, guitar

Reading Book List

Book	Lesson	Title
1	1 – 5	Emily and Elaine in the Dark
2	6 – 10	Dot and the Stopped Up Drain
3	11 – 15	The Day It Rained Bubbles
4	16 – 20	The Bear With Carrot Hair
5	21 – 25	Mary, Whiskers, and the Whale
6	26 – 30	Francis Dances
7	31 – 35	Benny's Pennies
8	41 – 45	Blue Shoe Canoes
9	46 – 50	Jonathan's Not-So-Great Great Week
10	51 – 55	Hedgehog Fudge
11	56 – 60	Bobcat Cowboys
12	61 – 65	The Kindness of Gnatty
13	66 – 70	Jonathan and Rosie
14	71 – 75	Connie the Caterpillar
15	81 – 85	Chocolate Mousse Stew
16	86 – 90	Ruff's Spy Plane
17	91 – 95	Walter's Warning
18	96 – 100	A Jewel For Paula
19	101 – 105	Jonathan's Unday
20	106 – 110	The Elephant and the Alphabet
21	111 – 115	Long John Featherhead
22	121 – 125	Lovey Dove and the Falcon
23	126 – 130	The Foozles of Loopation
24	131 – 135	What is Blizzy?
25	136 – 140	Ruff Returns
26	141 – 145	Jonathan's Musical Instrument
27	146 – 150	Hound Dog Hoedown
28	151 – 155	The Bobcat Cowboy Jellybean Train Robbery

Writing Skills Program

The Writing Skills Program was expanded in 2018 to include a new **Writing Skills Workbook**. It provides additional structure for the original writing lessons, as well as several new writing activities. These can be used in addition to or in place of the origninal writing assignments.

Creative Writing

Assignment in the regular lesson plans: The creative writing assignments are tied to the reading book in some way. The assignments are given on the fourth lesson of the week. Students are asked to write stories. They may even make books like the reading books. Students are asked to read their books in the following lesson. Teachers may want to alter the format presented in the lesson. You may want to assign a story on the fourth day of the week, but not have the students read them until the fifth day of the following week.

Students may then have time to go through the writing process: brainstorming, writing, rewriting, producing and illustrating the book. Since this can be rather involved, you may not want to do the creative writing exercise every week. You may choose not to go through every step of the process with every creative writing assignment. The process may be shortened to brainstorming, writing, and illustrating on most assignemts, then choosing to do the full process every quarter. The writing process is detailed on pages 19 and 20.

If students come up with ideas beyond what is presented in the teacher's manual, encourage them to develop those ideas. This can be in addition to or in place of creative writing assignments. The creative writing starters are meant as suggestions, not rigid guidelines.

Non-fiction Writing

Additional weekly writing assignment are given in this reference section of the teacher's manual. These can be found on pages 21 to 23 of this Teacher's Manual. These writing assignments emphasize opinion pieces, informative and explanatory texts, and narratives. These can be assigned at anytime during the week and can take the place of the creative writing assignments.

Writing Skills Workbook

The Writing Skills Program was expanded in 2018 to include a new **Writing Skills Workbook**. It provides additional structure for the original writing lessons, as well as several new writing activities. These can be used in addition to or in place of the origninal writing assignments.

Directions for the Writing Skills Workbook begin on page 24 of this teacher's manual. With the daily lesson plans, the materials section will note if a Writing Skills Workbook page is assigned to that lesson. It is suggested that you review available Writing Skills lessons for a week before teaching the first lesson of the week and decide which lessons you wish to use.

The Writing Process

The Writing/Publishing process may use the following steps:

The full writing process can involve many steps. You do not have to have students do every step for every assignment. You may use inventive spelling. This is fine, especially in the earlier part of the year, and if you do not have students continue through the full writing process. The emphasis here should be on creativity, not technical perfection.

Stories do not have to be long. They don't have to be complex. Students will evolve into better writers with practice. Some steps in the writing process may be too overwhelming for some younger students. If so, skip or adapt those steps by giving additional guidance or help. Creating a story should make the student feel empowered. It should be an experience for students that builds confidence. Children should learn to express themselves in new ways. Keep the process positive and fun, not overwhelming.

Brain Storming: In this step consider any and all ideas. Hopefully some of the ideas in the creative writing assignments will help begin this process. Make brief notes about any ideas that are brought up in this process. The notes can be one or two words or a short sentence. Using a chalkboard or white dry erase board (white board) is a good idea. In a classroom this may be a group activity.

Pre-Writing: In this step the student should choose the idea and begin to organize and develop thoughts more completely.

Write: Write the rough draft. This may be the final step for several of the assignments that you do not want to take to the publishing phase.

Processing: In this steps student are given critical feedback for their story. This can come from the teacher or other students. Students giving feedback should be instructed to do so in a helpful and thoughtful way. The idea should be to make the story better. This may include asking the author to clarify things they didn't understand. Students may also have ideas for adding to the story. Students receiving the feedback should be instructed in being open to receive the ideas of others. It shouldn't be a threatening process.

Students should be encouraged to consider the opinions of others, but they do not necessarily have to make changes they don't want to. The processing step is very good for developing language and communication skills and analytical skills. In a homeschool setting parents may want to get students together with other students outside their families for this step.

Edit: Students may rewrite any portion of the story that changes from the processing step. This can be done by marking out sections and penciling in the changes.

Technical changes: The student, then the teacher should evaluate the material for any technical mistakes such as spelling, punctuation, and grammar.

Rewrite: Copy the material with all the changes.

Proof: Check the rewritten material for any new mistakes. The student and the teacher may be involved in this.

Illustrate: Plan the pictures. Think about what to illustrate. Students should understand that not every idea in a story could or should be illustrated. The pictures are like snapshots of the action. Have students look at other books such as the book in the reading assignment and see what part of the text is illustrated and what isn't.

When the stories were developed for the curriculum, the text was broken into sections by length (approximate number of words). From that section of text, a decision was made about illustrating. What one thing could be illustrated from that page?

You may want students to make the pictures as line drawings, without color. This would allow them to be photocopied more easily. Students could then color the photocopies if they would like after publishing.

Publish: Put the story in a book form that can be shared with others. Again, this may be a single copy or it may be photocopied. If you plan on photocopying, put only one staple in the books while the students are creating them. Have the students number the pages. Take the staple back out to copy, then staple it again. You may also want students to use plain white paper for the cover instead of colored paper or construction paper if the cover is to be copied also.

The following two steps go beyond the publishing process. These two steps develop language skills to an even higher level. Not every work will be suitable for these steps, but they can be quite enjoyable for the students.

Playwright: Think of the story in terms of a play. How might the story be performed? What dialog would you use? When a book is adapted for a movie or play, it is changed to make it more presentable to an audience. For example, a character's thoughts have to be transformed to action or dialog for the audience to understand. This again is a brainstorming and writing process.

Perform: Perform a play adapted from the child's story. Maybe a single child will perform every part, maybe other children will be involved. Students may make costumes, props, and scenery as a part of the process. The plays may be recorded so students can see their own performances.

Additional Writing Assignments: The writing assignments below can be used in addition to or in place of the weekly writing assignments in the lesson plans. The writing assignments in the lesson plans are generally creative writing assignments. The writing assignments below are opinion pieces, informative or explanatory texts, or narratives. The assignments are based on words or groups of words that make up the weekly phonics themes. Some of these ideas are developed in the Writing Skills Workbook.

The stated lessons below are the first lessons of the week. The writing assignments can be given any time during the week, not necessarily the lesson number referenced. For example the Lesson 16 Ferrets assignment could be done in any of the lessons from 16 to 20. The writing assignment could also be extended beyond that time frame, especially if all the steps in the writing process are included.

The teacher should use discretion to assign or not assign the writing projects, resources used (For example the teacher may want to preselect some websites for research, supply basic facts and have students organize the information into an article), and the expected outcome based on student abilities as the year progresses (such as the length of the writing)

General writing instructions:

1. Use a variety of publishing tools including traditional pen and paper to computer programs and printers.

2. Do some writing assignments as single session writing assignments (opinion pieces may work best for this). Apply a more refined writing process to other projects (extended research, writing, proofing and correcting.) This would include revisions after received feedback from others.

3. Have peers of the teacher provide feedback on the writing. Ask questions of one another and make suggestions.

Lesson 16 Ferrets: What are they? What do they eat? Where do they live? Do they make good pets? Research to find out.

Lesson 21 Wheat: How is wheat used and grown? Research to find out.

Lesson 26 France: Research and write about France. It could be a historical perspective, or current such as cities, famous attractions and landmarks. Include your opinion about the country. Would you want to live or visit there? Why or why not?

Lesson 31 Hobbies: Tell about your hobby or a hobby you would like to take up. Include why you like the hobby and give steps to describe how to do the hobby. Include drawings or diagrams in your explanation.

Lesson 41 Fruit: Write about a fruit. In a classroom setting, produce a Fruit Book. Groups research different fruits and compile the work into a single classroom book. Research might include where and how it is grown and harvested. Include a fruit recipe that can include more than one fruit. Include drawings or illustrations. Include a survey with a graph of favorite fruits of classmates or family and friends.

Lesson 51 Badger: What is a badger? Where does it live? What does it eat? Research and write an article about badgers. Include drawings or pictures. Write captions for the pictures. Use headings in your article for the different topics such as *Where they Live* and *What they Eat.*

Lesson 56: Choose a topic based on a compound word such as baseball, goldfish, fireworks, or spaceship. Research the topic. Include pictures and definitions.

Lesson 61: Why do we have silent letters? Research to find out why words have silent letters. Provide examples of how words have changed.

Lesson 66 Tomorrow Land: Get out your time machine and travel twenty years into your future. What will your tomorrow be like? Put a special emphasis on using linking words such as: because, therefore, since, for example.

Lesson 71 Shield: In the time of knights and kings, ruling families decorated shields and armor with art that told about the family. This was called a coat of arms or a family crest. It told something about the family. It may have told about their values, their work, or what they think is important. For example it might have included a lion to represent kingship or fierceness. Sometimes the art was divided into four sections. Design a coat of arms for your family on a shield. You can use the Shield Sheet (in the Resource Pack) or make your own. Write an explanation for the art. What are you showing? You may find examples on-line to help you get some ideas.

Lesson 81 Stew or Soup: Make up a recipe for a stew or soup. Include a list of ingredients. Give step by step directions for making it, and estimated time to prepare it (prep time). Find recipes on-line for soups or stews as an example. In a classroom setting, the recipes could be combined into a workbook. You can also write a make-believe recipe like our example (see the Elephant Stew recipe example in the Resource Pack):

Lesson 86 Flies: Research the life cycle of flies. Write about it and include a life cycle diagram. Write a caption for your diagram. Organize your writing with subheadings for each part of the cycle.

Lesson 91 Water: Write about how water is used in your life. Include the three states of water (liquid, vapor, and solid). Include your opinion about your favorite use of water.

Lesson 96 Thought and Because: Write four or more sentences with this format: I once thought __________ because ___________________. The sentences can be real or made up.

Examples: I once wolves would make good pets because they look like dogs. I once thought the moon was made of cheese because it had holes like Swiss cheese. I once thought pineapples grew on pine trees because pineapple begins with pine. I once thought Dr. Pepper was good to drink when I was sick because it had doctor in it.

Lesson 101 Un: Have you ever been treated in an unfriendly way or been unforgiven for a mistake you made? Was it unjust? Were you unhappy? Were people understanding? If this hasn't happened to you, make an untrue situation that could happen or that you know happened to someone else. Write about it and include what you could do to undo the situation. Include your opinion about if you think you were treated unfairly or not. Use as many un words as you can. (The Resource Pack has a sheet with the Un- word list. Students may add words to the list. You may brainstorm additional words as a group.)

Lesson 106 Telegraph: research the history of the telegraph. Compare it to how we communicate today. Include at least one sentence or message in Morse Code. Use the Morse Code Alphabet sheet (Resource Pack).

Lesson 111 Breakfast: Plan a healthy breakfast. Write a breakfast plan. Include foods from different food groups. Tell why you chose them. Include your opinion about your favorite breakfast food. Answer the question: Why is it important to eat a good breakfast? Create and take a survey of favorite breakfast foods or favorite breakfast food restaurants. Include the survey results in a graph.

Lesson 121 Mammoth: Research and write an article about Wooly Mammoths. Organize your article by including section headings. Add drawings or pictures and write captions for them.

Lesson 126 Celebrations: Write about your favorite celebration. What do you do? Why is it fun? What is the history of the celebration? Include drawings or pictures. Create a survey or favorite celebrations and include the results in a graph.

Lesson 131 –ly: Choose a written piece such as an article, or a section of your favorite story. Add or change as many –ly adverbs to it as possible and rewrite it. (Resource Pack includes a copy master with this week's word list.) Students may think of other adverbs and add them to the list. You may have students brainstorm this before writing.

Lesson 136 Recall and retell: Recall and retell a recent news event. Write about the event. It can be a news event or an event that occurred at your school, or in your family or neighborhood. Use as many *re-* words as possible. (The Resource Pack has a sheet with the Re- word list. Students may add words to the list. You may brainstorm additional words as a group.)

Lesson 141 Instrument: Research and write about a musical instrument. What kind of instrument is it (stringed, percussion, woodwind, brass, electronics, etc.)? Choose an instrument that you play or would like to learn to play. Include your reasons for wanting to play that instrument. Include songs or types of music you would like to play. Research how much it might cost to buy the instrument. Include pictures or drawings of the instrument in your article. *Optional:* Take a survey of favorite musical instruments. Include the result in your article with a caption and a graph or table.

Lesson 146 Choose a topic based on a compound word in the word list. Research a topic, give an opinion, or tell a true experience you or someone else had based on the topic. Include pictures and definitions.

Lesson 151 (same as Lesson 146 with a new list): Choose a topic based on a compound word in the word list. Research a topic, give an opinion, or tell a true experience you or someone else had based on the topic. Include pictures and definitions.

Writing Skills Workbook Instruction

Lesson numbers are the suggested lesson to present the activity. The lesson numbers refer to the lesson numbers of the overall Second Grade SE Phonics and Reading Curriculum. Generally, you may shift the day for the activities for anytime during that week of lessons. Reading book related writing is usually presented after students have read the entire book. Students usually finish reading the book in the third lesson of the week. This would be lessons that end with 3 or 8.

Some pages are labeled story planning pages. These work with the creative writing assignments in the Teacher's Manual. Creative Writing assignments generally appear in the fourth lesson plan of the week. These are lessons that end with 4 or 9. If you use these, this will be the first step in the writing process. You can spread the completion of the writing assignment over several days, even extending into the next week. Some writing lessons refer back to these daily lesson plans in the teacher's manual.

As with other lessons in this manual, bold print usally indicates instruction that can be directly read to the student. Answers to questions are in parenthesis. Some Writing Skills Workbook pages ask questions using question words. You may want to make sure students are familiar with these words (who, what, where, when, why, how). There is a Question Words poster in the Resource Pack.

Lesson 3

The pictures are based on the story. Students will choose two pictures to write about. Students will answer the questions beginning with the sentence structures:

The scariest picture is ___________________, because ___________________.

I like the picture of the ___________________, because ___________________.

Students should not just fill in the blanks. They should copy the sentence starter on the lines adding their own descriptions of the pictures and their thoughts.

Students may not be able to read the word *because* (*au* digraph is not introduced until Lesson 96), so read the word for the students or help students decode. Students may need help with the words *scariest* and *picture*.

Students may relate their observations based on the story, *Emily and Elaine In the Dark*, or can just consider the pictures without the context of the story.

For example: In context of the story, the lightning may be the scariest, because it was the only choice of pictures that actually happened.

Out of context, the student might like the frog picture the best because they would like a pet frog.

Lesson 7

Introduction: **If you had to fix a stopped up drain, how would you do it? Maybe you would do it the way a plumber would. Maybe you would find some creative way to do it. Write four steps.**

Use words to show the order in your directions. The words are on the page. For example, you can begin the first step by writing:

The first step is to ___________.

On the fourth step you can use the word fourth or last.

The fourth step is to _________. Or

The last step is to __________.

Lesson 9

Students will write a story about alligators. See additional instructions in the 2nd SE Teacher's Manual Lesson 9. This sheet is most helpful if students are writing fictional stories instead of non-fiction (factual) so you may limit the original instructions in the Teacher's Manual to making up stories like the book, *Dot and the Stopped Up Drain*.

The page in the Writing Workbook provides further preparation to create the story. You may wish to expand the story writing assignment over several lessons and have students start by completing this sheet.

Students will list characters in the top section. Students will then write an order of events. Students should number the order. They don't have to list every step. Then, students will describe the ending. Using the book, *Dot and the Stopped Up Drain,* as an example:

Characters:

A woman named Beth, a dog named Dot, an alligator

Order of events:

1. Beth's sink was stopped up. 2. A dog named Dot came to fix it. 3. Dot found an alligator in the pipe. 4. The alligator had a tummy ache. 5. Dot helped the alligator feel better.

Ending

Dot and the alligator fixed the house. Dot took the alligator home for dinner.

Students will use this planning page to write their stories. Students should be encouraged to make changes from this plan as they write the story. Sometimes writers think of better ideas or make changes to their plans during the writing process.

Lesson 13

After reading the story, *The Day it Rained Bubbles*, students will describe the events for each picture on the page.

Lesson 14

This page may be used to help students plan to write the story described in Lesson 14 of the teacher's manual. The directions in the teacher's manual gives students the option to create a different "unnatural disaster", so this sheet would accommodate those ideas, too.

On this page students will make lists that will be expanded into ideas and sentences in the story. Since, these are lists, students should use as few of words as possible. Students should write at least two ideas for each list. Writing an idea is not limited to a single line, but the goal should be to use as few of words as possible.

On the bad and good things lists students will list things that would be bad and good about marbles raining out of the sky.

On the does not like and like lists students will write who or what would dislike or like marbles falling from the sky or having their neighborhood fill up with marbles. It can include people, animals, and even things (such as windows).

On the bottom section students will write a couple of possible ways to get rid of the marbles.

When writing the stories, students should refer to these ideas, but they are not limited by them. They may use items on the list or make up new items as they write.

Lesson 16

This lesson can be used as early as lesson 16, but could be used throughout lessons 16 to 20. Because a second writing assignment is given in Lesson 19, we suggest doing this activity earlier in the week.

This is a form for writing a short article about ferrets. Each part begins the statement. Students will research and write. The box at the top of the page is for a picture of a ferret. This can be a picture students draw or can be a picture students print and paste to the page.

The form:

The first space is for a general description of a ferret.

The second space is for students to describe the diet of ferrets.

The third space is for students to describe the habitat of ferrets.

The final space allows students to answer a question: Do ferrets make good pets? The first open space is for the words good or bad. Students will then express an opinion about keeping ferrets as pets. Students should explain their opinion.

Lesson 19

This is a sheet to help plan to write the story outlined in the Teacher's Manual in lesson 19. It presents many of the brainstorming questions from the Teacher's Manual. Read the questions with the students.

Choose four brainstorming questions from the top of the page and write answers for them. Choose questions with answers that may help you to write the story. On each set of lines is a box. Write the question number in the box. You do not need to write the questions, just write your answers.

If you think of a good question that is not on this page, make an X in the box and write details that will help you write your story.

Lesson 22

Introduce the activity to the students:

In the story, *Mary, Whiskers, and the Whale*, a creature from the sea needs to get home. Imagine if you had a visitor from the sea that came to live with you. Imagine you had a pet octopus!

What are some things you know about an octopus? Write a list of student responses that students will be able to see during the writing assignment.

If necessary give prompts or ask students to research:

How many arms to they have?
What do you think they would feel like?
Where would you keep an octopus?
What could it do with so many arms?
How do you think people would react to it?

On the workbook page, students will be given sentence starters. Require students to add at least three (or any other number you designate) words to each of the starters.

On additional paper, you may have students illustrate some or all of their sentences.

Lesson 24

Students will use this page to help organize facts about whales for the writing assignment in Teacher's Manual Lesson 24.

In that lesson, students will create a four page book about whales. Students will research and write.

Page 1: Baleen whales, Page 2 Toothed whales, Page 3 Dolphins, Page 4 Baby whales

The page in the Writing Workbook will organize facts for the content of the book.

As students research they may use the Whale Research Planning Page to record facts. Above each set of lines are the topics with circles in front of them. Students will write facts on the lines and fill in circles to indicate which page they would want to use that facts.

The facts can be stated as briefly as possible, such as: eats fish. More than one fact can be on a set of lines, but students wouldn't want to mix the topics (for example, put a baleen fact and dolphin fact on the same set of lines.)

Lesson 26

Students will write about France. The workbook page contains key words. Many of these may be out of the student's reading level, but should be able to use them with guidance from the teacher.

If a children's encyclopedia is a available, it will be a good source of information. On-line sources may be yield articles too complex for students to use. Therefore, the content will most likely need to be provided from information in this lesson.

There are more key words on the workbook page than will be used. Begin by reading all the key words and have students repeat them. Next, read the informational story about France. Then, ask students what they remember from what you've read. They may use the key words as reminders. Finally, ask students to write at least three facts about France. They will include the related key words.

France is a country in Europe. It is next to the Atlantic Ocean. The city with the most people in France is Paris. Paris is also the capital of France. If you go to France you may see a large, steel tower. It is called the Eiffel Tower.

One of the most famous leaders of France was named Napoleon. He was the emperor of France from 1804 to 1814. Today, France has a president.

People in France speak French. It is quite different from English. For example, their word for yes is spelled o-u-i. It sounds like our word, *we*.

France has been a friend to the United States. The Statue of Liberty was a gift from France to the United States. (Continued on the next page)

Lesson 26 Continued

The flag of France has the same colors as our flag. It is blue, white, and red. Instead of stars and stripes like the United States flag, it has a bar for each color.

Some wild animals that live in France include deer, rabbits, and foxes.

Students will choose three things to write about France from what you've just read. Students may want to circle the key words from their topics.

Have students tell you what they would like to write. Interact with students to help form their sentences. Each topic may only be one or two sentences. You may reread parts of the French facts as needed. Students should rephrase the ideas and not simply dictate what was said.

In a classroom setting, the refinement process would be done as a group, with all students writing the same thing after participating in developing the sentences.

Lesson 29

Students will use the first workbook page to plan the story. The first two lists, *I am good at* and *I want to*, brainstorm possible topics. The first list is for talents or skills the student already has. The second list is for talents or skills the student may want to develop. Students should try to think of at least two things for each list, stated as briefly as possible.

The next section has two questions. The question that is answered depends on if the students choose to write about a talent they would like to have or a talent they already have.

The next section is for the reaction of others to the talent.

The final section is to list ideas that might be the focus of the story like, *Francis Dances*. His talent came from being bitten by fleas.

On the next page, students will write their stories. The box is for an illustration. The first set of lines is for writing a title.

Lesson 31

Students can use this workbook page in lessons 31 to 33. You can have students write all five sentences in one lesson of spread it out over three lessons.

Students will simply write five sentences using as many of the -ies words from the list as possible. If students know other words that end with -ies, they may use those, too. Each sentence should contain at least one of the words, but challenge students to include two of the words in each sentence.

Lesson 34

This page can be used to plan the story assigned in the Teacher's Manual for Lesson 34. Students do not need to write in complete sentences on this page. Students may write multiple ideas for each set of lines for brainstorming.

The first lines are for possible recipients of the gifts. The second lines (because) is for possible reasons for the gift.

How will I get it? Students can brainstorm ideas for how they would get it. If they pay for it, how would they earn the money?

Where will I get it? Students can think of creative places to find the gift.

Will it be liked? Students can brainstorm ideas about the reaction the gift will get.

How will it be helpful? What would the receiver do with it?

Other. Students can write notes for any other ideas they have for the story.

Lesson 43

Introduce the activity: **A caption is a short description of a picture. It is usually just one or two sentences that can help someone quickly tell how the picture relates to the story.**

Look for examples of captions in books, magazines, and online sources.

Write captions for the three pictures from the story, *Blue Shoe Canoes*. You can look at the reading book to help remember what happened in the story when that picture was used.

Lesson 44

This page can be used to plan the picnic creative writing assignment presented in Lesson 44 of the Teacher's Manual. Students can make notes to help brainstorm and organize their story.

Students do not need to write in complete sentences. Multiple possible ideas can be written on each set of lines. Students can change the details as they choose to when writing the actual story.

Place: Where did the picnic take place? Are there any other places in the story?

Foods: What foods were at the picnic? Are they important to the story?

Who?: Who was at the picnic? Who is the main character?

Activities: What did you do at the picnic?

Problem and Solution: Did something happen on the picnic that caused a problem? What was or could be the solution?

Other: Students can make notes of any other ideas for the story.

Lesson 48

The story, *Jonathan's Not-So-Great Great Week*, takes place over a one-week period. After reading the story, students will summarize what happened each day of the week.

Lesson 49

Students will plan their one-week story by making notes for each day. Students will use these notes to create a story. The notes can be real or students may make up events.

Lesson 52

This is a form for a research paper about badgers. Students will write a general description of a badger, their habitat, and diet. Students will draw or print, cut, and paste illustrations in the boxes.

Lesson 54

This writing activity can be used in place of the creative writing activity in the Teacher's Manual Lesson 54. Students will create their own candy recipe.

The page is a form that can be used for writing it. The candy recipe does not have to be a real recipe. It can be quite creative and imaginary, and most likely something you wouldn't want to actually try cooking.

The top line is for a title. There are two columns to write a list of ingredients. This should include the measurement of each ingredient. If measuring utensils are available, let students look at them to help decide on quantities of ingredients. You may familiarize students with abbreviations such as tsp for teaspoon and tbsp or T for tablespoon.

The last section is for writing cooking directions.

The Language and Reading workbook page for Lesson 54 has the recipe for Hedgehog Fudge. Students can use this for an example or any recipe book.

Lesson 56

Students will write sentences with at least two compound words. Five sentences can be written on the page. You may have students complete the activity in one lesson or over multiple lessons. The activity can be presented in any of the lessons from lesson 56 to 58.

Lesson 59

This workbook page can be used in addition to or in place of the creative writing exercise in Lesson 59. Students will write captions for the four pictures from the story, *Bobcat Cowboys.*

A caption can describe what is happening in the picture, or who is in the picture and what are they doing, it can describe what is happening in the story that matches the pictures. Students can reference the reading book to help write the captions.

Lesson 63

Students will write about characters from the book, *The Kindness of Gnatty.* Students can write descriptions or write about the character's role in the story.

Students should write at least two sentences for each character.

Lesson 64

The workbook page can be used to help develop the creative writing assignment from Lesson 64 of the Teacher's Manual. Students can use this for notes and brainstorming. Students do not need to write in complete sentences. Students can modify, add to, or ignore these ideas as they write.

The fifth question can apply to the character that is helping or the character being helped, or notes for both.

Lesson 68

After reading the story, *Jonathan and Rosie*, students will write the effects of the causes on the workbook page.

You might introduce some simple cause-effect relationships as examples.

Cause: Flip a light switch. Effect: The light goes off or on.
Cause: Drop a glass vase on concrete floor. Effect: The vase shatters.

Lesson 69

This writing assignment may be used in addition to or in place of the creative writing assignment in the Teacher's Manual for Lesson 69. This lesson may also be completed in Lesson 70 instead of Lesson 69 if you wish students to do both activities.

Students will write about traveling twenty years into the future in a time machine. They will write at least 4 sentences. Each sentence will use different linking words: because, therefore, since, and for example.

Each linking word functions differently. You may discuss the differences and give examples before introducing the activity.

Because: This linking word connects an effect to a cause. Effect: my toe hurts. Cause: I dropped a rock on my foot. My toe hurts because I dropped a rock on my foot. The words after the word *because* is the cause. (See the word cause in because). The word *because* is with the part of the sentence that is the cause.

Therefore: This linking word connects a cause and effect, too. It functions differently than the word *because* by being a part of the sentence that is the effect.

Cause: It rained Effect: the picnic was cancelled.

It rained, therefore, the picnic was cancelled.

Since: The word *since* also links cause and effect. It is used like the word *because*. It is a part of the cause, not the effect.

Cause: It rained Effect: the picnic was cancelled.

Since it rained, the picnic was cancelled. Or The picnic was cancelled since it rained.

The words *for example* links a sentence to facts or ideas that can add details.

I like many kinds of fruit, for example; apples, oranges, and peaches.

There are punctuation rules that are likely to apply, especially with commas. You may ignore those for the time being. They are out of the scope of this curriculum. If you want the sentences punctuated with commas correctly, you can simply tell students where to add them.

Introduce the activity. Get out your time machine and travel twenty years into your future. What will your tomorrow be like? Write 4 sentences. Use the linking words somewhere in each sentence.

Lesson 71

This activity can be done anytime during the week. There is a Resource Pack page that features a larger shield and no handwriting lines. You may use that shield and plain paper in place of this page. The workbook page was created to add the convenience of not having to make a copy.

In the time of knights and kings, ruling families decorated shields and armor with art that told about the family. This was called a coat of arms or a family crest. It told something about the family. It may have told about their values, their work, or what they think is important. For example, it might have included a lion to represent kingship or fierceness. Sometimes the art was divided into four sections. Design a coat of arms for your family on a shield. You can use the Shield Sheet (in the Resource Pack) **or make your own. Write an explanation for the art. What are you showing? You may find examples on-line to help you get some ideas.**

Lesson 73

Write captions for the pictures from *Connie the Caterpillar*.

Lesson 81

Students will arrange a poem into two different rhyming patterns. This activity can be done during any lesson from 81 to 85, but probably not Lesson 84. The LAR workbook page for Lesson 84 features a stew recipe writing activity, so no other writing activity for this week is in this workbook.

Introduce the activity.

The lines in poems do not have to rhyme, but they often do. Usually those rhymes will fit a pattern. For lines in a poem to rhyme, only the last word in the line has to rhyme. We can label these patterns with letters. Each time a line doesn't end with a word that doesn't rhyme with the ending word of the last sentence, a new letter labels that word in the rhyming pattern. When any other ending word rhymes with that word, it is labeled with the same letter.

For example, listen to this poem. (Read the complete poem, then discuss.)

There was a little frog
It waited for a fly
It sat upon a log
When will a lunch zip by?

The four ending words are frog, fly, log, and by. The first label will be A. The first rhyming word is frog. All words that rhyme with *frog* will be labeled with the letter A. The next ending word is *fly*. Does the word *fly* rhyme with *frog?* (no) So words that rhyme with fly will be labeled B. Does the next ending word, log, rhyme with frog or fly? (Yes, it rhymes with frog.) **Words that rhyme with frog are labeled A in this poem. So our pattern so far is ABA. Now test the next ending word, by. Does it rhyme with frog and be labeled A, or fly and be labeled B? If it doesn't rhyme with either it will be labeled with the letter C.** (It rhymes with fly. It is labeled B) **So this poem has a rhyme pattern of A, B, A, B.** (Continued on the next page)

Notes:

Lesson 1

Lesson Objectives

1. Students will review beginning blends (sn, sp, br, cr, dr, fr, pr, tr, bl, cl, gl, fl, pl, sl). (P & L)
2. Students will learn spelling words. (S)
3. Students will read words and definitions. (L)
4. Students will prepare to read the story *Emily and Elaine in the Dark*. (R)
5. Students will copy sentences neatly and correctly. (H)

Materials

Language and Reading (LAR) workbook page
Spelling and Phonics (SAP) workbook page
Book: *Emily and Elaine in the Dark*

Teaching

1. Write each blend or have students look at the row of blends at the bottom of the SAP page. Have students think of words that begin with the blends. Have students match blends to the endings on the bottom of the SAP page to complete the words. Look at the spelling list and find other words that begin with each beginning blend.

2. Use the SAP page. Have students read and spell each word.

   snow, spider, clay, glove, plant, blink, flavor, sleeve, brain, treat, crash, drawer, frost, prince

   Next students will alphabetize the list. **The spelling words have been put into two groups to alphabetize. Look at the first group. Do any words begin with a?** (no) **Do any words begin with b?** (yes) **Two words begin with b. Look at the second letter to see which one comes first in alphabetical order.** (blink) **Before you write any words on the lines, number all the words in the word list in the order you will write them. That way if you make mistakes, they will be easier to fix.**

   Bottom section of SAP: **Add a blend to the beginning of each word to make another word.**

3. Use the LAR page. **Complete the crossword puzzle. A word list is provided, but not all the words in the list will be used.**

4. *Emily and Elaine in the Dark* focuses on reviewing words used in about the first third of the first grade program. In addition to those words, the following words may be new to students and will require some instruction: answer (answered), heard, lightning.

   The following are some suggestions to help children remember the words:

The word *answer:*	the w is silent. Also, familiarize the students with the suffix -ed added (answered)
The word *heard:*	It's as if the a is silent and it was spelled h-er-d. Compare to the word hear. In this word -ea- makes the long e sound.
The word *lightning:*	separate the word light-ning.

   The following words were used in the first grade curriculum, but additional review may be helpful: baseball, beautiful, asleep, nothing, outside, sometimes, would.

   Next, have the children read the word list on the back of the book. Students will begin reading the book in Lesson 2.

5. Use the handwriting sheet or have the children write the following sentences:

   The black snake floated in the water.
   The toy train crashed and broke.

LAR Answers

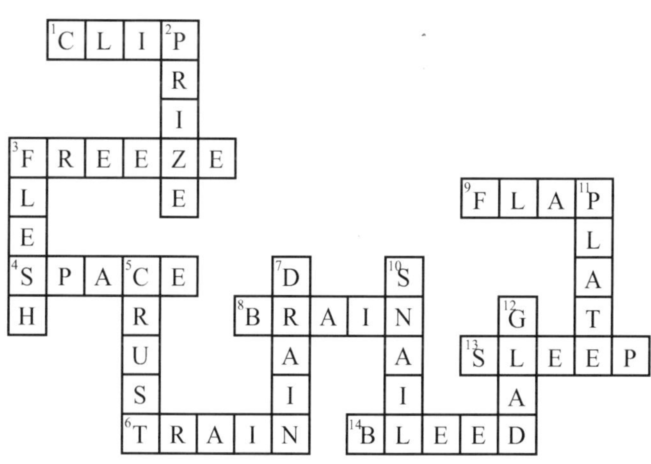

SAP Answers

Alphabetizing

1. blink	5. drawer
2. brain	6. flavor
3. clay	7. frost
4. crash	8. glove

1. plant	4. snow
2. prince	5. spider
3. sleeve	6. treat

Adding blends: answers vary (many different blends may complete words for each ending)

Emily and Elaine in the Dark

Second Grade Phonics & Reading

Book 1
Lessons 1 to 5

Emily and Elaine
In the Dark

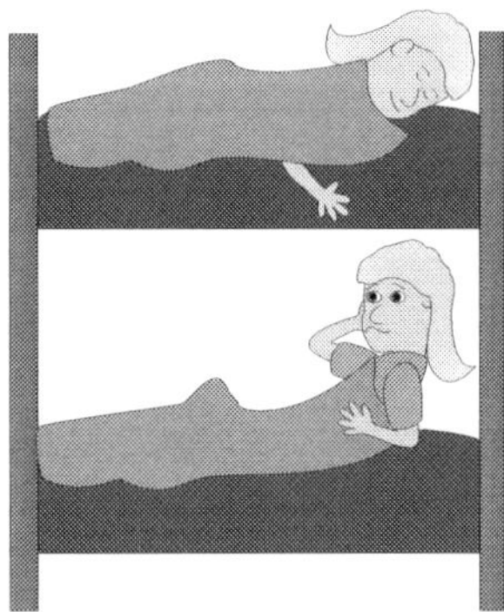

Written and illustrated by
Brian Davis

Emily and Elaine Rose were in their bunk beds. Elaine could not sleep.

"Are you awake?" Elaine asked her twin sister.

"No," spoke Emily. "I'm asleep."

"You can't be sleeping," said Elaine. "You just spoke to me."

Emily leaned over the top bunk. "OK., I'm awake. But, I would like to be asleep. So, please stop talking and go to sleep."

Emily looked at the clock. "It's after eleven o'clock."

1

2

Emily and Elaine in the Dark

"I can't sleep. I think a long snake is in the room. It's behind the drum," said Elaine.

Emily slid out of bed.

"Grab the baseball bat," blurted Elaine. "Club the snake on the head."

Emily walked to the drum. She flipped on the light.

"It's just a cord," said Emily. "It's plugged into the wall."

"I'm just glad you're alive," said Elaine. "It could have been a snake. It could have harmed us."

3

4

Emily flipped off the light. She slipped back into bed.

"You need to do what I do," said Emily. "Sometimes I am afraid of the dark. I just pretend there are good things in the room. See the shadow of the tree branch?"

"Yes," answered Elaine. "It looks like a flesh eating lion. It's looking for twin girls to snack on."

5

"No," said Emily. "It's a pretty horse trotting. I pretend I am riding it."

"Yes!" cried Elaine. "I see it now. Can I ride next, please?"

"Yes," answered Emily. "Just put her in the barn after your ride."

6

Emily and Elaine in the Dark

Emily drifted off to sleep.

"Are you awake?" Elaine asked. "Emily, are you awake?" Elaine asked again.

She shook the bed.

"What now?" asked Emily. "You woke me up again."

"I can't sleep. I heard a sound," said Elaine. "I think it was an ape grunting. He's in the tree."

"It's just the wind," answered Emily. "It's blowing the branch. The branch is hitting the house."

"That's not the only sound I hear," said Elaine.

"The other sound is a frog croaking," said Emily.

7

8

"The croaking frog is keeping me awake," said Elaine.

"You're keeping me awake," said Emily. "Just pretend that the frog is waiting for a kiss. He's really a prince. He's climbed a tower to save you."

"Yuck!" said Elaine. "I think I'll just pretend it's a frog in a tree."

9

Emily drifted back to sleep.
Then, it started to storm outside.
Rain crashed into the house.
The wind rocked the trees in the yard.
Lightning flashed.

Emily slipped out of bed.

"Are you awake?" Emily asked Elaine.

Elaine did not answer.
All she did was snore.
The lightning flashed again.

Emily ran to her mother and father's room.

10

Emily and Elaine in the Dark

She snuggled up in their bed and fell asleep. The next day, her mother and father woke up. They were very quiet.
Emily was still asleep. They slipped out of the room.

Elaine came out of her room.

"Emily is not in her bed," said Elaine.

"She's asleep in our room," said her mother.

"I think the storm scared her," said her father.

"There was a storm?" asked Elaine.

Her mother and father giggled.

"Nothing scares you," said her father.

"You should teach Emily to be brave,"added her mother.

11

8

Emily and Elaine in the Dark word list:

added	dark	hitting	put	stop
after	drifted	horse	quiet	storm
alive	drum	house	rain	talking
answered	eating	keeping	really	teach
asked	Elaine	leaned	riding	their
asleep	eleven	light	rocked	there
awake	Emily	lightning	room	things
barn	father	lion	scared	tower
baseball	flashed	long	scares	tree
beds	flesh	looked	shadow	trotting
been	flipped	looks	shook	twin
behind	frog	mother	should	very
blowing	giggled	next	sister	waiting
blurted	girls	nothing	sleep	walked
branch	glad	now	spoke	wall
brave	good	out	sleeping	were
bunk	grab	outside	slid	what
can't	grunting	over	slipped	wind
climbed	harmed	o'clock	snack	woke
clock	have	please	snake	would
club	head	plugged	snore	yard
cord	hear	pretend	snuggled	your
could	heard	pretty	sometimes	you're
crashed	her	prince	sound	yuck
croaking	he's			

Lesson 2

Lesson Objectives

1. Students will review vowel +r. (P)
2. Students will review the suffix -ed. (S & L)
3. Students will complete analogies with spelling words.
4. Students will read the story *Emily and Elaine in the Dark.* (R)
5. Students will copy sentences neatly and correctly. (H)

Materials

LAR workbook page
SAP workbook page
Emily and Elaine in the Dark

Teaching

1. Write the words ban, bid, bun, Bet, and won. Have the students review the vowel sounds in each word. **The "a" in ban makes what sound?** (*a*) Repeat for the other words.

   Next, add an r after the vowel. Have students read the new words: barn, bird, burn, Bert, worn. **Did the vowel sounds change?** Have students isolate the vowel + r sounds (ar-barn, ir-bird, etc.). Ask: **What vowel + r sounds are pronounced the same?** (ir, er, ur).

   Write the words horse, were, large, and purse. Point out that the silent e does not make the first vowel long. Have students read the words.

   Top of the LAR workbook page: **Complete the sentences using the vowel + r words. Write the numbers from the word list in the blanks.**

2. Write the words mail, need, float, name, trim, pant, dress, farm, star and force. **Add a suffix to each of these words. Can you tell a definition for the word suffix?** (letters added to the end of words) Also review the term root word (the word before a suffix was added). Review the spelling rules for adding suffixes:

   For long vowel words that do not end with a silent e, simply add -ed: mailed, needed, floated.

   For words that end with silent e, drop the silent e and add thesuffix -ed: named, forced.

   For one-syllable short vowel words, if the last two letters in a word are a vowel and consonant, double the consonant and add ed (except for the letter x): trimmed, starred.

   Add the suffix to words that end with two consonants:
   panted, dressed, farmed.

   Bottom of the LAR workbook page: **Add the suffix -ed to the words in the boxes. Write the word on the lines.**

3. Use the top of the SAP page. **In the purple box is a list of words. Look at the columns of red words and green words. Find the word in the word list that is *spelled* almost like the words in red. On the green side, match the spelling word that has a *meaning* that is related to green word.**

   On the bottom section, fill in the boxes with letters of spelling words. All the spelling words will fit in the boxes. Two clues have been given. The number of boxes in each word is also a clue.

4. Introduce the story *Emily and Elaine in the Dark*. For students who were taught using the first grade program, ask if they remember Emily and Elaine from last year. Ask if they can remember what happened in the stories. For other students ask: **Have you ever been afraid in the dark?** (Allow students to respond.) **If you have a good imagination, you may think there are all kinds of things to be afraid of in the dark. What are some things someone might imagine in the dark? Do you think those things are really there?**

   This story is about two sisters and one of them is afraid of the dark.

   Review the additional reading vocabulary: answer (answered), heard, lightning.
   Students will now read pages 1 to 6.

   Next, ask the following questions:

   Who was afraid of the dark? (Elaine)
   What was the first thing she thought was in the room? (a long snake)
   What did the snake really turn out to be? (a cord plugged into the wall)
   What did Emily do to keep from being afraid in the dark? (She pretended there are good things in the room.)
   What are some things you might pretend are in your room if you are afraid?
   (Answers vary.)
   What did Elaine see to make her think a lion was in the room? (a shadow of a tree branch)
   What did Emily pretend was in her room? (a horse)

5. Use the handwriting sheet or have the children write the following sentences:

   The horse in the barn jerked Curt's arm.
   The girl had a purse made of yarn.

LAR Answers

Top	Bottom
1. 5,8	1. printed
2. 2,7	2. trotted
3. 3,9	3. spilled
4. 10,1	4. rained
5. 6,4	5. dropped
	6. shaved

SAP Answers

Top

1. sleeve	6. spider
2. glove	7. plant
3. crash	8. flavor
4. snow	9. brain
5. frost	10. prince

										f	
					s	p	i	d	e	r	
					l					o	
					e					s	
			c		e		b			t	
		f	l	a	v	o	r				
			a		e		a				
			y				i				
				p	r	i	n	c	e		d
				l				r			r
		g		a				a			a
	b	l	i	n	k			s	n	o	w
		o		t				h			e
		v									r
t	r	e	a	t							

Lesson 3

Lesson Objectives

1. Students will review ending blends (rd, rn, rm, rk, rt, nd, ng, nt). (L & P)
2. Students will review contractions. (L)
3. Students will review the spelling list. (S)
4. Students will read the story *Emily and Elaine in the Dark.* (R)
5. Students will copy sentences neatly and correctly. (H)

Materials

LAR
SAP
Emily and Elaine in the Dark
Writing Skills Workbook page is available (See TM page 25)

Teaching

1. Write the words far, bar, hut, won, and had. Have students read the words. Add an m to the end of the word far. **Read the new word.** (farm). Add a k to bar and have students read the word (bark).

   Next, have students read the words hut, won, and had. **Make three more words by adding an r before the last consonant.** (hurt, worn, hard) **Did the r change the vowel sounds?** Have students make the vowel + r sounds in isolation.

   Finally, write the words hug, bad, wet. **Read the words.** Have students add an n before the last consonant to make three more words (hung, band, went). **Read the words.**

   Top of the LAR workbook page: **Some words in the sentences are missing letters. Circle the words that are wrong. Write the words correctly on the lines. Add either *d, g, k, m, n, r* or *t.***

2. Review the term contraction. **It's when we put two words together.** Write the words did not and didn't. Point to the apostrophe. **Can you remember the name of this punctuation mark? What does it do in the word didn't?** (It show that letters were taken out.) **What letter was left out when we turned did not into the contraction didn't?** (o) Say each of the following words and have students write the two words that were contracted on a piece of paper.

   Aren't, can't, isn't, wasn't, weren't

   Use the bottom of the LAR workbook page. **Read the sentences. Find words that can be made into contractions. Write the contractions on the lines.**

3. Review adding the suffixes *ing* and *ed.* **Sometimes suffixes are added to words to make them the correct tense for a sentence. The suffix e-d is added to verbs to make them past tense. That means the sentence happened in the past. The suffix i-n-g is added to verbs to make them present tense. That means the sentence reads like it is happening now.**

Use the top of SAP page 3. **Choose the right suffix to add to the spelling words to complete the sentences.**

Use the bottom of SAP page 3: **Match the spelling words to the clues.**

4. Review the first half of the book *Emily and Elaine in the Dark*. Next, read the second half of the book. After completing the story ask the students the following questions:

   What did Elaine think was grunting in a tree? (an ape)
   What was really making the sound? (a frog croaking)
   What did Emily pretend the frog was? (a prince)
   Why do you think Elaine didn't want to pretend the frog was a prince? (Answers vary.)
   Who was afraid of the storm? (Emily)
   What did she do? (She went to her parent's room.)
   Who did the parents think was brave? (Elaine)
   Why? (Answers vary.)

5. Use the handwriting sheet or have the children write the following sentences:

   Kent's bird can't stand too long.
   The shark didn't turn to harm Bert.

LAR Answers

1. art
2. sting
3. yard
4. dent
5. bend

1. weren't
2. aren't
3. can't
4. isn't
5. didn't
6. wasn't

SAP Answers

1. snowed
2. planting
3. frosted
4. blinking
5. flavored

sleeve	glove
clay	brain
crash	spider
drawer	treat
	prince

Lesson 4

Lesson Objectives

1. Students will review spelling words. (S)
2. Students will review prefixes (a-, be-). (L)
3. Students will read *Emily and Elaine in the Dark.* (R)
4. Students will write a story. (CW)
5. Students will copy sentences neatly and correctly. (H)

Materials

LAR
SAP
Emily and Elaine in the Dark

Teaching

1. Use the top of the SAP workbook page. **The letters in the boxes are supposed to spell a spelling word, but letters have been added. Color in the boxes that contain letters that do not belong.**

   Use the bottom of the SAP workbook page. **You can sometimes see shorter words in longer words. The spelling words can be found in the longer words at the bottom of the workbook page. Find the spelling word in each word and write it on the lines.**

2. Review the term suffix (letters added to the end of the word). Ask students if they know the definition of a prefix. If not, tell students it is the opposite of a suffix. It is letters added to the beginning of the word. Also, review the term root word (the word before a suffix or prefix is added).

   Write the words side, and cross. Have students read the words. Add the prefix be to side. Have students read the new word (beside). Ask students to say the prefix (be). What is the root word of beside? (side) Add the letter a to cross. What is the new word? (across) What was the prefix? (a) What is the root word? (cross)

3. Read the book *Emily and Elaine in the Dark* a second time. Next, have students look at the back of the book and answer the following questions about the word list. You may do this orally or have students write answers:

   What word means beautiful? (pretty)
   What words are contractions? (can't, he's, you're, technically o'clock is too - of the clock.) You may ask students to write the words that were contracted.
   What words have the -ed suffix? (added, answered, asked, blurted, climbed, crashed, drifted, flashed, flipped, giggled, harmed, leaned, looked, plugged, rocked, scared, slipped, snuggled, walked) You may ask students to write the root words.
   What are things that happen during a storm? (rain, lightning)
   What words are animals? (frog, horse, lion, snake)
   What words have a prefix? (alive, asleep, awake, behind) You may have the students write the root words.

   Top of the LAR workbook page: Fill in ovals to answer questions about the story.

4. The students will write a story. As a beginning writing exercise, students will basically complete sentences.

   Introduce the activity: **Emily and Elaine were afraid of some things. What was Elaine afraid of?** (the dark) **What scared Emily?** (a storm) **Are there things you are afraid of or have been afraid of? You will make your own story like Emily and Elaine in the Dark.** (Options are in parenthesis.)

   Use the bottom of the LAR workbook page. The sentences below are printed on the workbook page along with lines for completing the sentences.

   Sometimes I am afraid of __________.
   I think it might _______.
   It makes me want to __________.
   I don't want to __________.
   My (mother, father) tells (told) me to _________.
   My (friend, brother, sister) told me to ________.
   I will _______ the next time I am scared.
   If ______ (name of a person) is afraid I will ___________.

   Save the stories. Students will read them in the next lesson.

5. Use the handwriting sheet or have the children write the following sentences:

   The rain began to fill the red pail.
   The snail crawled across the steel rail.

LAR Answers

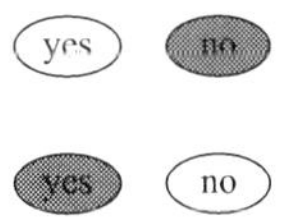

SAP Answers

s	■	p	i	■	■	d	e	r	■
■	■	c	■	l	a	■	y	■	■
■	d	■	r	■	a	w	■	e	r
■	p	l	■	■	a	■	n	t	■
s	■	l	e	■	■	e	■	v	e

shirtsleeves — sleeve
mistreatment — treat
eggplant — plant
gatecrasher — crash
princess — prince
unflavored — flavor
permafrost — frost
unblinking — blink
snowmobile — snow
scatterbrained — brain
foxglove — glove

Lesson 5

Lesson Objectives

1. Students will be tested on phonics concepts. (P)
2. Students will be test on language concepts. (L)
3. Students will read the story they have written. (R)
4. Students will take a spelling test. (S)
5. Students will copy a sentence neatly and correctly. (H)

Materials

Creative writing assignment from Lesson 4
Lesson 5 assessment (copy master)

Teaching

1. Use the top of the assessment as a phonics test. Have the students fill in the circles next to the words that answer the questions.

2. Use the bottom of the assessment. Read the words. Write the root words on the lines.

3. Have students take turns reading the stories that were written during the creative writing section of Lesson 4.

4. Have students number their papers from 1 to 14. Give the following words as dictation. Spelling word list:

   1. blink, 2. sleeve, 3. spider, 4. flavor, 5. glove, 6. treat, 7. frost, 8. crash, 9. drawer, 10. snow, 11. prince, 12. clay, 13. brain, 14. plant

5. Use the handwriting sheet or have the children write the following sentences:

   Craig's snake belongs in the glass jar.
   Barb agreed to paint the barn.

Assessment Answers

1. flute
2. shark
3. tent
4. tail
5. clock

1. plan	6. stay
2. clamp	7. spot
3. spell	8. flash
4. stain	9. croak
5. snore	10. store

Lesson 6

Lesson Objectives

1. Students will review ending blends (sk, lk, nk, ft, ld, lf, lt, lp). (P)
2. Students will spell words correctly. (S)
3. Students will prepare to read *Dot and the Stopped Up Drain.* (R)
4. Students will copy sentences neatly and correctly. (H)

Materials

LAR
SAP
Dot and the Stopped Up Drain

Teaching

1. Write each blend (sk, lk, nk, ft, ld, lf, lt, lp). Have students think of words that end with the blends. Have students write a word that ends with each blend on a piece of paper.

   Students will complete the crossword puzzle on the LAR workbook page using words that end with these blends. A word list is provided, but not all the words in the list will be used.

2. Use the SAP workbook page. Have students read and spell each word.

   skill, scout, swift, smell, after, held, self, salt, loud, poodle, cool, pillow, bottom, twinkle

   Alphabetize the two groups of spelling words. Write small numbers by each word to show the line you will write them on. Next, write the words on the lines.

   Bottom section: **Look at the four words at the bottom of the page. We can change words by just changing the vowels. Change the vowel in each of these words to make a different word. You may have a choice of making more than one word with some of the words.**

3. *Dot and the Stopped Up Drain* focuses on reviewing words used in the first grade program. In addition to those words, the following words may be new to students and will require some instruction: ache, alligator, basement, bathroom, bathtub, problem, swiftly, yahoo.

   The following are some suggestions to help children remember the words. The words and directions are printed on the bottom of the LAR workbook page:

   The word *ache:* The a is long. The ch makes the k sound. The e is silent.

   The word *alligator:* Break into syllables, al-li-ga-tor. The -ga- has a long a sound.

   The word *basement:* Break into syllables, base-ment

   The word *bathroom* and *bathtub:* Divide the words. bath room, bath tub

   The word *problem:* Break into syllables, pro-blem. The vowels are short.

   The word *swiftly:* Take off the suffix (swift). The y makes a long e sound.

   The word *yahoo:* Break into syllables. The a makes a short o sound. The -oo- sound is as in moose.

   The following words were used in the first grade curriculum, but additional review may be helpful: kitchen, skiing, thought, wild

   Next, have the children read the word list on the back of the book. Students will begin reading the book in Lesson 7.

4. Use the handwriting sheet or have the children write the following sentences:

   I helped paint the old shelf pink.
   We took the colt for a walk at dusk.

LAR Answers

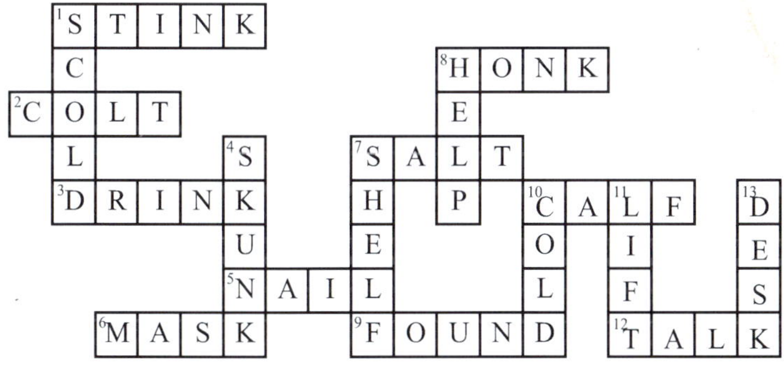

SAP Answers

1. after	4. held
2. bottom	5. loud
3. cool	6. twinkle

1. pillow	5. self
2. poodle	6. skill
3. salt	7. smell
4. scout	8. swift

skull hold
small lad, led or lid

Dot and the Stopped Up Drain

Beth was in the kitchen. She wanted to get a drink of cool water. The water did not go down the drain.

"There is still water in the sink," thought Beth.

Beth walked down the hall. She turned on the water in the bathtub. The water didn't go down the drain.

"It seems I need some help. The drains are stopped up."

1

She called Dot the dog to fix the pipes in the house. Soon, Dot came to help.

"I checked the bathroom and the kitchen," said Beth.

"The drains do not work. I need to go to the mall to eat lunch. It will take some time. I will be back after noon."

Beth left Dot at her house.

2

3

Dot and the Stopped Up Drain

Dot checked the drain in the kitchen. She checked the drain in the bathtub. She thrust a broom down the bathtub drain. She heard a loud crunch.

The end of the broom had been bitten off. This did not scare Dot.

"I found the problem," said Dot.

She went to her truck. She came back with a ladder.

4

5

Dot went into the basement. She set the ladder up under the bathtub drain. She took a large wrench from her tool belt. She loosened the pipe.

Swish! Down came the water from the bathtub. That's not all that fell out. There on the floor was a very angry alligator.

6

This did not scare Dot. She sat on top of the ladder. A smile came on Dot's face. She reached for a rope on her tool belt. She made a lasso.

She made one swift throw. The rope looped around the alligator's snout. The alligator went wild.

7

Dot and the Stopped Up Drain

This did not scare Dot. The alligator bolted up the steps. The alligator was very swift.

Dot held the rope. She bounced off the ladder. She went skiing across the basement.

Dot did not let loose. Dot hopped on the alligator's back.

8

They were in the kitchen next. The alligator twisted. The alligator twirled.

"Yahoo!" hooted Dot.

She thrived on alligator riding. Milk jugs spilled. A shelf was knocked down.

Bowls scooted across the room. The kitchen became very cluttered.

This lasted for about an hour. Dot held on.

9

The alligator gave up. Dot smiled. She scolded the alligator.

"What were you doing in that pipe?"

The alligator sat up. He was not in a good mood. He rubbed his belly.

"I see," said Dot softly. "You had a tummy ache."

The alligator nodded yes.

"Have you been eating hot peppers?" asked Dot.

The alligator nodded yes.

"I see," said Dot. "You need a pill for your tummy ache."

10

11

Dot and the Stopped Up Drain

Dot left the room. She came back soon.

"My tummy aches if I eat hot peppers, too."

Dot pulled off the lasso. She offered the alligator some tummy ache pills. The alligator munched the pills. The pills soothed the alligator's belly.

12

Dot and the alligator had a big task to do. The house was a mess. Beth would be back after noon.

They worked swiftly. The alligator cleaned the kitchen.

13

They fixed the shelf.

They put back the bathtub drain pipe. Dot was very pleased. So she took the alligator home for dinner. Her pups were cooking a nice meal.

14

Dot's pups came out with round bowls.

The bowls were filled with hot stuffed peppers.

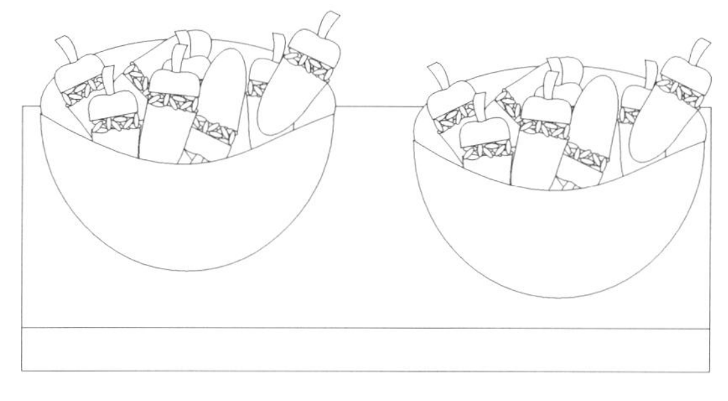

15

Dot and the Stopped Up Drain

Dot and the Stopped Up Drain

Dot and the Stopped Up Drain word list:

about
ache
across
after
alligator
angry
around
basement
bathtub
bathroom
belly
belt
Beth
bitten
bolted
bounced
bowls
broom
checked
cleaned
cluttered
cool

crunch
didn't
dinner
Dot
down
drain
drink
eat
eating
end
fixed
floor
found
good
heard
held
help
home
hooted
hopped
hour
house

into
kitchen
knocked
ladder
large
lasso
lasted
left
looped
loose
loosened
loud
lunch
mall
mess
milk
mood
munched
next
nodded
noon
now
offered

one
out
peppers
pills
problem
reached
room
round
rubbed
scare
scolded
scooted
shelf
sink
skiing
smile
snout
softly
soon
soothed
spilled
steps
still

stopped
swift
swiftly
swish
task
this
thought
thrived
throw
thrust
tool
truck
tummy
twirled
twisted
under
very
wanted
water
wild
work
wrench
yahoo

Lesson 7

Lesson Objectives

1. Students will review beginning blends (sk, sc, sw, sm, tw). (P)
2. Students will review the suffix -ing. (L & S)
3. Students will review spelling words. (S)
4. Students will read the story *Dot and the Stopped Up Drain.* (R)
5. Students will copy sentences neatly and correctly. (H)

Materials

LAR
SAP
Dot and the Stopped Up Drain
Writing Skills Workbook page is available (See TM page 25)

Teaching

1. Write the words bunk, man, king, cash, and big. Have the students read each word.

   Write the five beginning blends: sw, tw, sc, sm, sk. Have students replace each beginning consonant with one of the blends to make five new words. (skunk, scan, swing, smash, twig)

   Top of LAR workbook page 6: **Read the sentences. The underlined word does not belong in the sentence. Replace the beginning consonant with a blend to complete the sentences. Write the correct word on the lines at the end of the sentences.**

2. Introduce the suffix -ing. Review the rules for adding suffixes:

   For long vowel words that do not end with a silent e, simply add -ing: mailing, needing, floating.

   For words that end with silent e, drop the silent e and add the suffix -ing: naming, forcing.

   For one syllable words, if the last two letters in a word are a vowel and consonant, double the consonant and add ing: trimming, starring.

   Add the suffix to words that end with two consonants: panting, dressing, farming, painting.

   Have students add -ing to these spelling words: **scare, switch, smile, ask, milk, melt, help**. (scaring, switching, smiling, asking, milking, melting, helping)

   And these words: **flop, skip, sweep, thin, crow, zoom.** (flopping, skipping, sweeping, thinning, crowing, zooming)

   Use the bottom of the LAR workbook page. **Choose the correct form of the words to complete the sentences. Fill in the circle to mark your answer.**

3. Review the spelling list. Choose spelling words and have students spell them. Spelling list: **skill, scout, swift, smell, after, held, self, salt, loud, poodle, cool, pillow, bottom, twinkle.**

   Use the top of the SAP workbook page. **Complete the sentences with spelling words.**

   Use the bottom of the SAP page. **Unscramble the spelling words.**

4. Introduce the story *Dot and the Stopped Up Drain*. In this story, Dot the plumber helps out a customer and an animal. Find out how in this story.

   Review the additional reading vocabulary: **alligator, basement, bathroom, problem, swiftly, yahoo.**

   Students will now read pages 1 to 8. Next, ask the following questions:

   Where did Beth go after Dot came to fix the pipes? (to the mall)
   What happened to the broom handle? (It was bitten off.)
   Where did Dot take the ladder? (to the basement)
   What was stuck in the drain? (an alligator)
   Why do you think the alligator was angry? (Answers vary.)
   Was Dot scared of the alligator? (no)
   How did she catch the alligator? (She lassoed him.)

5. Use the handwriting sheet or have the children write the following sentences:

   She wore a blouse, a skirt, and a scarf.
   The twelve children smelled the swine.

LAR Answers

1. swim
2. smile
3. twin
4. skate
5. scored

SAP Answers

1. poodle, pillow
2. loud
3. smell
4. held
5. scout

1.	○ milk	○ milked	● milking
2.	○ bounce	● bounced	○ bouncing
3.	● smell	○ smelled	○ smelling
4.	● ask	○ asked	○ asking
5.	○ mow	● mowed	○ mowing
6.	○ skid	● skidded	○ skidding
7.	○ shout	○ shouted	● shouting

salt	skill
cool	swift
bottom	after
twinkle	self

Lesson 8

Lesson Objectives

1. Students will review vowel digraphs (ow as in snow, ou as in out, oo as in moon). (P)
2. Students will review contractions. (L)
3. Students will review the spelling list. (S)
4. Students will read the story *Dot and the Stopped Up Drain*. (R)
5. Students will copy sentences neatly and correctly. (H)

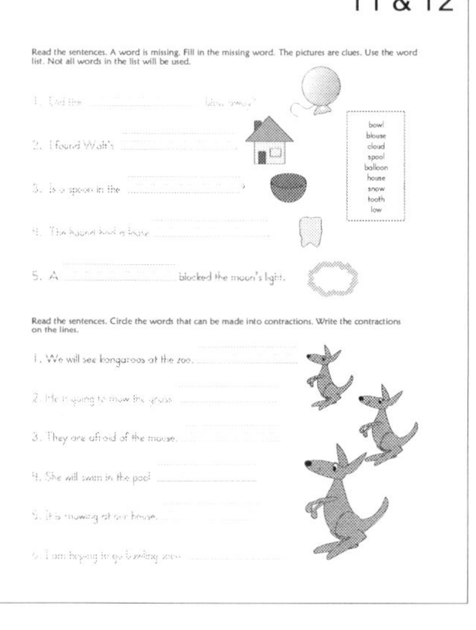

Materials

LAR
SAP
Dot and the Stopped Up Drain

Teaching

1. Write the words snow, flown, found, house, moose, spoon. Have the students find the letters that make the vowel sounds.

   For the words snow, and flown, the w acts like a silent vowel. It makes the o long. Ask students if they know the other sound ow makes. **It makes the *ow* sound as in *brown* and *cow*.**
   For the words *found*, and *house*, the o-u work together to make a different vowel sound. It is the same sound that o-w makes in *cow*.
   For the words *moose* and *spoon*, the two o's make the long oo sound that is similar to a long u sound. Remind students that oo has another sound, oo as in *book*. In this lesson only the oo sound as in *moose* will be used.

   Top of the LAR workbook page: **Choose a word from the list to complete the sentences. Write the words on the lines.**

2. Review the term contraction. It's when we put two words together. Write the words I will and I'll. Point to the apostrophe. Ask students if they can remember the name of this punctuation mark. Ask what it does in the word I'll. (It shows that letters were taken out.) Ask what letters were left out when we turned *I will* into the contraction *I'll*. Say each of the following words and have students write the two words that were contracted on a piece of paper.

   He'll, she'll, we'll, they'll

   Introduce contracting with be verbs. Write: he is, she is, it is, we are, they are, I am. Ask students to find the contractions for the sets of words (he's, she's, it's, we're, they're, I'm). The word *is* can also be contracted with proper nouns: Beth is, Beth's, Walt is, Walt's, Mitch is, Mitch's.

   Use the bottom of the LAR workbook page. **Find two words in each sentence that can form a contraction. Write the contractions on the lines at the end of the sentences.**

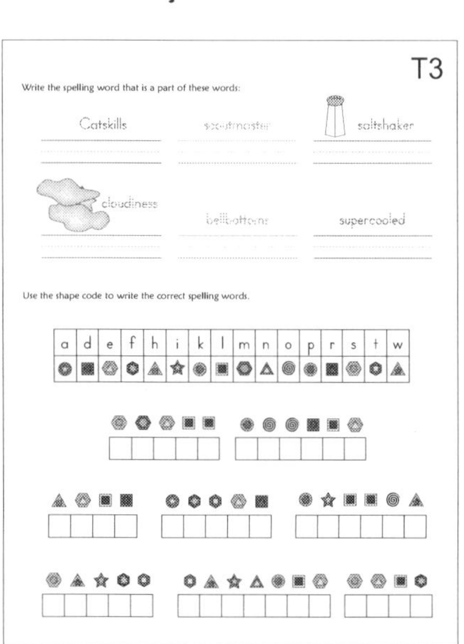

3. Use the top of the SAP workbook page. **Write the spelling word that is a part of each longer word.**

   Use the bottom of the SAP page. **The spelling words are written in code. Use the code key to decode the spelling words. Write the letters in the boxes.**

4. Review the first half of the book *Dot and the Stopped Up Drain*. Next, read the second half of the book. After completing the story ask the students the following questions:

   How long did Dot ride the alligator? (an hour)
   What was wrong with the alligator? (He had a tummy ache.)
   What did the alligator eat? (hot peppers)
   How did Dot know the alligator had a tummy ache? (It rubbed it's belly.)
   What did Dot give the alligator? (tummy ache pills)
   Who cleaned up the kitchen? (the alligator)
   Where did they go after leaving Beth's house? (to Dot's house)
   Why did Dot want to help the alligator? (Answers vary - She knew what it was like to have a tummy ache.)
   Do you think this is a true story? (Answers vary.)
   What was there in this story that probably couldn't happen? (Answers vary.)

5. Use the handwriting sheet or have the children write the following sentences:

   I found the broom in the house.
   She'll show us her pet raccoon.

LAR Answers

Top

1. balloon
2. house
3. bowl
4. tooth
5. cloud

Bottom

1. We'll
2. He's
3. They're
4. She'll
5. It's
6. I'm

SAP Answers

Top

skill scout salt
cloud bottom cool

Bottom

smell poodle
held after pillow
swift twinkle self

Lesson 9

Lesson Objectives

1. Students will review words with the ch and th consonant digraphs. (P)
2. Students will review spelling words. (L & S)
3. Students will read the story *Dot and the Stopped Up Drain.* (R)
4. Students will answer questions based on observations. (L)
5. Students will write a story. (CW)
6. Students will copy sentences neatly and correctly. (H)

Materials

LAR
SAP
Dot and the Stopped Up Drain
Writing Skills Workbook page is available

Teaching

1. Write the digraphs th and ch.

   For the digraph th: T-h has two sounds. **The t-h sometimes uses your voice, *that.* Sometimes you do not use your voice, *think.* The t-h sound can come at the end of words *too, with, cloth,* math. The t-h sound can also be in the middle of words, *mother, brother, father.***

   Ask students to think of words that have t-h in them. Have students identify the t-h sound (voiced or unvoiced). Have students identify where the t-h sound is in the word (beginning, middle, end).

   For the digraph ch: It has several sounds, but only the c-h sound as in *child* will be used in this lesson. The ch can also be at the beginning (chain), middle (kitchen), or end (couch) of the word. Ask students to think of words that have ch in them. Have students identify where the ch sound is in the word (beginning, middle, end).

2. Use the SAP page. **Match a spelling word to each description. Write the words on the lines.**

3. Read the book Dot and the Stopped Up Drain a second time. Next, have students look at the back of the book and answer the following questions about the word list. You may do this orally or have students write answers:

   What words are places in a house? (basement, bathroom, kitchen)
   What words have the suffix -ing? (eating, skiing) Ask students to write the root words.
   What words have a prefix? (about, across, around) Ask students to write the root words of across and around.
   What words have the -ed suffix? (bolted, bounced, checked, cleaned, cluttered, fixed, hooted, hopped, knocked, lasted, looped,loosened, munched, nodded, offered, reached, rubbed, scolded, scooted, soothed, spilled, stopped, thrived, twirled, twisted, wanted) You may ask students to write the root words.
   What are things that Dot had on her tool belt? (lasso, wrench)
   What words have the digraph c-h? (ache, checked, crunch, kitchen, reached, wrench)
   Which one does not have the c-h sound you hear in chair? (ache)

   Top of LAR page: **Fill in ovals to answer questions about the story.**

4. Use the bottom of the LAR page. **Look at the photograph and the drawing of the alligators. Read the statements about alligators at the bottom of the page. All the statements are true. Which statements can you know are true from the pictures on the page? Answer yes or no if the pictures show that the statement is true.** Students may interpret the pictures differently. Allow for some variance in the given answer if students can explain their choice.

5. The students will write a story. You may have students write the story on a piece of paper or make a book that can be illustrated. Books will again need a cover sheet and two additional sheets. Students may illustrate the pages. Students may make up titles to the story.

   Introduce the activity: **Today you will make up a story about alligators. It can be a true story that just talks about alligators, or it can be made up, like the story *Dot and the Stopped Up Drain.***

   Read about alligators to prepare the students to write. You may read a book, an encyclopedia entry, or you may read this summary:

   Alligators are reptiles that live in lakes, marshes, rivers, and swamps. Most of the alligators in the United States are found in the southern states from Texas to Florida. Some alligators are raised on alligator farms. People eat the alligator meat and use the skins to make shoes, belts, handbags, and other things. Some people buy baby alligators for pets.

   An alligator is full grown at about ten years old. Most are about six feet long. Some alligators may be up to 19 feet long. Female alligators weigh about 120 pounds. Male alligators weigh about 250 pounds.

   When an alligator is born it is only about nine inches long. Alligators hatch from eggs. The mother alligator lays about 30 to 60 eggs in the springtime. It takes about ten weeks for the eggs to hatch.

   Alligators eat snakes, frogs, and fish. Young alligators eat insects and small animals that live in water. Sometimes alligators eat bigger animals like pigs or birds that live in the water. Alligators do not usually attack people.

6. Use the handwriting sheet or have the children write the following sentences:

   Beth gave her mother that thin cloth.
   The chimp on the branch munched on cheese.

LAR Answers

Top

- **yes** no
- **no**
- **yes** no
- **yes** no
- yes **no**

Bottom

1. **yes** no
2. yes **no**
3. **yes** no
4. **yes** no
5. yes **no**
6. yes **no**
7. yes **no**
8. **yes** no

SAP Answers

bottom	swift
smell	loud
poodle	pillow
twinkle	skill
held	salt
scout	cool
after	self

Lesson 10

Lesson Objectives

1. Students will be tested on phonics concepts. (P)
2. Students will be tested on language concepts. (L)
3. Students will read the story they have written. (CW)
4. Students will take a spelling test. (S)
5. Students will copy a sentence neatly and correctly. (H)

Materials

Creative writing assignment from Lesson 9
Assessment for Lesson 10 (copy master)

Teaching

1. Use the assessment page as a phonics test. Have the students fill in the circles next to the words that complete the sentences at the top of the page.

2. Use the bottom of the assessment page. Have the student read the pairs of words. Write the contractions on the lines.

3. Have students take turns reading the books or stories that were written during the creative writing section of Lesson 9.

4. Have students number their paper from 1 to 14. Give the following words as dictation.

   Spelling word list:
   1. swift, 2. salt, 3. bottom, 4. held, 5. skill, 6. pillow, 7. loud,

   8. smell, 9. poodle, 10. twinkle, 11. scout, 12. self, 13. cool, 14. after

5. Use the handwriting sheet or have the children write the following sentences:

   Walt found the pink chalk on the stool.
   Mother stitched twelve gold skirts.

Assessment Answers

Part 1

1. snout
2. smoke
3. mouse
4. crow
5. spoon

Part 2

1. he'll
2. she's
3. we're
4. I'm
5. they'll
6. he's
7. she'll
8. they're
9. I'll
10. we'll

Lesson 11

1. Students will review silent letters. (L & P)
2. Students will review vowel digraphs (oo as in book, ow as in town). (L & P)
3. Students will spell words correctly. (S)
4. Students will prepare to read *The Day It Rained Bubbles*. (R)
5. Students will copy sentences neatly and correctly. (H)

Materials

LAR
SAP
The Day It Rained Bubbles

Teaching

1. Write the words **night, knock, lamb,** and **wrench.** Say: **All these words have something in common. Can you tell me what it is?** Give students the opportunity to respond. **They all have silent letters. We've read several words with silent e. But in these words the letters are not vowels. The silent letters are consonants.** Ask students to read each word. Have students tell you which letters are silent.

   Top of the LAR workbook page: **Read the sentences. In each sentence are words that have silent letters. Circle the silent letters that are consonants.**

2. Write the words book, moon, crown, and bowl. Have students look at the words *book* and *moon*. Underline the two oo's in each word.

   Ask: **Do these two words have the same vowels?** (Yes) **Do they have the same vowel sounds?** (No) **Some words have the same vowels, but different vowel sounds. The two o's make different sounds in these two words. If you are not sure which sound is used in a word, try them both. You may also be able to tell by reading other words in a sentence.**

   The two o's make one more sound. Write the word **door. In this word you simply follow the rule for vowel + r. It's pronounced like there is only one o. It has the *or* sound. There are two other words you may use that are spelled this way. They are *floor* and *poor*.**

   Point to crown and bowl. **Now let's talk about these two words. The o's work with the w's to make the vowel sounds in these words. The -ow can make the long o sound as in snow and blow. Which one of these words has the long o sound?** (bowl) **The -ow can also make the sound you hear in the word *now. Crown* has the same sound.**

   Bottom of the LAR workbook page: **Read the sentences. A word is underlined. Fill in the circle at the end of the sentence by the picture of a word that has the same vowel sound.** (The choices will be three of the following: book, moon, crown, bowl, and door.)

3. Use the SAP page. Have students read and spell each spelling word. Spelling list: poison, loyal, happy, beetle, shook, cookie, floor, night, knife, limb, write, tower, jaw, scream, shrink

   Top part: **Alphabetize the spelling words.**

   Bottom part: **Write the spelling words that have silent consonants.**

4. *The Day It Rained Bubbles* focuses on reviewing words used in about the first third of the first grade program. In addition to those words, the following words may be new to students and will require some instruction: airport, hairdos, arrested, awfully, everyone, factory, officer, smokestack, together.

The following are some suggestions to help children remember the words:

The word *airport:* the ai sound as in air has not yet been taught, but students can come close to the sound by making the long a sound and combining the -ir in one syllable. Students should be able to read the last syllable (port).

The word *hairdos:*	Take off the s and break into parts hair-do. The ai is the same as in the word airport. D-o is the word do. Add the s to make it plural.
The word *arrested:*	Underline the root word (rest). Point out the suffix (ed). Point out the prefix (a).
The word *awfully:*	Break into syllables aw-ful-ly. The students learned the aw sound in first grade and it will be reviewed this week. Point out the suffix. The y makes a long e sound.
The word *everyone:*	Separate the words every and one. Break the word every into parts ev-er-y. The y makes the long e sound.
The word *factory:*	Break into parts fac-tor-y. The y makes the long e sound.
The word *officer:*	Break into parts off-i-cer. The i is short. The c makes the s sound because it is followed by an e.
The word *smokestack:*	Break into two words smoke and stack.
The word *together:*	Break into parts to-ge-ther. The *e* in -ge- is short.

The following words (and abbreviations) were used in the first grade curriculum, but additional review may be helpful: Mr., Mrs., cookies, frightened.

Next, have the children read the word list on the back of the book. Students will begin reading the book in Lesson 12.

5. Use the handwriting sheet or have the children write the following sentences:

The comb is right by the brown book.
I need a wrench to fix the door knob.

SAP Answers

1. beetle	5. jaw
2. cookie	6. knife
3. floor	7. limb
4. happy	8. loyal

1. night	4. shook
2. poison	5. shrink
3. scream	6. tower
	7. write

Bottom section in any order:
night, knife, limb, write

LAR Answers

1. The comb is bright yellow.
2. Use a wrench to twist the tight bolt.
3. Don't cut your thumb with the knife.
4. Do you write with your right hand?
5. He wrestled the frightened lamb.

The Day it Rained Bubbles

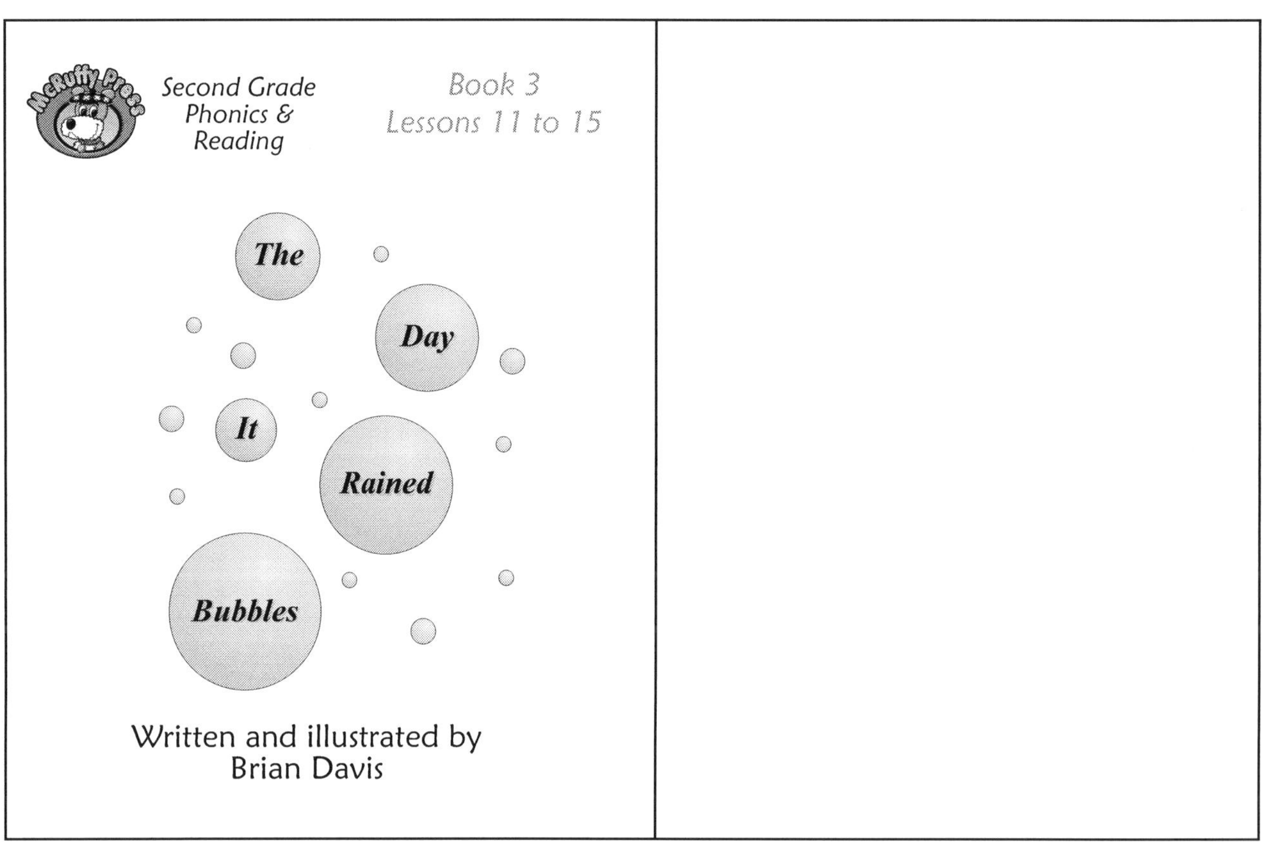

Something was wrong at the soap factory. The bubble maker was squealing. The boiler was making a screeching noise.

Pipes were spraying. Steam streamed from kettles. Lights were flashing. Sirens were squawking. People were running out the doors.

1

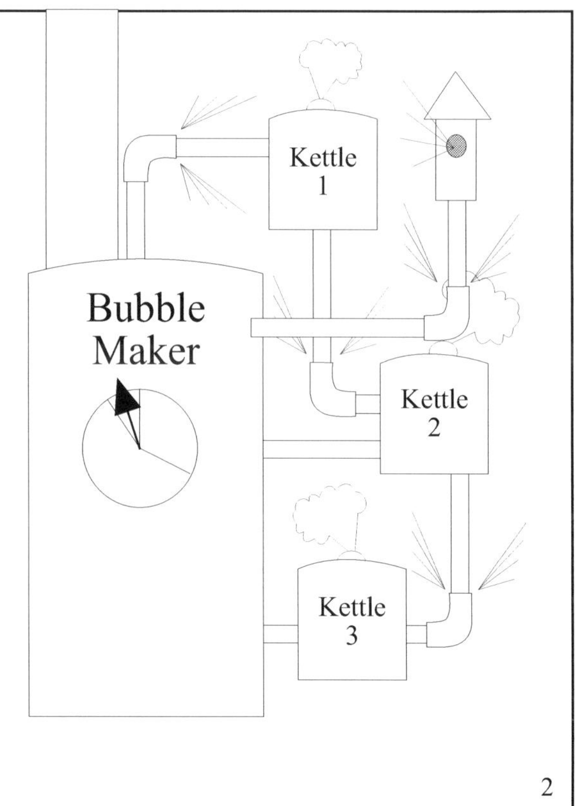

2

The Day it Rained Bubbles

Huge bubbles
came out of the smokestack.
They flew up into the sky. The bubbles floated higher and higher. The biggest bubble nudged a cloud.

Boom! It popped. The sound rumbled like thunder. The ground shook.

It made a mighty fright in the town. Billy fell off his bike. Kathy tumbled from her bed. She landed on the floor.

3

Soon the sky was filled with little bubbles. A squirrel sprung from a tree branch. It landed in a bubble.

The bubble scraped a chimney and popped. The squirrel tumbled into Mrs. Little's house. It was covered with soot.

The squirrel frightened Mrs. Little. Her screaming scared the squirrel. It ran right back up
the chimney.

4

The bubbles pleased Mrs. Dean.

"Will that be one bubble or two?" asked Mrs. Dean at her tea party.

Everyone looked so silly. They had bubble beards. They had bubble hairdos.

They ate bubble cookies and bubble jelly. The kitty made them chuckle the most. Mrs. Dean's kitty looked just like a poodle.

5

6

The Day it Rained Bubbles

The bubbles got together. They made bigger bubbles. Randy Brown got stuck in a huge bubble. He almost floated to the moon.

Randy Brown floated over the town. Quite a crowd began to watch. The bubble scraped the church steeple.

It sliced the bubble like a knife. Randy was left seated on the tower. He sat there for hours.

7

Popping bubbles made the streets slippery. Some cars squealed to a stop. The bubbles squirted from their tires. At least there were no wrecks.

Mr. Cook had a boat. He rowed to tow the cars. It was quite a sight. He made lots of money.

8

The mayor was eating a meal. Bubbles landed on his noodles. Bubbles fell down on the meat.

"I don't know what to do," sighed the mayor.

"Call the police!" shouted the cook.

The police arrested car loads of bubbles. Soon, the jail was crawling with bubbles. The bubbles squeezed right between the bars. They floated out the door. The jail was left squeaky clean.

9

10

The Day it Rained Bubbles

"I don't know what to do now," sighed the mayor.

"Call the dump trucks!" said the police officer.

The dump trucks plowed into the bubbles. Loaders filled the dump trucks. Trucks began to carry the bubbles from the town.

The bubbles blew out over the highway. The bubbles drifted back to town. The dump trucks were left bubbly clean.

"Look!" pointed a little boy.

About ninety bubbles became one big bubble. It filled the mayor with fear.

"Oh, no!" sighed the mayor. "I don't know what to do."

11

12

"Call the airport," said the dump truck driver.

The mayor did just that. Roy the pilot lassoed the big bubble in no time.

"Boy, this is an awfully big bubble," said Roy. "This may take a heap of power."

He towed it back to the soap factory. A fleet of choppers stuffed it into the smokestack. They lowered a huge cork. That kept it from squeezing out again.

13

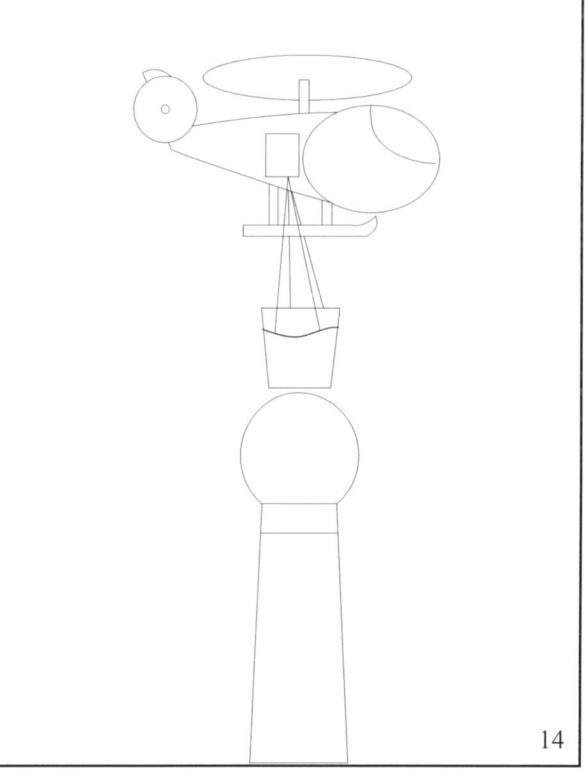

14

The Day it Rained Bubbles

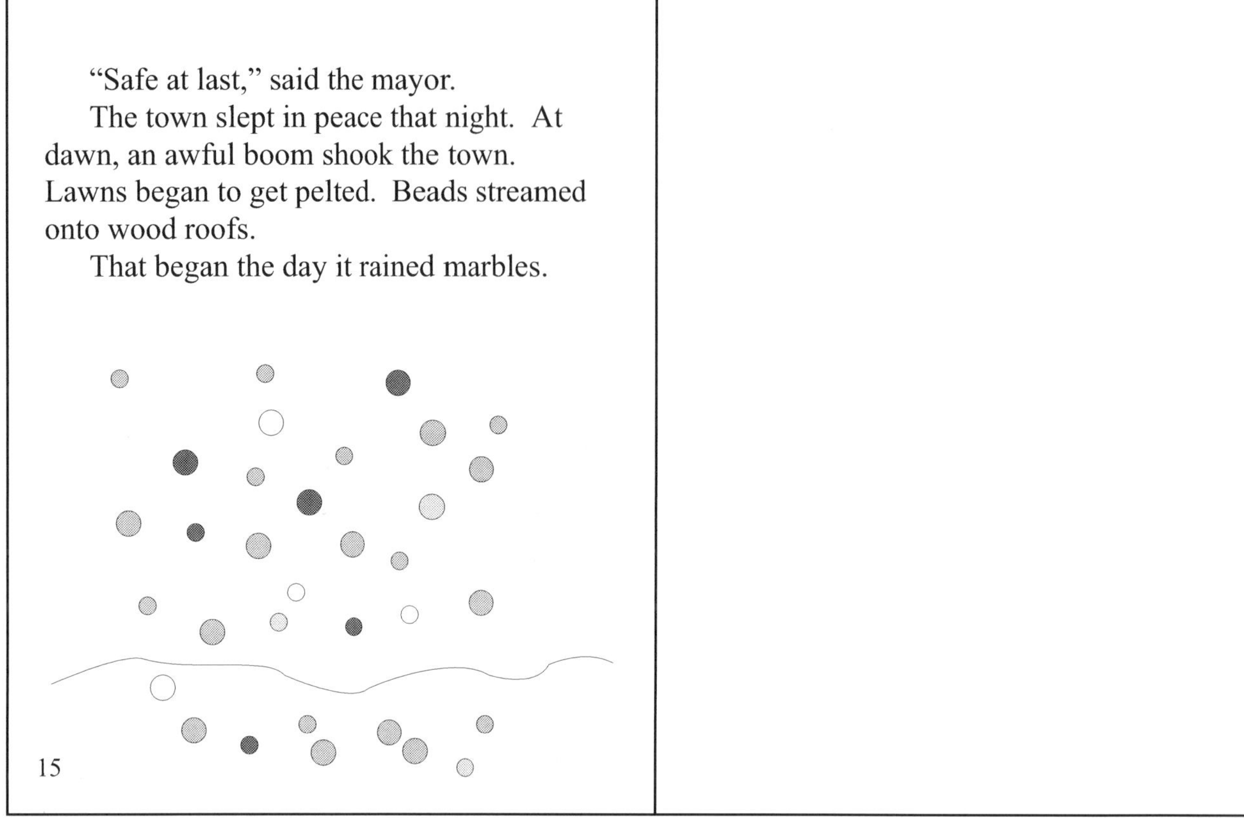

"Safe at last," said the mayor.

The town slept in peace that night. At dawn, an awful boom shook the town. Lawns began to get pelted. Beads streamed onto wood roofs.

That began the day it rained marbles.

15

The Day it Rained Bubbles

again
airport
almost
arrested
awful
awfully
beads
beards
became
began
between
bigger
biggest
Billy
boilcr
boom
boy
branch
Brown
bubble
bubbly
chimney
choppers
chuckle
church
clean
cloud
Cook
cookies
cork
covered
crawling
crowd
dawn
Dean
don't
doors
down
drifted
driver
dump
eating
everyone
factory
fear
filled
flashing
flcct
flew
floated
floor
fright
frightened
from
ground
hairdos
heap
higher
hours
house
huge
jelly
Kathy
kept
kettles
kitty
knife
know
landed
lassoed
last
lawns
least
left
lights
little
loaders
looked
lowered
maker
making
marblcs
mayor
meal
meat
mighty
money
moon
Mr.
Mrs.
ninety
noise
noodles
now
nudged
officer
out
party
peace
pelted
people
pilot
pipes
pleased
plowed
pointed
police
poodle
popped
power
praying
quite
rained
Randy
right
roofs
rowed
Roy
rumbled
running
scared
screeching
seated
shook
shouted
sighed
sight
silly
sirens
sky
slept
sliced
slippery
smokestack
soap
something
soot
sound
sprung
squawking
squeaky
squealed
squealing
squeezed
squirrel
squirted
steam
steeple
strcamcd
streets
stuck
stuffed
tea
them
there
they
thunder
together
towed
tower
town
trucks
tumbled
watch
what
wood
wrecks
wrong

Lesson 12

Lesson Objectives

1. Students will review three-letter beginning blends (scr, shr, spl, spr, squ, str). (P)
2. Students will review the suffix -er and learn the suffix -est. (L)
3. Students will review spelling words. (S)
4. Students will read the story *The Day It Rained Bubbles*. (R)
5. Students will copy sentences neatly and correctly. (H)

Materials

LAR
SAP
The Day It Rained Bubbles

Teaching

1. Put a matching exercise on the chalkboard. Write the blends scr, shr, spl, spr, squ, and str in a column. In a second column write the ending parts of the words: ice, eak, inkle, eam, eet, unk. Have students match beginning blends to the ends of words.

   Top of the LAR workbook page: **Correctly complete the words with missing letters. Add three letter beginning blends.**

2. Review the suffix -ed and introduce the suffixes -er and -est. Review the rules for adding suffixes:

   For long vowel words that do not end with a silent e, simply add the suffix: mean, meaner, meanest.

   This is also true for other vowel digraphs: round, roundest.

   For words that end with silent e, drop the silent e and add the suffix: wise, wiser, wisest.

   This is also true for other vowel digraphs: loose, looser, loosest.

   For one syllable words, if the last two letters in a word are a vowel and consonant, double the consonant and add the suffixes: big, bigger, biggest.

   Bottom of the LAR workbook page. **Add the suffixes -er and -est to each of the words.**

3. Use the top part of the SAP workbook page. **Fill in the boxes to make the spelling words. Start with the clue space, the letter o.**

   Use the bottom of the SAP workbook page. **Read the sentences. Letters are missing from spelling words. Add the missing vowels.**

4. Introduce the story *The Day It Rained Bubbles*. In this story, a soap machine goes crazy and creates all kinds of problems in a town.

   Review the additional reading vocabulary: airport, hairdos, arrested, awfully, everyone, factory, officer, smokestack, together. Students will now read pages 1 to 8.

   Next, ask the following questions:

   What caused Billy to fall off his bike? (The bubble popped.)
   What scared Mrs. Little? (a squirrel)
   How did the squirrel get in her house? (It fell down a chimney.)
   Why did people look silly at Mrs. Dean's tea party? (They had bubble beards and hairdos.)
   What kept Randy Brown from floating to the moon? (a church steeple)
   How did Mr. Cook make a lot of money? (He towed cars with his boat.)
   Who do you think liked the bubbles? (Mr. Cook, Mrs. Dean)

5. Use the handwriting sheet or have the children write the following sentences:

   The spring on the screen door squeaks.
   The striped cloth shrunk and split in half.

LAR Answers

Top

1. scraped
2. sprinkle
3. squirrel, shrub
4. splashed, stream
5. street, squeaked
6. sprayed, screen

Bottom

1. hotter, hottest
2. slower, slowest
3. cuter, cutest
4. wilder, wildest
5. louder, loudest

SAP Answers

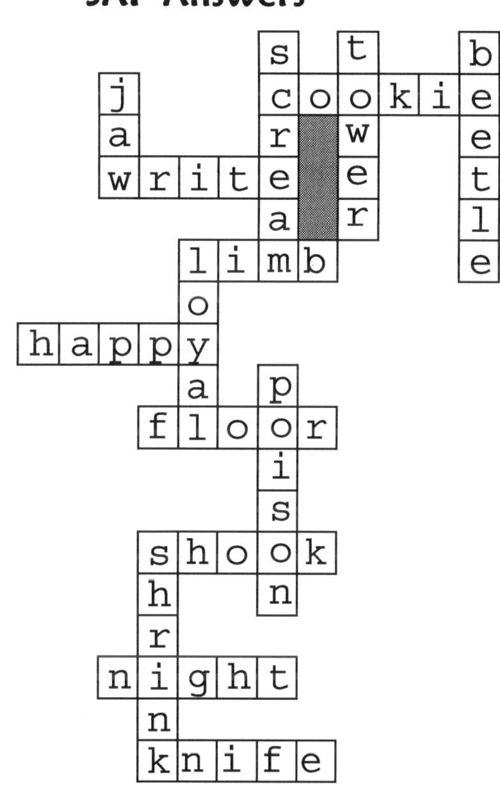

The beetle crawling on the floor made me scream.

A tree limb fell on the tower last night.

The loyal dog was so happy it shook its tail.

The poison made the weeds shrink.

We will slice the cookie with a knife

Lesson 13

Lesson Objectives

1. Students will review two syllable words. (P)
2. Students will review opposites. (L)
3. Students will review the spelling list. (S)
4. Students will read the story *The Day It Rained Bubbles*. (R)
5. Students will copy sentences neatly and correctly. (H)

Materials

LAR
SAP
The Day It Rained Bubbles
Writing Skills Workbook page is available

Teaching

1. Two syllable words that end with -le and the long e sound of y will be reviewed in this lesson. Review the term syllable. **Syllables are parts of a word that are said together. A syllable must have a vowel sound. Syllables are typically divided between consonants, especially double consonants. For example: penny is divided between the n's. Although each syllable has one of the double consonants, the sound of the consonant is only pronounced once. Syllables are never divided between digraphs (such as th in mother).**

   Write the words bubble, bottle, puppy, and donkey. Clap the syllables.

   Top of the LAR workbook page: **Choose the correct words from the list to complete each sentence.**

2. Review the term opposite. **Another name for an opposite is antonym.** Have students say the opposites for the following:

   hot (cold), **short** (tall), **wet** (dry)

   Bottom of the LAR workbook page: **Find the opposites of the words. Write the words on the lines. Choose words from the list.**

3. Use the SAP page. Write the word roof. **Look at the spelling words that are numbered in the box. The word *roof* has the letters r-o-o-f. What spelling word has an r, two o's, and an f?** (floor) **What number is next to it?** (7).

   On this page are short words that can be made from the spelling words. Find the spelling word that can be made from it and write the number for that spelling word on the lines. Find the word *wet.* It has two spaces. Two spelling words have the letters w-e-t. The number of sets of lines next to each word shows how many spelling words you need to find that contain those letters. Write numbers for each set of lines.

   Use the bottom of the SAP workbook page. **Read the seven sentences. A word is underlined in each sentence. Find a spelling word to take the place of the underlined word. Choose the word that changes the meaning of the sentence the least.**

4. Review the first half of the book *The Day It Rained Bubbles*. Next, read the second half of the book. After completing the story ask the students the following questions:

   What did the bubbles do to the mayor's meal? (Bubbles fell on the meat and noodles.)
   How did the bubbles get out of jail? (They squeezed through the bars.)
   Who did the police say to call? (the dump trucks)
   How did the bubble get back to the smokestack? (Roy towed it with his plane.)
   What did the choppers do? (stuffed the bubble in the smokestack and put a cork on it.)
   What happened the next day? (It rained marbles.)
   What are some other ways they might have gotten rid of the bubbles? (Answers vary.)
   What would you do if it rained bubbles? (Answers vary.)
   Do you think this could be a true story? (Answers vary.)
   What was there in this story that probably couldn't happen? (Answers vary.)

5. Use the handwriting sheet or have the children write the following sentences:

   Cathy can carry the candy apples.
   A thistle is on the saddle in the stable.

LAR Answers

Top

1. flower
2. nibbled
3. fluffy
4. monkey
5. buggy
6. tumbled

Bottom

1. girl
2. happy
3. light
4. grow
5. lumpy
6. big
7. far
8. day
9. down
10. weak

SAP Answers

Top

ice 6 or 7,12 wet 11,12

in 1,8,9,15 pay 3

let 4, I'm 10, all 2 ram 14 his 15

a 2,3,13,14 hit 8 race 14

fin 9 ears 14 so 1,5

Bottom

1. knife
2. scream
3. limb
4. poison
5. happy
6. cookie
7. beetle

Lesson 14

Lesson Objectives

1. Students will review words with vowel digraphs and diphthongs (-ea- long e, -oi-, -oy, and -aw-). (P)
2. Students will review synonyms. (L)
3. Students will review spelling words. (S & L)
4. Students will write a story. (CW)
5. Students will read the story *The Day It Rained Bubbles*. (R)
6. Students will copy sentences neatly and correctly. (H)

Materials

LAR
SAP
The Day It Rained Bubbles
Writing Skills Workbook page is available

Teaching

1. Write the words toy, noise, draw, and teach. **What letters make the vowel sounds in each word? The word *toy* and *noise* contain diphthongs. These are combinations of vowels that start as one vowel sound and slides to another. The word *teach* contains the long e sound.**

   LAR: **Solve the crossword puzzle.**

2. Review the term synonym. **Synonyms are words that have similar meanings.** Use the following examples: **What is a synonym for bunny?** (rabbit) **What is a synonym for huge?** (big, giant, jumbo, etc.)

   Write the following word list: little, law, lawn, noise, moist, clean, speak, dirty, bawl, joy.

   Students will need a piece of paper numbered to 10. You will say a word. The students will write the synonym from the list.

   1. damp, 2. tidy, 3. rule, 4. sound, 5. muddy,
   6. gladness, 7. weep, 8. small, 9. say, 10. yard

3. Use the SAP workbook page. **Match the spelling words to the descriptions. Write the words on the lines.**

4. The students will write a story. You may have students write the story on a piece of paper or make a book that can be illustrated. Students may illustrate the pages. Students may make up their own titles to the story.

   Introduce the activity: **Today you will make up a story about the day it rained marbles like at the end of the story *The Day It Rained Bubbles.***

   Have students think of some of the good things that could have happened if the ground was covered with marbles. What are some of the bad things? How did the marbles get there? How will the town get rid of them? Who might like the marbles? Who or what wouldn't like the marbles?

   It doesn't have to be a story with a plot. Maybe each page can tell what would be good or bad about the day it rained marbles.

   Story Option: Students may make up their own "unnatural disaster" instead of the one about marbles.

5. Read the book *The Day It Rained Bubbles* a second time. Next, have students look at the back of the book and answer the following questions about the word list. You may do this orally or have students write answers:

   What word is a synonym for scared? (frightened)
   What word is a synonym for roads? (streets)
   What word ends with -est? (biggest) **What is the root word?** (big)
   What words are foods you can eat? (cookies, jelly, meat, noodles)
   What word is a building where things are made? (factory)
   Find the words that begin with silent consonants. (knife, know, wrecks, wrong)
   Find the words that end with -le. (bubble, chuckle, little, people, poodle, steeple)
   What word is the opposite of whispered? (shouted)

6. Use the handwriting sheet or have the children write the following sentences:

   The boy oiled the joint that made the noise.
   We saw a seal crawl onto the beach.

LAR Answers

[1]B	E	A	C	H		[5]S	T	R	I	[17]P	E			[11]H	A	[12]P	P	Y
O						P				L				E		O		
T		[3]P	U	D	D	L	E			U				A		I		[16]B
T		A				A				[9]M	O	I	S	T		N		O
[2]L	A	W	[4]N			[7]S	H	R	U	B					[15]S	T	A	Y
E			I			H				E		[6]P				S		
			G		[13]C			[10]T	U	R	K	E	Y					
			H		O			O				E						
			T	O	W	N		Y			[14]C	L	A	W				

SAP Answers

beetle
knife
night
tower
loyal
shook
jaw
floor

shrink
limb
happy
write
scream
poison
cookie

Lesson 15

Lesson Objectives

1. Students will be tested on phonics concepts. (P)
2. Students will be tested on language concepts. (L)
3. Students will read the story they have written. (R)
4. Students will take a spelling test. (S)
5. Students will copy a sentence neatly and correctly. (H)

Materials

* Creative writing assignment from Lesson 14
* Assessment for Lesson 15

Teaching

1. Use the assessment for Lesson 15 as a phonics test. Have the students fill in the circles next to the words that complete the sentences.

2. Use the bottom of the assessment page. Read the words. Add the suffixes er and est to each word.

3. Have students take turns reading the books or stories that were written during the creative writing section of Lesson 14.

4. Have students number their papers from 1 to 15. Give the following words as dictation.

   Spelling word list:

   1. cookie, 2. tower, 3. shrink, 4. loyal, 5. knife, 6. beetle, 7. scream, 8. floor,

   9. happy, 10. shook, 11. limb, 12. poison, 13. jaw, 14. write, 15. night

5. Use the handwriting sheet or have the children write the following sentences:

   Did Sally eat the apples and peanut butter?
   Billy crawled across the floor on his knees.

Assessment Answers

1. squirted
2. knife
3. clown
4. cook
5. fuzzy

1. wetter, wettest
2. deeper, deepest
3. wider, widest
4. quicker, quickest
5. older, oldest

Lesson 16

Lesson Objectives

1. Students will read words with the -air sound. (P)
2. Students will learn about homophones. (L)
3. Students will spell words correctly. (S)
4. Students will prepare to read *The Bear With Carrot Hair.* (R)
5. Students will copy sentences neatly and correctly. (H)

Materials

LAR
SAP
The Bear With Carrot Hair
Writing Skills Workbook page is available

Word List Lessons 16 to 20:
air, aircraft, airport, airplane, affair, bare, barrel, bear, Blair, blare, care, careful, careless, carrot, carry, chair, cherry, Clair, dare, downstairs, fair, fare, flare, flair, ferret, glare, hair, hare, Harry, Kerry, lair, mare, marry, Mary, merry, pair, parrot, pear, prepare, rare, repair, scare, share, snare, spare, square, stair, stare, swear, tear, Terry, their, there, upstairs, very, ware, wear, where

Teaching

1. The sound the letters -air combine to make are a special sound. The a is blended with *ir* into a sound that acts like a diphthong. (Diphthongs are vowel combinations that begin as one sound and slide to another.) Names and other two-syllable words such as Terry, Jerry, marry, etc. have a similar sound although it is technically not the same. These words will be included in this grouping. No distinction will be made in this curriculum.

   Write the words scare, air, bear, Harry, Terry, and parrot. Students should be familiar with the word scare. Tell students that all the words have the same vowel sound. In the two syllable words, the vowel sound is used in the first syllable. Have students try to pronounce each of the words. Have students find the letters that make the -air sound.

   Top of the LAR workbook page: **Read the sentences. A word is missing. Fill in the missing word. The picture is a clue. A word list is given. Not all words will be used.**

2. Introduce the term homophone. **Homo means one and phone means sound. Homophone means one sound. Homophones are words that sound alike but have different spellings. For example: two, too, to. They each have different meanings.** Write the name Kerry. Ask students if they can think of a homophone for the name Kerry. (carry)

   Bottom of the LAR workbook page: **Read the pairs of sentences. In each pair of sentences are words that are homophones. Circle the homophones.**

3. Use the SAP workbook page. Have students read and spell each word. Spelling list: there, pear, cherry, hair, rare, very, pair, bear, marry, chair, fair, square, carry, airplane

   Alphabetize the two groups of words. At the bottom of the page, write the spelling words that are homophones of the six words.

4. *The Bear With Carrot Hair* focuses on reviewing words with the -air sound. In addition to those words, the following words may be new to students and will require some instruction: bought, careful, careless, downstairs, prepared, where.

   The following are some suggestions to help children remember the words:

The word *bought:*	The letters ough make the short o sound in this word. It rhymes with thought.
The words *careful* and *careless:*	Divide the words. Have students compare the two words.
The word *downstairs:*	Break into two words.
The word *prepared:*	Have students find the suffix and prefix. The e is long in pre-.
The word *where:*	The h can be pronounced, or it could be considered silent. The word has the air sound.

   Next, have the children read the word list on the back of the book. Students will begin reading the book in Lesson 17.

5. Use the handwriting sheet or have the children write the following sentences:

   Terry climbed the stairs to the airplane.
   Did Mary wear that pair of socks?

LAR Answers

1. parrot's
2. airplane
3. chair
4. pear
5. stairs

1. bear, bare
2. fair, fare
3. where, wear
4. hare, hair
5. marry, Mary, merry

SAP Answers

1. airplane	5. cherry
2. bear	6. fair
3. carry	7. hair
4. chair	8. marry

1. pair	4. square
2. pear	5. there
3. rare	6. very

hair	there
very	fair
marry	bear

The Bear With Carrot Hair

Second Grade
Phonics &
Reading

Book 4
Lessons 16 to 20

The Bear
With
Carrot
Hair

Written and illustrated by
Brian Davis

Clair the bear fell in love. So did Jerry the bear. All the bears thought they made a cute pair. One day, Jerry went to Clair's house.

He seemed kind of scared. Jerry knelt on one knee. Clair sat on a chair.

"I am prepared to marry you," said Jerry. "I want to share my life with you. I have a ring. Will you wear it?"

Clair was very happy.

"A bear like you is rare,"she said to Jerry. "I would love to marry you. Where is the ring? I want to wear it."

Jerry gave her the ring.

"I must tell my sister, Blair," said Clair. She ran up the stairs. She zoomed away like an airplane.

1

2

The Bear With Carrot Hair

The next few months they began to prepare. Clair and Blair shopped for clothes to wear. Clair bought a long white dress.

Jerry asked the baker to make a cake. "I would like a carrot cake," said Jerry.

"Yes," said the baker. "The cake will be square. It will have cherry icing."

3

4

It was the day before the wedding.

"We are all prepared," said Clair.

"Good," said Jerry. "Let's go to the town square. The Pear Fair is there."

The happy bear pair got on the bus. Jerry paid the fare. The bus took them to the Pear Fair.

The bears had so much fun. They rode a twirling barrel. They played games.

Clair won a toy parrot. Jerry won a stuffed hare. Jerry ate cherry pie. Clair ate pear pie.

5

6

The Bear With Carrot Hair

Next, they saw a ferret on a stage. A pretty bear was with him. Jerry stopped and stared.

"That bear has pretty hair," said Jerry.

Clair glared at Jerry.

"Your hair is pretty too," said Jerry.

7

"This bear wears my Bear Hair Spray," said the ferret. "Would you like a bottle?"

He held a bottle of Mr. Ferret's Bear Hair Spray.

"Yes," said Clair.

"Good," said Mr. Ferret. "Be careful. Don't use too much."

8

That night, Clair sprayed her hair. She wanted Jerry to stare at her hair. Clair was too careless.

"My hair will be very pretty," thought Clair.

She sprayed on more of Mr. Ferret's Bear Hair Spray. The next day, Clair looked at her hair. She was scared.

Her hair was not there! Her scalp was bare.

Blair came up the stairs.

"Clair, where is your hair?" asked Blair.

Clair began to cry. "Jerry will not want to marry me."

"He's waiting downstairs," said Blair.

"Tell him I can't marry him today," Clair said. Then she began to cry harder. Her bare bear scalp was too much to bear.

9

10

The Bear With Carrot Hair

Blair found Jerry downstairs.

"Clair will not marry you today," said Blair.

"Is she too scared?" asked Jerry.

"Clair was careless," said Blair. "She used too much Bear Hair Spray. Her hair fell out. Her scalp is bare."

"Oh no," said Jerry. "I must go talk to Mr. Ferret."

Jerry found Mr. Ferret. He was at the Pear Fair.

"Clair's hair fell out. Her scalp is bare," said Jerry.

"I told her to be careful," sighed Mr. Ferret. "It will grow back. For now, I think I can help. I know a clown. His name is Carrot. He is a friend of mine."

Mr. Ferret took Jerry to Carrot. The clown gave him a large box. Mr. Ferret helped carry the box.

11

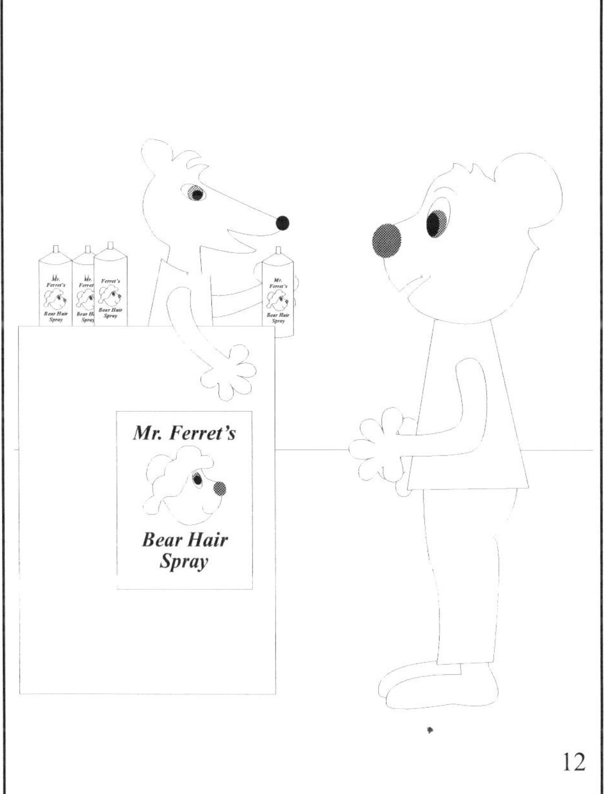

12

Blair went to Clair. "Jerry has something for you," said Blair. "Now you can marry him."

In Blair's hand was a wig. It was as orange as a carrot.

"I will look silly," said Clair. "All my friends will stare."

"But, Jerry wants to marry you," said Blair. "You have a big carrot cake. It has cherry icing.

There are bears downstairs. They are sitting in chairs. They were very merry. They want to see you marry Jerry."

Clair sighed, "I will wear the carrot orange wig. I will marry Jerry."

13

14

The Bear With Carrot Hair

Clair was very scared. She looked silly in carrot orange hair.

Clair came into the room. All she could do was stare.

Suddenly, Clair began to giggle. Bears were standing next to chairs. All the bears were wearing wigs. All the bears had carrot orange hair.

15

The Bear With Carrot Hair

airplane
baker
bare
barrel
bear
began
Blair
bottle
bought
careful
careless
carrot
carry
cherry
Clair
clothes
clown
cry
downstairs
dress
fair
fare

ferret
found
friend
games
giggle
glared
good
grow
hair
happy
harder
hare
house
icing
Jerry
knee
knelt
large
long
love
marry
merry
months
much

next
night
now
orange
paid
pair
parrot
pear
pie
played
prepared
pretty
rare
scalp
scared
share
shopped
sister
sitting
something
sprayed
square
stage

stairs
standing
stare
stared
stuffed
suddenly
talk
there
thought
today
took
twirling
very
waiting
wanted
wear
wearing
wears
wedding
where
white
wig
zoomed

Lesson 17

Lesson Objectives

1. Students will identify words that have the -air sound. (P)
2. Students will proofread sentences. (L)
3. Students will review spelling words. (S)
4. Students will read *The Bear With Carrot Hair.* (R)
5. Students will copy sentences neatly and correctly. (H)

Materials

LAR
SAP
The Bear With Carrot Hair

Teaching

1. Write the words dear and swear. Ask students to identify thelast three letters in each word. Read the words to the students. Ask which word has the -air sound. Ask what sound is in the other word (dear-long e).

   Top of the LAR workbook page: **Read the sentences. In each sentence is a word in bold print. Fill in the circle next to the airplane if the word has the *air* sound (as in the word air and swear). Fill in the circle next to the gear if it has the *ear* sound (as in the word gear and ear).**

2. Use the bottom of the LAR page. **Look for mistakes such as missing ending punctuation (periods, question marks, apostrophes) and capitalization (beginning and names). Fill in the missing punctuation and circle the words that need to be capitalized.**

3. Use the SAP workbook page. **All the spelling words have the letter r in them. Fit the words in the boxes at the top of the page.**

   Bottom section. **Look at the pictures. The words in the sentences that describe the pictures are all mixed up. Write the sentences in the correct order.**

4. Introduce the story *The Bear With Carrot Hair.* **In this story, two bears fall in love. They decide to get married. Something terrible happens the day of the wedding. Read the book to find out how the bears solved their problem.** Review the additional reading vocabulary: bought, careful, careless, downstairs, prepared, where.

   Students will read pages 1 to 8. Next, ask the following questions:

   Why was Jerry scared at the beginning of the story? (He was going to ask Clair to marry him.)
   Why do you think that scared him? (Answers vary.)
   What was the wedding cake like? (square, carrot cake, cherry icing)
   Where did Blair and Jerry go the day before the wedding? (the Pear Fair)
   What did they do there? (rode a barrel ride, won prizes, ate pie)
   What was the ferret selling? (Mr. Ferret's Bear Hair Spray)
   Why do you think Clair wanted a bottle? (Answers vary.)
   Why do you think Clair glared at Jerry? (Answers vary.)
   What does it meant to glare? (to stare at angrily)

5. Use the handwriting sheet or have the children write the following sentences:

   Kerry has strawberry blond hair.
   Did Larry repair the tear on the chair?

LAR Answers

1. ● ○
2. ● ○
3. ○ ●
4. ● ○
5. ○ ●

1. kerry the hare was very fast.
2. the barrel rolled down the stairs.
3. can clair fly Terry's airplane?
4. jerry didn't repair larry's car.
5. did mary feed Harry's parrot?

SAP Answers

Top section: answer order may vary within each box shown below.

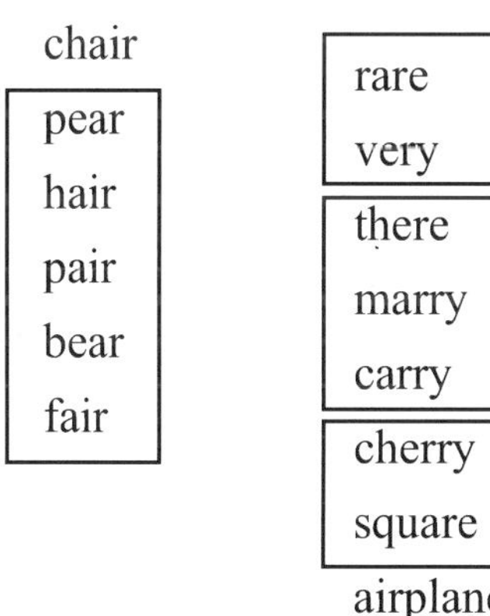

Bottom section
The bear ate from the cherry tree.
The square chair is very light.

Lesson 18

Lesson Objectives

1. Students will review words spelled with -air. (P)
2. Students will read about prairie dogs. (R & L)
3. Students will add suffixes to spelling words. (S)
4. Students will complete analogies with spelling words. (S & L)
5. Students will read the story *The Bear With Carrot Hair*. (R)
6. Students will copy sentences neatly and correctly. (H)

Materials

LAR
SAP
Question Words poster (Resource Pack)
The Bear With Carrot Hair

Teaching

1. Use the top of the LAR workbook page: **Complete the sentences using one of the words spelled with the letters a-i-r.**

2. Use the bottom of the LAR workbook page. **Look at the pictures of the animals. What can you tell me about them just by looking at the pictures?** (answers vary)

   Students will read about prairie dogs and answer the questions. Help students read the word prairie dog. Have them find the letters that make the -air sound.

   After students have finished, ask: What was the main topic of the first paragraph? (Prairie dogs bark to warn other prairie dogs.) What is the main topic of the second paragraph? (Prairie dogs build towns.)

   Use the question words poster. **Look at the poster. Questions begins with words such as: who, what, where, when, why, or how. Think of any question that begins with who.** (Example: Who is you mother?) Repeat with the other question words.

   Make up 3 questions about prairie dogs from the information you read. Next have students write their own questions about prairie dogs that are answered in the article.

   Display the poster where it can be seen for future reference.

3. Introduce adding suffixes to words ending with y. Use the top of the SAP workbook page and work through the examples with the students. **We know that sometimes you have to change the spelling of words before you add a suffix like ed or ing. That's true with words that end with y. The y is dropped and an i is added when adding ed or s to words that end with y. When adding s, also add an e. Look at the example. Puppy becomes puppies. The y is changed to i and es is added.**

   Look at the example with hurry. The y is dropped and i is added with the suffix ed to make the word *hurried.*

   Apply the spelling rules and add suffixes to cherry, carry, and marry.

4. Use the bottom of the SAP page. **Use spelling words to complete the analogies. An analogy is when we compare two different sets of things. Such as big is to little as hot is to cold. Compare the first two things and then compare the last two things the same way. Big and little are opposites, so you would compare hot to its opposite.**

   What if I had said small is to little as big is to ____.
   What might fill in the blank? (large)

   Sometimes the relationship might be a grouping such as one is to number as A is to (letter).

   The relationship could be a part to whole relationship.
   Arm is to person as tire is to (car).

   Complete the analogies on the workbook page using spelling words.

5. Review the first half of the book *The Bear With Carrot Hair.* Next, read the second half of the book. After completing the story ask the students the following questions:

   What happened to Clair's hair? (It fell out.)
   What caused it to fall out? (She used too much Bear Hair Spray.)
   Did Jerry still want to marry her? (Yes)
   Who did Jerry find to help him? (Mr. Ferret)
   Who gave Jerry the box? (Carrot the Clown)
   What was in the box? (carrot orange wigs)
   How did Jerry solve Clair's problem? (He gave her a wig)
   How did the wig help Clair? (Answers vary.)
   Do you think this could be a true story? (Answers vary.)
   What was there in this story that probably couldn't happen? (Answers vary.)

6. Use the handwriting sheet or have the children write the following sentences:

   The barrels were filled with carrots and pears.
   The parrot glared at the ferret.

LAR Answers

1. hair
2. chair
3. fair
4. air
5. pair

1. ○ yes ● no
2. ● yes ○ no
3. ● yes ○ no
4. ○ yes ● no
5. ○ yes ● no

SAP Answers

Top

cherries	
carried	carries
married	marries

Bottom

airplane	pear
square	chair
bear	there

Lesson 19

Lesson Objectives

1. Students will choose the correct form of a word. (L)
2. Students will read the story *The Bear With Carrot Hair.* (R)
3. Students will practice writing spelling words. (S)
4. Students will write a story. (CW)
5. Students will copy sentences neatly and correctly. (H)

Materials

LAR
SAP
The Bear With Carrot Hair
Writing Skills Workbook page is available

Teaching

1. Review suffixes -ing and -ed. Have students add ing to the word wear. Have students add ed to spare. Next, use the top of the LAR workbook page. **Fill in the oval next to the correct form of the word that completes the sentences.**

2. Read the book *The Bear With Carrot Hair* a second time. Next, have students look at the back of the book and answer the following questions about the word list. You may do this orally or have students write answers:

   What words can be things you eat? (cake, carrot, cherry, icing, orange, pear, pie)
   Find the words that have homophones in the list. (bare, bear, fair, fare, hair, hare, marry, merry, pair, pear, wear, where)
   What word is the opposite of standing? (sitting) **What is the root word?** (sit)
   What word is the opposite of upstairs? (downstairs)
   What words begin with silent letters? (knee, knelt)
   Find the words that have the suffix -er. (baker, harder) Note: sister ends with er but the er is not a suffix in this word.
   What words are synonyms of the word looked? (glared, stared)

   Use the bottom of the LAR page. **Answer the questions about the story. Fill in the ovals, yes or no.**

3. Use the SAP page. **Write the spelling words the match each description.**

4. The students will write a story. You may have students write the story on a piece of paper or make a book that can be illustrated. Books will again need a cover sheet and two additional sheets. Students may illustrate the pages. Students may make up their own titles to the story.

   Introduce the activity: **Today you will make up a story about an airplane ride.** Students can make themselves the main character, other people, or an animal. They can even use Jerry and Clair. They may be flying somewhere on their honeymoon.

   The following questions can be used for brainstorming:

   Have students think of where the airplane is going. What will they see? What will they do? Did anything unusual happen at the airport? or on the airplane? Was someone special on the airplane? Maybe the character will have to fly the plane. Why is the character on the plane? Maybe the airplane is one that the character built. What was it made of? How did the character build it?

5. Use the handwriting sheet or have the children write the following sentences:

   Did Sherry or Kerry marry Harry?
   I was very scared of the bear.

LAR Answers

1. ● share ○ shared ○ sharing
2. ● stared ○ staring ○ stare
3. ○ repaired ● repairing ○ repair
4. ○ care ● caring ○ cared
5. ○ glaring ○ glare ● glared
6. ● air ○ airing ○ aired
7. ○ prepare ● preparing ○ prepared

1. ○ yes ● no
2. ● yes ○ no
3. ○ yes ● no
4. ● yes ○ no
5. ● yes ○ no
6. Answers vary. Sample answer:

She wanted to have nice hair like the bear at the fair.

SAP Answers

bear	very
pear	chair
square	cherry
hair	marry
carry	rare
pair	fair
airplane	there

Lesson 20

Lesson Objectives

1. Students will be tested on phonics concepts. (P)
2. Students will be tested on language concepts. (L)
3. Students will take a spelling test. (S)
4. Students will read the story they have written. (R)
5. Students will read a poem. (L & R)
6. Students will copy a sentence neatly and correctly. (H)

Materials

LAR
Creative writing assignment from Lesson 19
Assessment for Lesson 20

Teaching

1. Use part A of the assessment as a phonics test. **Fill in the circles next to the words that complete the sentences.**

2. Use part B of the assessment page. **Alphabetize the list of words. Write a number to show the order in the box before each word.**

3. Because so many of the words have homophones, a spelling dictation test would be confusing. The test this week will be written. *Use part C of the assessment page.* Students will fill in the circle next to the correctly spelled word in each set.

4. Have students take turns reading the books or stories that were written during the creative writing section of Lesson 19.

5. Prepare students to read the poem. It may contain some words students have not learned to read such as frightening, pajamas, and tomorrow.

   Have you every been afraid to go to bed at night? Have you ever thought something could be hiding in the dark? Today you'll read a poem about something that is hiding upstairs in a house.

   Before you read let's talk about poetry a little. There are many forms and kinds of poetry. Some poems rhyme and some don't. This is a rhyming poem. See if you can pick out the pattern of rhymes.

   It's also arranged in groups of four sentences. This is called a quatrain. It is a common way to organize a poem.

   The poem is reprinted on the next page. After reading the poem discuss the content and style.

   What was the rhyming pattern in each quatrain (four sentences)? (The first two sentences rhymed and the last two sentences rhymed in each quatrain.)

   What was the person afraid of? (his or her brother)

   What do you think will happen the next night? Do you think the brother will be scared? Why or why not?

What is a grizzly lair? (A lair is the home of a wild animal. A grizzly is a kind of bear.)
It really has a double meaning. Grizzly is a kind of bear, it can also mean *a terrible thing*. So it can mean a bear's den or a very terrible place to go.

What phrases let you know the person going up the stairs was afraid?

A poem can be a short way to tell a story. Tell the story of the poem in another way that doesn't rhyme. Tell what happened in the poem.

6. Use the handwriting sheet or have the children write the following sentences:

   I saw Mary wearing that pair of pants.
   Where is their pet hare, Blair?

Assessment Answers

Part A
1. carrot
2. Where
3. share
4. hare
5. carry

Part B
2 5 1 4 3

Part C

1. ○ baar	● bear	○ baer		8. ○ earplane	● airplane	○ airplaine
2. ○ rair	● rare	○ rere		9. ● very	○ vairy	○ bery
3. ● square	○ sqaure	○ squair		10. ○ karry	● carry	○ cairy
4. ○ tere	○ threre	● there		11. ○ mery	○ mairry	● marry
5. ○ hiar	○ haire	● hair		12. ○ payre	○ piar	● pair
6. ● chair	○ chere	○ chare		13. ○ charry	○ cheiry	● cherry
7. ○ fiar	● fair	○ farre		14. ● pear	○ paer	○ peair

Upstairs Scare

There's something lurking up the stairs
With beady eyes, a frightening glare
Soon my fear I'll have to face
To my bed I'll have to race.

Mom says it's time that I prepare
With the pajamas I will wear
Then I hear a little growl
I think the beast is on the prowl

"Don't make me go, show that you care
Don't send me to the grizzly lair"
With that my mom just had to smile
"The beast has waited quite awhile"

So one by one the stairs I climb
The beast will pounce most any time
It's my brother's turn, it's only fair
But, tomorrow *I* get to be the bear

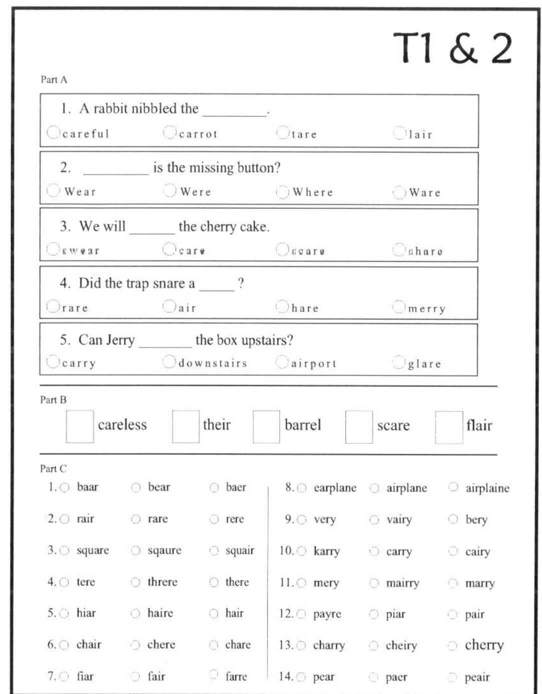

T1 & 2

Part A

1. A rabbit nibbled the ________.
○ careful ○ carrot ○ tare ○ lair

2. ________ is the missing button?
○ Wear ○ Were ○ Where ○ Ware

3. We will ______ the cherry cake.
○ swear ○ care ○ scare ○ share

4. Did the trap snare a _____?
○ rare ○ air ○ hare ○ merry

5. Can Jerry ______ the box upstairs?
○ carry ○ downstairs ○ airport ○ glare

Part B

☐ careless ☐ their ☐ barrel ☐ scare ☐ flair

Part C

1. ○ baar	○ bear	○ baer	8. ○ earplane	○ airplane	○ airplaine
2. ○ rair	○ rare	○ rere	9. ○ very	○ vairy	○ bery
3. ○ square	○ sqaure	○ squair	10. ○ karry	○ carry	○ cairy
4. ○ tere	○ threre	○ there	11. ○ mery	○ mairry	○ marry
5. ○ hiar	○ haire	○ hair	12. ○ payre	○ piar	○ pair
6. ○ chair	○ chere	○ chare	13. ○ charry	○ cheiry	○ cherry
7. ○ fiar	○ fair	○ farre	14. ○ pear	○ paer	○ peair

Lesson 21

Lesson Objectives

1. Students will read words with the wh digraph. (P)
2. Students will spell words correctly. (S)
3. Students will prepare to read *Mary, Whiskers, and the Whale*. (R)
4. Students will copy sentences neatly and correctly. (H)

Materials

LAR
SAP
Mary, Whiskers, and the Whale

Word List Lessons 21 to 25:
whack, whale, wham, whap, what, wheat, wheel, wheeze, when, where, whether, which, whiff, while, whim, whimper, whine, whip, whir, whirl, whisk, whisker, whisper, whistle, white, whither, whittle, whiz, whoa, whoops, whoosh, why

Teaching

1. The w-h digraph is traditionally pronounced hw. Making the h silent is also acceptable. Use whichever you prefer. Choose words from the list on the next page and have children try to read them.

   Top of the LAR workbook page: **Read the sentences. A word is missing. Fill in the missing word. The picture is a clue. A word list is given. Not all words will be used.**

2. Use the SAP workbook page. Have students read and spell each spelling word. **Today we're not going to alphabetize the list. You're going to sort the words by vowel sounds. You'll write each word one time. One word has the sounds you hear in the word air. Write it on the first line. The vowel sound is spelled differently.**

   Two words have two vowel sounds. Write those words on the next lines. Finish sorting the other words on the page. Write a word on each set of lines.

3. *Mary, Whiskers, and the Whale* focuses on words that begin with the wh- digraph. In addition to those words, the following words may be new to students and will require some instruction: corner, good-bye, library, woman.

   The following are some suggestions to help children remember the words. The words are on the LAR page. Have students read the words using the pronunciation guides. **Read the words. Complete the sentences using the words.**

   The word *corner:* Break the word into syllables, cor-ner
   The word *good-bye:* The -ye in bye makes the long i sound.
   The word *library:* Break into syllables. li- the i is long. -brar- has the *air* sound. Y makes the long e sound.
   The word *woman:* Wo-man. The o is long.

   Introduce the story: Ask a student to read the title of the book. Ask what words have the wh digraph. (Whiskers, Whale) Tell students that the story is about a whale with a problem. Ask students what they know about whales.

   Beginning this week, students will first read the story silently. Students will read as much of the story as they can in the time allowed.

4. Use the handwriting sheet or have the children write the following sentences:

   Whack the bug with a whisk broom.
   The wheat flour was white.

LAR Answers

1. white
2. whiskers
3. whale
4. wheel
5. whip

1. woman
2. library
3. corner
4. goodbye

SAP Answers

order can vary for categories with two or more answers

air sound where

two vowel sounds whisker, whimper

Long e wheat, wheel

Long a whale

Long i while, white, why

Long o whoa

One vowel: Vowel + r whirl

Short o what

One vowel: short i which, whip

Mary, Whiskers, and the Whale

One day, Barry was fishing. The line whirled off the spool. Barry sat down and waited.

Wham! Something bit the hook.

"What is that?" thought Barry.

The fishing pole almost bent in half.

"It feels like a baby whale!"

He wheeled in the line. Barry stared at the end of his fishing pole.

"It looks like a baby whale, too!"

Barry loaded the whale onto his car. He was careful not to hurt the whale. Still, the whale began to whimper.

"We will be home soon," said Barry.

Barry whirled around a corner. The whale flew off the car. Barry didn't know the whale was gone. He kept driving.

1

2

Mary, Whiskers, and the Whale

The whale landed in a swimming pool.

"Ahh," whispered the whale.

It was glad to be back in the water. The whale was as big as the pool. A white dog started barking at the whale. Its name was Whiskers.

The whale waved at the dog. Its fin made a splash. A wave of water soaked Whiskers. Whiskers the white dog whimpered. He ran to the house.

3

4

"What are you scared of Whiskers? Why are you so wet?" asked the little girl. Her name was Mary.

"Arf, arf, arf," said Whiskers the white dog.

"A whale is in the swimming pool?" asked Mary.

"Arf, arf, arf," answered Whiskers.

"And it splashed you. I see," said Mary.

"Arf, arf?" asked Whiskers.

"I don't know what to do," answered Mary. "I'll go ask my mom."

Mary ran into the house. Her mom was upstairs.

"Mom!" yelled Mary. "A whale is in the the swimming pool. What should I do?"

Her mom was working. "Get a net. Whisk it away."

"OK.," said Mary. She ran back to Whiskers.

"How did a snail get in the pool?" thought mom.

5

6

Mary, Whiskers, and the Whale

Mary got a net. The whale wouldn't whisk away.

"I don't think this is going to work," said Mary. "Baby whale, you can't stay here. What will we do?"

7

The whale wheezed. Water whooshed out of its top. The water whacked Whiskers the white dog. Whiskers whimpered.

"Arf, arf," barked Whiskers.

"That's a good idea," said Mary. "Help me carry the skates."

8

Mary, Whiskers, and the whale put on skates. They wheeled down the street. They went to the library. Mary looked for a book about whales.

"Where are the whale books?" Mary asked a woman behind a desk.

The woman didn't look up. She just pointed to a shelf.

"Thank you," said Mary.

9

10

Mary, Whiskers, and the Whale

She found a book. Mary looked inside the book.

"It says that your home is the sea."

The whale nodded yes. As the whale nodded it bumped the shelf. Wham! The shelf toppled over.

The woman at the desk looked up. She pointed to a sign. It said: "No whales or dogs in the library".

Whiskers and the whale whimpered. Mary, Whiskers, and the whale left.

11

12

The whale whiffed the air. It wheeled down the street.

"Come back!" yelled Mary. "Where are you going?"

Whiskers and Mary chased the whale. They came to a store. A sign on the store said: "Mr. Whittle's Fresh Fish."

The store was a wreck. A man had a broom. He was whipping the whale.

"Bad whale! Bad whale!" yelled Mr. Whittle. "You ate all my fish. You wrecked my store!"

The whale whimpered. Mary, Whiskers, and the whale repaired the store.

13

14

Mary, Whiskers, and the Whale

"That is better," said Mr. Whittle. "But I have no fish."

"Why don't you take the whale fishing?" asked Mary. "He's good at it."

"Why not," said Mr. Whittle. "I have nothing left to sell."

They got into a truck. Mr. Whittle drove to the sea. The whale was happy. It scooped up some fish. The whale filled Mr. Whittle's truck with fish.

"Thank you, whale," said Mr. Whittle.

"You are a good whale," said Mary.

"Arf, arf," said Whiskers the white dog.

The whale waved good-bye. Its fin whacked the water. Whoosh! The wave of water whacked Whiskers again.

15

Mary, Whiskers, and the Whale

about
almost
answered
arf
around
away
baby
Barry
began
bent
better
book
broom
bumped
careful
carry
chased
come
corner
desk
didn't
down
fishing
flew
found
going
gone
good-bye
half
he's
hook
its
kept
know
left
library
loaded
looks
Mary
nothing
over
pointed
pool
repaired
scared
scooped
sea
shelf
sign
some
something
splashed
spool
stared
swimming
thank
think
thought
toppled
truck
upstairs
waited
water
whacked
whale
wham
what
wheeled
wheezed
where
whiffed
whimper
whimpered
whipping
whirled
whisk
Whiskers
whispered
white
Whittle
whoa
whoosh
whooshed
why
woman
work
wouldn't
wreck

Lesson 22

Lesson Objectives

1. Students will complete questions using wh words. (P)
2. Students will complete sentences using opposites. (L)
3. Students will use spelling words in sentences. (S)
4. Students will read the story *Mary, Whiskers, and the Whale.* (R)
5. Students will copy sentences neatly and correctly. (H)

Materials

LAR
SAP
Mary, Whiskers, and the Whale
Writing Skills Workbook page is available

Teaching

1. **Questions begin with certain words that ask something. Many of these words begin with wh.** Write the words where, what, when, and why. **Read these words. Each word indicates the kind of information a question is asking. Where is asking for a place. What is asking what happened or what was used. When asks for a time. Why asks for a reason.**

   Top of the LAR workbook page: **Read the sentences. Complete them with the correct word for the question. Fill in the oval next to either where, what, when, or why to complete each question.**

2. **Name two words that are opposites. Use the bottom of the LAR page. Read the first sentence. A word is in black print. Complete the second sentence using the opposite of the black word.**

3. Use the SAP page. **Complete the sentences using spelling words.
   The list is at the top of the page.**

4. Review the additional reading vocabulary: corner, good-bye, library, woman

   Students will read pages 1 to 8 out loud. Next, ask the following questions:

   How did Barry get a whale? (He caught it while fishing.)
   **What do you think Barry did when he discovered the whale
   was missing?** (Answers vary.)
   What do you think Barry was going to do with the whale? (Answers vary.)
   How did Whiskers get wet? (The whale splashed him.)
   What did Mary's mother think was in the swimming pool? (a snail)
   Why did the mother misunderstand Mary? (She was busy working)
   Why do you think the whale couldn't stay in the pool? (Answers vary.)

5. Use the handwriting sheet or have the children write the following sentences:

   The whirling wind whooshed.
   Did she use a whisk to whip the cream?

LAR Answers

Top

1. What
2. Where
3. Why
4. When
5. Where
6. Why
7. What

Bottom

1. down
2. white
3. whispered
4. little
5. hard

SAP Answers

1. white
2. whiskers
3. Which, wheat
4. whale
5. whip
6. whoa
7. Why, whimper
8. Where, wheel

Why and Where may be switched in answers 7 and 8.

Lesson 23

Lesson Objectives

1. Students will review rhymes and spelling words. (L & S)
2. Students will read about whales. (R & L)
3. Students will read the story *Mary, Whiskers, and the Whale.* (R)
4. Students will copy sentences neatly and correctly. (H)

Materials

LAR
SAP
Question Poster
Mary, Whiskers, and the Whale

Teaching

1. **Say and spell the spelling word that rhymes with these words:**

   1. night, 2. temper, 3. dry, 4. bear, 5. pitch, 6. crow, 7. feel, 8. chip, 9. file, 10. pail, 11. feet, 12. brisker, 13. pearl, 14. bought

   Answers: 1. white, 2. whimper, 3. why, 4. where, 5. which, 6. whoa, 7. wheel, 8. whip, 9. while, 10. whale, 11. wheat, 12. whisker, 13. whirl, 14. what

   Next, use the SAP page. **Look at the words at the top of the page. The spelling words are written without vowels. Fill in the missing vowels.**

   On the second part of the page, five sentences are written with mistakes. Words are spelled wrong and the ending punctuation mark is missing. Circle the misspelled words and write them correctly on the lines. You will write more than one word on each line. Write the correct punctuation mark at the end of each sentence. It will be a period or a question mark.

2. Use the LAR workbook page. **Look at the pictures on the page. What can you tell me just by looking at the pictures and reading the captions?**

   Read about whales and answer the questions. Write words to complete the sentences about whales. After students have finished continue the discussion:

   What is the author trying to teach? (Information about whales)
   What are flukes? (the two parts of the tail)
   What in the text can help you find the meaning of flukes quickly? (Look forflukes on bold print.)
   What is the main topic of the article? (Whales)
   What are the topics of the first paragraph? (The size ofwhales and how they swim.)
   What is the main topic of the second paragraph? (How whales breathe)
   What is the main topic of the third paragraph? (What whales eat)

   Use the Question Poster. **Write three questions about whales. Use the question words to begin the questions.**

   Pick one kind of whale and do more research. Compare your information to the information in the workbook.

3. Review the first half of the book *Mary, Whiskers, and the Whale*. Next, read the second half of the book. After completing the story ask the students the following questions:

   Where was the first place the whale went on skates? (the library)
   How did the shelf get tipped over? (The whale bumped it.)
   Where did the whale go next? (to Mr. Whittle's fish store)
   How did the whale get back home? (in Mr. Whittle's truck)
   How did the whale help Mr. Whittle? (It caught him some fish.)
   Do you think this could be a true story? (Answers vary.)
   What was there in this story that probably couldn't happen? (Answers vary.)

4. Use the handwriting sheet or have the children write the following sentences:

   The white dog whiffed the air. Where is the truck's wheel?

LAR Answers

1. milk
2. water
3. whistle
4. fish, squid (or birds)
5. flukes

SAP Answers

Answers in the box may be switched.

whale	wheat wheel where which
while	whip white whoa why

whirl what whisker whimper

1. whip white period
2. Which whimper question mark
3. Where wheat question mark
4. What whale question mark
5. why whiskers period

Lesson 24

Lesson Objectives

1. Students will unscramble sentences. (L & P)
2. Students will read the story *Mary, Whiskers, and the Whale*. (R)
3. Students will review spelling words. (S)
4. Students will write a story. (CW)
5. Students will copy sentences neatly and correctly. (H)

Materials

LAR
SAP
Mary, Whiskers, and the Whale
Writing Skills Workbook page is available

Teaching

1. Write a mixed up sentence: the stop? will car When. **Look at the words and rearrange them into a sentence. What word comes first?** (write a 1 above the word When). Continue with the other words. (When will the car stop?)

   Use the top of the LAR page. **Number the words in each sentence in the correct order.**

2. Read the book *Mary, Whiskers, and the Whale* again. Next, have students look at the back of the book and answer the following questions about the word list. You may do this orally or have students write answers:

   What words have the vowel + r sound you hear in bear? (Barry, careful, carry, library, Mary, where)
   What word means to speak quietly? (whisper)
   What word is things that can grow on a face? (Whiskers)
   What word means to have hit something? (whacked)
   What word rhymes with night? (white)
   Find three words that some questions begin with. (what, where, why)
   What word means a place to find lots of books? (library)

   Use the bottom of the LAR workbook page. **Fill in circles to answer the questions about the story.**

3. Use the SAP workbook page. **Match the spelling words to the descriptions.**

4. The students will write a non-fiction story about whales. You may have students write the story on a piece of paper or make a book that can be illustrated. Books will again need a cover sheet and two additional sheets. Students may illustrate the pages or find and print pictures.

   Introduce the activity: **Today you will write about whales.** Read information about whales. Help students line out the book page by page. Four pages can be illustrations. One page can tell about baleen whales. One page can tell about toothed whales. One page can tell about dolphins. One page can tell about what whales eat, or baby whales.

5. Use the handwriting sheet or have the children write the following sentences:

   Why is Whiskers whimpering?
   Which whale does funny tricks?

LAR Answers

4 2 1 3 5

3 1 5 4 2

3 2 4 6 1 5

3 6 4 1 5 2

3 1 4 2

SAP Answers

whimper	whirl
wheat	why
whoa	whale
white	whip
where	whisker
while	what
wheel	which

Lesson 25

Lesson Objectives

1. Students will be tested on phonics concepts. (P)
2. Students will be tested on language concepts. (L)
3. Students will take a spelling test. (S)
4. Students will make a graphic organizer. (R & L)
5. Students will read the story they have written. (R)
6. Students will copy a sentence neatly and correctly. (H)

Materials

LAR
Creative writing assignment from lesson 24
Assessment for lesson 25

Teaching

1. Use part A of the workbook page as a phonics test. Have the students fill in the circles next to the words that complete the sentences.

2. Use part B of the workbook page. Alphabetize the list of words. Write a number to show the order in the box before each word.

3. Have students number their papers from 1 to 14. Give the following words as dictation.

   Spelling word list: 1. wheat, 2. why, 3. whip, 4. where, 5. whale, 6. whisker,
   7. wheel, 8. whimper, 9. white, 10. which, 11. whoa, 12. while
   13. what, 14. whirl

4. Use the LAR page. **Today you'll complete a graphic organizer for the story, *Mary, Whiskers, and the Whale.* A graphic organizer is a way to diagram a story. There are all kinds of ways it can be done. It will help you see important parts of the story very quickly.**

   Look at the workbook page. This graphic organizer divides the story into five parts. At the bottom of the page are ten numbered sentences. These are details about the story. Write a number in each circle that tells the part of the story that the detail happened.

5. Have students take turns reading the books or stories that were written during the creative writing section of Lesson 24.

6. Use the handwriting sheet or have the children write the following sentences:

   The man whittled on the wood.
   Why do I need to whisper?

Assessment Answers

1. wheel
2. whack
3. whisper
4. white
5. whimper

1. 2, 3, 5, 1, 4
2. 4, 2, 1, 3, 5
3. 5, 3, 2, 4, 1

LAR Answers

Answers may be switched between sides.

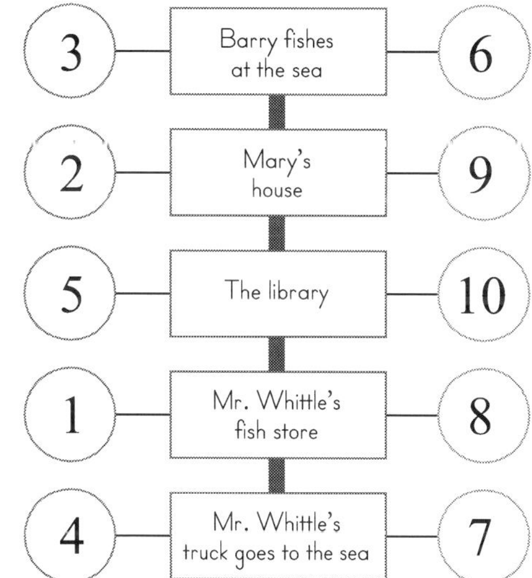

Lesson 26

Lesson Objectives

1. Students will read words spelled with -nc- and -ns-. (P)
2. Students will learn the meanings of words. (L)
3. Students will spell words correctly. (S)
4. Students will prepare to read the story *Francis Dances*. (R)
5. Students will copy sentences neatly and correctly. (H)

Materials

LAR
SAP
Francis Dances
Writing Skills Workbook page is available

Word List Lessons 26 to 30:
bounce, dance, lance, chance, France, Francis, glance, ounce, pounce, prance, stance, trance, fence, since, sense, mince, rinse, dunce, dense, hence, once, wince, prince, princess

Teaching

1. Write the letters ance, ence, ince. Have students read the endings. **Think of words with these sounds.** If they can't write some of the beginning letters or blends and have them try them on the word endings.

   Three spelling words replace the c with an s. Point these out as exceptions: rinse, sense, dense.

2. Have students read the words on the LAR workbook page dense, dunce, glance, lance, pounce, prance, stance, wince. After each word is a simplified definition. Next, the students will write the word that answers the questions.

3. Use the SAP page. Have students read and spell each spelling word. Spelling list: bounce, pounce, dance, sense, wince, balance, glance, ounce, fence, rinse, once, princess, cleanse, immense.

   On the top section, alphabetize the word lists. On the bottom section, two syllable words have been written in parts. The syllables are mixed up. Put the words together to make three spelling words.

4. *Francis Dances* focuses on words that end with -nce or -nse. In addition to those words, the following words may be new to students and will require some instruction: caused, talent.

   The word *caused:* au makes the same sound as aw.
   The word *talent:* tal-ent, the a makes the short a sound.

   You may also review the words *anything* and *everyone*.

   Introduce the story: Ask a student to read the title of the book. Ask: **Do you have a special talent? Maybe you do and don't know it. Francis discovers his special talent in *Francis Dances*.**

   Students will silently read as much of the story as they can in the time allowed.

5. Use the handwriting sheet or have the children write the following sentences:

The prince and princess danced.
Lance has a chance to go to France.

LAR Answers

1. pounce
2. wince
3. dense
4. lance
5. prance
6. glance
7. stance
8. dunce

SAP Answers

1. balance	4. dance
2. bounce	5. fence
3. cleanse	6. glance

1. immense	5. princess
2. once	6. rinse
3. ounce	7. sense
4. pounce	8. wince

Bottom - any order:

balance princess immense

Francis Dances

Second Grade Phonics & Reading

Book 6
Lessons 26 to 30

Francis Dances

Written and illustrated by
Brian Davis

A big dog lived in the big white house. That dog had just gotten a fancy collar. It was a flea collar.

That caused quite a problem for Mincy. You see, Mincy was a flea. He saw the collar. Mincy called a meeting of all the dog's fleas.

"We have to flee this dog at once," said Mincy the flea.

One by one, the fleas bounced to the ground.

1

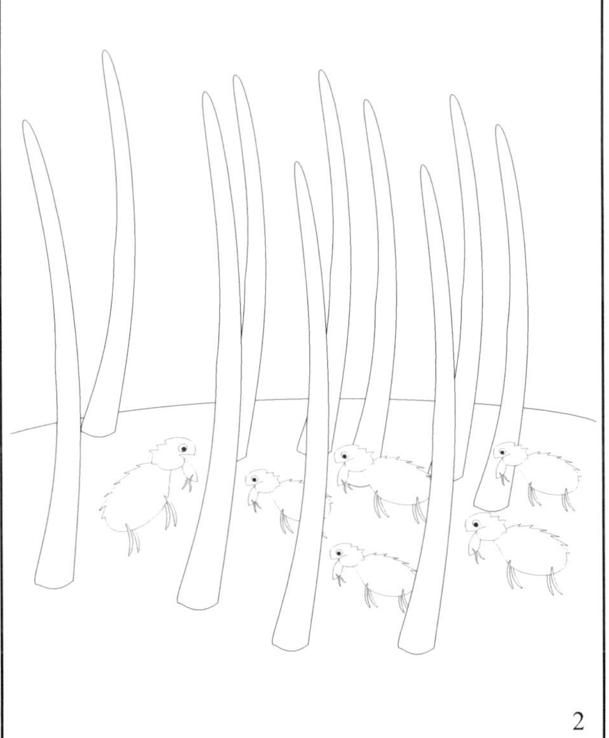

2

Francis Dances

A dog named Francis was walking by the white house. He rested by the fence. Mincy sensed a dog was near.

"This way," yelled Mincy the flea.

The fleas pounced on Francis. Francis winced.

"What was that," he thought.

Mincy and the fleas climbed the dog.

"This seems like a nice dog. He will be our new home," announced Mincy.

The fleas began to crawl into the dense fur.

3

4

Francis watched the other dogs. Princess the fancy poodle was pretty. She pranced down the street.

Lance could do tricks. People stopped and glanced at Lance. Francis felt like a dunce. He couldn't do anything.

"I don't have talent," moaned Francis. That upset the fleas.

"Our dog is a dunce," said a flea.

"He has no talent," said another flea.

"Let's pounce on the poodle," said a third flea. "You are what you eat."

"Wait," said Mincy. "Give this dog a chance. He doesn't need talent. He has us."

5

6

Francis Dances

Mincy had a plan. He made a map of the dog. He sent fleas to all parts of Francis.

"Go to work," announced Mincy.

The first flea bit Francis on the leg. Francis winced. Francis bounced up. Another flea bit Francis. The dog twisted. Mincy bit him twice. Francis twirled.

"Look!" announced a little boy. "That dog is dancing."

"That's a real fancy dance," said the boy's mother.

Princess the poodle stopped prancing. Lance stopped doing tricks. They glanced at Francis. Then, they stared at Francis.

7

The fleas kept biting. Francis kept dancing. A TV truck pulled up. A man started filming Francis.

8

Soon, everyone knew about Francis the dancing dog. Mincy wanted to keep his dog happy. Biting Francis made the fleas happy. Francis got his own TV show.

"He is a very talented dog," everyone said.

Princess the poodle began to like Francis. Everyone treated Francis like a prince. Francis began to think he was very talented, too.

9

10

Francis Dances

One day, a man came to Francis.

"We make flea collars," said the man. "Wear ours on TV. We will pay you."

That sounded good to Francis. That did not sound good to Mincy. He called a meeting of all the fleas.

"Our dog is getting a flea collar," announced Mincy. The fleas winced.

"Not our dog," said the fleas.

"He needs us," said another flea.

"We have one chance," said Mincy. "We must tell Francis that we make him dance."

So the fleas bounced up to the dog's ear.

"Francis," Mincy yelled into the dog's ear. "We are your fleas. When we bite, you dance."

"I am a talented dog," said Francis. "I don't need fleas."

So Francis got the flea collar. The fleas fled Francis.

11

12

The next day, Francis was on TV. He began to dance. He bounced a little. He twisted a little. It was an awful dance.

"This dog has no talent," said the flea collar man.

He took his flea collar back.

"I thought you had talent," said Princess the Poodle. She pranced away.

Francis was sad. "I am a dunce," said Francis. "My fleas were my friends. I made them leave."

13

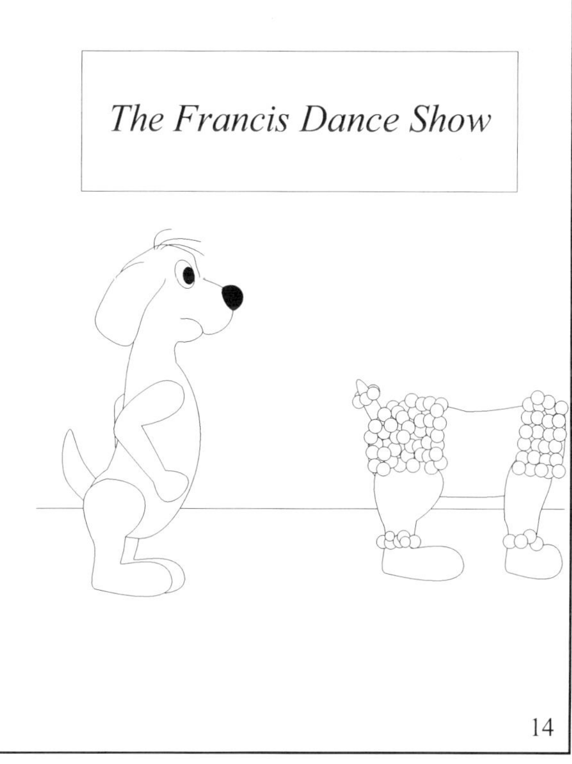

14

Francis Dances

The next day, Francis was sad. He sat by a fence. Mincy and the fleas bounced up to him.

"Are you OK., Francis?" asked Mincy.

"No," answered Francis. "I have no talent. I also made you fleas flee."

"You do have talent," said Mincy.

"We've been biting dogs all day," said another flea.

"None of them danced as well as you," said a third flea.

Mincy pounced on the dog's nose. "We need each other,"said Mincy. "So can we have this dance?"

Francis smiled, "Please, fleas."

The fleas pounced on Francis. Francis and the fleas danced all day. They were very talented.

15

Francis Dances

announced	dunce	Mincy	stared
another	eat	moaned	street
answered	everyone	near	talent
anything	fancy	once	third
awful	fence	other	thought
bounced	first	ounce	TV
boy	flea	own	twice
caused	flee	please	twirled
chance	Francis	pounced	twisted
climbed	glanced	pranced	upset
collar	good	pretty	very
couldn't	gotten	prince	wanted
dance	ground	Princess	watched
dancing	happy	problem	wear
dense	knew	quite	what
doesn't	Lance	sensed	when
down	leave	show	white
	little	sound	winced

Lesson 27

Lesson Objectives

1. Students will complete a sentence using a word that contains -nce or -nse. (P)
2. Students will review synonyms. (L)
3. Students will review spelling words. (S)
4. Students will turn statements into questions. (S & L)
5. Students will read the story *Francis Dances.* (R)
6. Students will copy sentences neatly and correctly. (H)

Materials

LAR
SAP
Francis Dances

Teaching

1. Use the top of the LAR workbook page: **Fill in the circle next to the word that best completes the sentence.**

2. **What is a synonym for the word *big?*** (large, huge, etc.) Use the bottom of the LAR page. **Read the first sentence. A word is in bold print. Complete the second sentence using a synonym of the bold word.**

3. Use the top of the SAP page. **Fit all the spelling words in to the grid. Start with the clue spaces. You can also count squares as clues.**

4. Write the sentence: The loud sound did make you wince. **This is a statement. Rearrange the words to make it into a question.** (Did the loud sound make you wince?)

   Use the bottom section of the SAP page. **Turn the two sentences into questions by moving words. Remember to use a question mark at the end.**

5. Review the additional reading vocabulary: caused, talent.

   Students will read pages 1 to 8 out loud. Next, ask the following questions:

   Why did the fleas leave their dog? (It got a flea collar.)
   What word on page 3 means lots of fur that is close together? (dense)
   What did Francis feel like he didn't have? (talent)
   Why did Francis start dancing? (The fleas were biting him.)
   Who thought of a way to make Francis dance? (Mincy the flea)

6. Use the handwriting sheet or have the children write the following sentences:

   The ball bounced over the fence.
   It makes sense to rinse the dish.

Lesson 27

LAR Answers

1. ● fence ○ ounce ○ glance
2. ○ stance ○ prince ● dance
3. ● princess ○ fence ○ mince
4. ○ dense ● since ○ dunce
5. ○ chance ● pranced ○ winced
6. ● pounced ○ glanced ○ lanced
7. ○ sensed ● winced ○ pranced

1. glanced
2. dense
3. lance
4. rinsing
5. bounced

SAP Answers

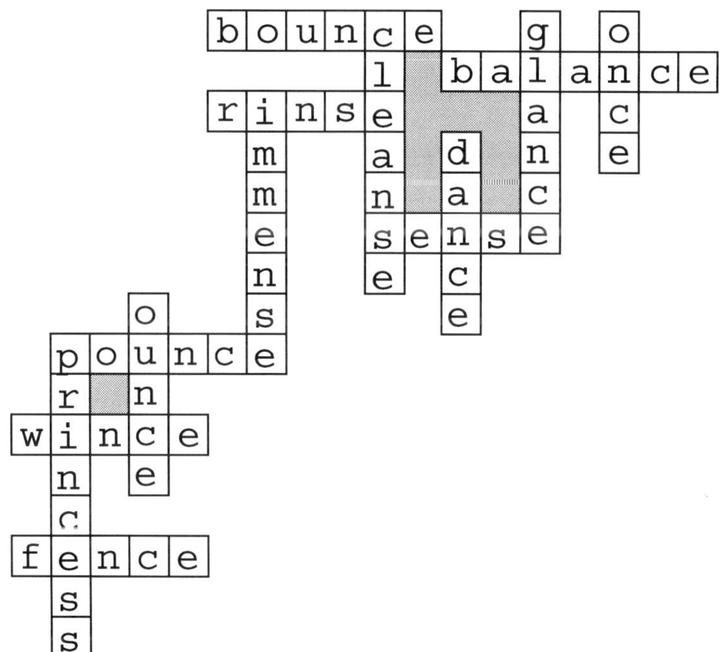

1. Does it take good balance to dance on ice?

2. Will the balls bounce off the fence?

Lesson 28

Lesson Objectives

1. Students will read a story and answer questions. (L)
2. Students will read spelling words. (S)
3. Students will read the story *Francis Dances*. (R)
4. Students will copy sentences neatly and correctly. (H)

Materials

LAR
SAP
Francis Dances

Teaching

1. Use the LAR workbook page. **Read the story. Answer the questions at the bottom of the page. Write complete sentences.**

2. Use top of the SAP workbook page. **Use the shape code to decode the spelling words.**

   Bottom section: **Look at he long words. In each of these words is a spelling word. Write the spelling words on the lines.**

3. Review the first half of the book Francis Dances. Next, read the second half of the book. After completing the story ask the students the following questions:

   How did everyone hear about Francis? (He was on TV.)
   Why do you think the other dogs and people treat Francis like a prince? (Answers vary.)
   What do you think it means to treat someone like a prince? (Answers vary.)
   Did Francis think the fleas helped him dance? (no)
   How do you know? (He said he didn't need fleas.)
   What happened after the fleas left Francis? (He couldn't dance.)
   What did Francis and the fleas learn? (They needed each other.)

4. Use the handwriting sheet or have the children write the following sentences:

   The cat glanced at the dog once.
   Francis has been waiting since noon.

LAR Answers

Answers may vary in wording from the following.
You may or may not have students answer questions with complete sentences.

1. The princess was trapped in a tower.
2. The knight was riding a prancing horse.
3. The knight tossed the princess a rope and lance.
4. The tower was too high.
5. The princess forgot the key to the tower.

SAP Answers

Top

glance	wince	sense
bounce	dance	ounce
fence	rinse	pounce
balance	once	cleanse
immense	princess	

Bottom

balance	dance	
fence	sense	
once	glance	ounce

Lesson 29

Lesson Objectives

1. Students will review nouns. (L)
2. Students will review spelling words. (S)
3. Students will write a story. (CW)
4. Students will read the story *Francis Dances*. (R)
5. Students will copy sentences neatly and correctly. (H)

Materials

LAR
SAP
Francis Dances
Writing Skills Workbook pages are available

Teaching

1. Introduce the term noun. At this point we will work with only more tangle nouns. Nouns are people places, or things. Many words are dependent on context to determine if they are nouns. Words will be presented in context for this reason.

   Use the top of the LAR workbook page. **At the end of the sentence are two words. Fill in the circle next to the word that is used as a noun in the sentence.**

2. Use the SAP page. **Match the spelling words to the descriptions. Write the words on the lines.**

3. Students will write a story about a special talent. It can be a talent they have or a talent they would like to have. They may replace themselves as the character with anyone or anything else. Students will think about how other people like the talent. How did they get this talent? How does it make them feel?

4. Read the book *Francis Dances* again. Next, have students look at the back of the book and answer the following questions about the word list. You may do this orally or have students write answers:

   What words can mean children of a king? (prince, Princess)
   What two words are homophones of each other? (flea, flee)
   What words are contractions? (couldn't, doesn't) **What words are they made of?** (could not, does not)
   What word is a synonym of hopped? (bounced)
   What word means to have looked quickly*?* (glanced)
   What three words begin with the same two letters as whale? (what, when, white)
   What word is a look you might get on your face if you get hurt? (wince)

   Use the bottom of the LAR page. **Fill in the circles to answer questions about the story.**

5. Use the handwriting sheet or have the children write the following sentences:

   The lion pounced on the deer.
   The prince tossed the lance.

LAR Answers

1. ● princess ○ dance
2. ○ rinsed ● shirt
3. ○ burked ● fence
4. ○ win ● prize
5. ● fox ○ ran
6. ● lion ○ pounced
7. ○ dropped ● lance
8. ○ winced ● whiskers

1. Was Mincy a poodle? yes **no**
2. Was Francis on TV? **yes** no
3. Could Lance do tricks? **yes** no
4. Did the fleas talk to Francis? **yes** no
5. Did Francis juggle pins? yes  **no**

SAP Answers

princess	sense
balance	once
bounce	dance
rinse	cleanse
glance	fence
immense	ounce
pounce	wince

Lesson 30

Lesson Objectives

1. Students will be tested on phonics concepts. (P)
2. Students will be tested on language concepts. (L)
3. Students will take a spelling test. (S)
4. Students will read the story they have written. (R)
5. Students will answer questions about Francis Dances. (R)
6. Students will review nouns.
7. Students will copy a sentence neatly and correctly. (H)

Materials

LAR
Assessment Lesson 30
Francis Dances

Teaching

1. Use part A of the workbook page as a phonics test. Have the students fill in the circles next to the words that complete the sentences.

2. Use part B of the workbook page. Students will fill in the oval next to the word that is the noun in the sentence.

3. Have students number their papers from 1 to 14. Give the following words as dictation.

   Spelling word list: **1. pounce, 2. wince, 3. bounce, 4. ounce, 5. sense, 6. once, 7. rinse, 8. cleanse, 9. princess, 10. glance, 11. fence, 12. dance 13. balance, 14. immense**

4. Have students take turns reading the books or stories that were written during the creative writing section of Lesson 29.

5. Use the top of the LAR page. **Number the sentences in the order they happened. You may use the book, *Francis Dances,* to help you.**

6. **There is a sport of sword fighting. It is called fencing. Many words have more than one meaning. Sometimes the different meanings are used in different ways. A fence that is around a yard is a noun. If you fence with swords, fence is a verb.**

   Use the bottom of the LARworkbook page. **Words are in bold print. Spelling words were used two different ways in the sentences. Fill in a circle to mark your answers.**

7. Use the handwriting sheet or have the children write the following sentences:

   The weeds along the fence were dense.
   Did Francis mince the apple?

Assessment Answers

1. lance
2. fence
3. rinse
4. dance
5. winced

1. prince
2. bike
3. horse
4. pan
5. airplane

LAR Answers

6
8
3
7
9
1
2
4
5

1. ● noun ○ verb
2. ○ noun ● verb
3. ○ noun ● verb
4. ● noun ○ verb
5. ● noun ○ verb
6. ○ noun ● verb

Lesson 31

Lesson Objectives

1. Students will decode words that end with -ies and -ied. (P)
2. Students will unscramble sentences. (L)
3. Students will spell twelve words correctly. (S)
4. Students will prepare to read the story *Benny's Pennies*. (R)
5. Students will copy sentences neatly and correctly. (H)

Materials

LAR
SAP
Benny's Pennies
Writing Skills Workbook page is available

Word List Lessons 31 to 35:
armies, babies, bellies, berries, bodies, buggies, bunnies, candies, carries, cherries, cities, copies, daddies, families, fifties, forties, grannies, hobbies, hurries, jellies, kitties, mommies, nineties, parties, pennies, puppies, sixties, stories, thirties, carried, hurried, copied, tried, cried, pried

Teaching

1. Write the words puppy, story, and copy. Ask: **What letter do all these words end with?** (y) **What sound does it make?** (long e) **Is the letter before them a vowel or consonant?** (consonant)

   Say: **Today we will add an s to words like these. The rule is to drop the y and add ies.** Demonstrate this with the word puppy. Erase the y and add ies to make puppies. Ask how it changed the meaning of the word. (It now means more than one puppy.)

   Next repeat with the words **try** and **cry**. Point out that the y makes a long i sound in these words. The rule still applies. **Try** becomes **tries. Cry** becomes **cries. Changing the words *try* to *tries*, and *cry* to *cries* makes it something that is happening now. The cat will cry for its mother. The cat cries for its mother.**

   The spelling rules are the same for adding ed to words that end with y. Write the word carry. **Carry becomes carried. How did the word change?** (Drop the y and add ied.)

   Use the top of the LAR page. **Read the sentences. A word is missing. Fill in the circle to choose the correct word.**

2. Use the bottom of the LAR worksheet. **Unscramble the sentences by writing numbers in the boxes.**

3. Use the SAP page. Have students read and spell each word.

   Spelling list: jellies, babies, puppies, families, bunnies, hobbies, pennies, thirties, hurried, copied, worried, fried, tried, cried.

   SAP top section: **Alphabetize the spelling words in each box.**

   Bottom section: **Write the root words to the four words at the bottom of the page. Take off the suffix and i. Add a y in its place.**

4. *Benny's Pennies* focuses on words that end with ie.

   Introduce the story: Ask a student to read the title of the book. Ask: **Have you ever wanted to buy a special gift for someone? In this story, Benny wants to buy his grandfather a gift. Read the story to find out how Benny gets a special birthday present for his grandfather.** Students will silently read as much of the story as they can in the time allowed.

5. Use the handwriting sheet or have the children write the following sentences:

   The puppies were in the box.
   The babies were in the buggies.

LAR Answers

1. ● puppy ○ puppies
2. ○ party ● parties
3. ○ penny ● pennies
4. ● bunny ○ bunnies
5. ○ story ● stories

3 5 2 4 1 or 3 2 5 4 1

5 3 4 2 1

4 1 5 3 2

2 4 1 3 5

6 5 2 1 4 3

SAP Answers

1. babies	5. families
2. bunnies	6. fried
3. copied	7. hobbies
4. cried	8. hurried

1. jellies	4. thirties
2. pennies	5. tried
3. puppies	6. worried

baby try
family worry

Benny's Pennies

Second Grade Phonics & Reading

Book 7
Lessons 31 to 35

Benny's Pennies

Written and illustrated by
Brian Davis

Benny and his grandfather were going to a store. Benny had a pocket full of pennies. He was going to surprise his grandfather.

Benny was going to buy a gift. It was his grandfather's birthday. Grandfather was in his sixties now.

They hopped into an old green truck. Grandfather turned the key.

"What do you want for your birthday?" asked Benny.

The truck whirred, but did not start. Grandfather tried again. It still did not start.

"What I would like is a new truck," answered Grandfather.

Benny counted his pennies.

Grandfather sighed, "You can't buy a truck for pennies."

1

2

Benny's Pennies

The truck would not start. So Benny got his wagon. He began to walk to a store.

Benny walked by a house. Outside was a cage. In the cage were puppies.

A sign said, "Free puppies."

So, Benny took two.

"My grandfather likes puppies."

The wagon carried the puppies. Benny walked back to his grandfather.

"I got you two puppies," said Benny.

"That is very nice," said Grandfather. "But, puppies bark at night. I need my sleep."

So Benny put the puppies back in the wagon.

3

4

Benny walked by a pet shop. A sign said, "Kitties on sale!"

"Kitties don't bark," said Benny. "Grandfather would like some kitties."

He pulled out his pennies. A woman came out. Benny held out the pennies.

"Can I buy some kitties?"

The woman smiled. "Those are nice puppies. I'll trade you two kitties for the puppies."

"O.K.," said Benny.

His wagon now carried two kitties.

5

Nora's Ark Pet Store

6

Benny's Pennies

Benny came to a farmer. He had a load of apples on his truck. They were for sale.

"I have some pennies," said Benny. "May I buy some apples?"

"Those look like nice kitties," said the farmer.

The kitties ran to a barn. They each came back with mice.

7

"I could use some kitties like those," said the farmer. "Give me your kitties. I'll give you a wagon load of apples."

"O.K.," said Benny.

8

Benny walked by a store. It sold yummy candies, jellies, and pies. They made Benny hungry. He took a bite out of an apple. It tasted good.

"Mm...Mm," said Benny.

A man came out of the store.

"Those look like good apples," said the man.

"They are," said Benny.

He gave one to the man. Benny pulled out his pennies.

"Can I get a pie. It's for my grandfather."

The man bit the apple.

"I will trade you two pies. They are made from fresh berries. Give me these apples."

"O.K.," said Benny.

9

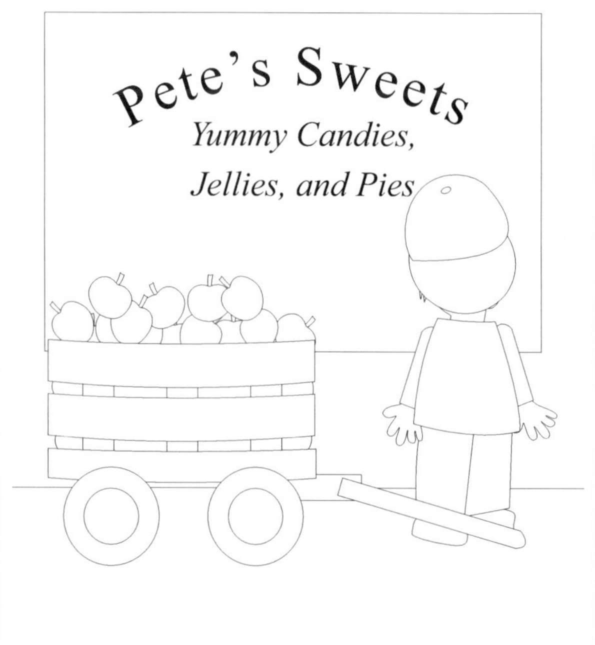

10

Benny's Pennies

Benny walked by a house. A sign said, "Yard Sale".

Benny began to look around. He found an old box of baseball cards. He pulled out his pennies.

"Can I get these cards?" asked Benny.

The lady at the table said, "I haven't eaten today. I'll trade you the pies for the cards."

"O.K.," said Benny.

11

12

Next, Benny came to a big car lot. He pulled out his pennies.

"Sir, may I get a truck. It's for my Grandfather."

The man giggled. "A truck costs a lot. You can't buy a truck for pennies."

The man looked at the wagon.

"What's in the box?" asked the man.

"Old baseball cards," said Benny.

"Baseball cards are one of my hobbies," said the man.

Benny let him look at the cards.

"Oh my!" yelled the man.

He held a card.

"This is a very rare card. Will you trade a truck for this card?"

"O.K.," said Benny.

13

Big Bert's
New Cars and Trucks
Great deals on wheels!

14

Benny's Pennies

Benny went inside his Grandfather's house.

"Come outside," said Benny. "I have your birthday present."

"It's not more puppies, is it?" asked his grandfather.

Grandfather and Benny walked to the street. Benny pointed to a new truck.

"Happy Birthday, Grandfather."

"You got this with your pennies?" asked Grandfather.

Benny shook his head no.

"It took two puppies. It took two kitties.

It took a wagon full of apples. It took two pies made with berries. It took one baseball card."

"You were right Grandfather. You can't buy a truck for pennies."

15

Benny's Pennies

apples
around
baseball
Benny
berries
birthday
buy
candies
card
carried
costs
counted
eaten

farmer
fresh
gift
giggled
going
grandfather
hobbies
hungry
inside
jellies
kitties
new
night
now

outside
pennies
pies
pocket
pointed
present
puppies
shook
sir
sixties
some
street
surprise

table
today
took
trade
tried
two
very
wagon
what
whirred
would
yard
yummy

Lesson 32

Lesson Objectives

1. Students will add the suffix -ed to words that end with y. (P)
2. Students will recognize categories of words. (L)
3. Students will review spelling words. (S)
4. Students will write number words. (S)
5. Students will read the story *Benny's Pennies*. (R)
6. Students will copy sentences neatly and correctly. (H)

Materials

LAR
SAP
Benny's Pennies

Teaching

1. Write the words carry and try. Ask students how they would change them to carries and tries. (Drop the y. Add -ies.) Ask: **How do you think you would change them to carried and tried?** Students may be able to determine that they drop the y and add -ied. If not introduce that as the rule.

   Top of the LAR workbook page: **Replace the word that ended with -ies with the same root word ending with -ied. Write the new word in the sentence.** Have students try to describe how it changed the meaning of the sentences.

2. Say the words apple, orange, banana. Ask students how they are alike. Use the bottom of the LAR workbook page. Students will read the three words. Students will write a sentence to tell how the three words are alike. You may give them a format that they will write. For example: **They are all _______.**

3. Use the top of the SAP workbook page. **Look at the four boxes of letters on the workbook page. Each box has letters to make some of the spelling words. The letters in the boxes can be used more than once, even in the same word.**

   The first word in the spelling list is *jellies*. What group has the letters to spell *jellies*? J is an unusual letter. Look for a box with the letter j. (purple box) **Does the box have all the letters to write the word *jellies*?** (yes, the letters j e l i s) **Write the word jellies on one of the purple lines. Find where all the other words belong. Write the words on the lines.**

4. **One of the spelling words is a number. Which word?** (thirties). **The word thirties means all or any of the numbers from 30 to 39. It's the word thirty with the *s* ending. To spell it, we drop the y and add ies.**

   Use the bottom of the SAP page. **Add the s ending to these numbers. Don't forget to use the spelling rules.**

5. Review the additional reading vocabulary: caused, talent. Students will read pages 1 to 8 out loud. Next, ask the following questions:

   Why didn't Benny's Grandfather drive to the store? (The truck wouldn't start.)
   What did his grandfather want for his birthday? (a new truck)
   Do you think he expected Benny to get him the truck? (Answers vary.)
   Why didn't the grandfather want the puppies? (They bark at night.)
   What did Benny trade the puppies for? (two kitties)
   Why did the farmer want the kitties? (They caught mice.)
   What do you think Benny was going to do with the apples? (Answers vary.)

6. Use the handwriting sheet or have the children write the following sentences:

   The babies cried for their mommies.
   Some daddies like candies.

LAR Answers

Top

1. hurried
2. copied
3. tried
4. cried
5. carried

Bottom
Wording may vary.

1. They are all animals.
2. They can be made from berries.
3. They are all members of families.
4. They are all coins.
5. They are all numbers.

SAP Answers

Order can vary in each box.

copied worried cried	babies bunnies pennies puppies
tried thirties hurried hobbies	families fried jellies

sixties fifties nineties
twenties eighties

Lesson 33

Lesson Objectives

1. Students will review the rule for sounds of the letter c. (P)
2. Students will review nouns. (L)
3. Students will complete analogies with spelling words. (S & L)
4. Student will proofread sentences. (S)
5. Students will read the story *Benny's Pennies*. (R)
6. Students will copy sentences neatly and correctly. (H)

Materials

LAR
SAP
Benny's Pennies

Teaching

1. Review the rule for c sounds. **If c is followed by an e or i it has the s sound. If c is followed by a, o, or u, or a consonant such as l, r, or k** (except h) **it has the k sound.**

   Use the top of the LAR workbook page. **Apply the rule. If the first c in the word has the s sound, write an S in the box. If the first c in the word has the k sound, write a K in the box.**

2. Review the term noun. Nouns are people places, or things. Use the bottom of the LAR workbook page. **At the end of the sentences are two words. Fill in the circle next to the word that is used as a noun in each sentence.**

3. Use the top of the SAP page. **Complete the analogies with spelling words.**

4. Use the bottom of the SAP page. **Proofread the sentences. Circle the words that are misspelled. Write them correctly on the lines. You will write more than one word on each set of lines. Add an ending punctuation mark, a period or question mark.**

5. Review the first half of the book Benny's Pennies. Next, read the second half of the book. After completing the story ask the students the following questions:

   Were the pies apple pies? (No) **What kind were they?** (berry pies)
   What do you think the man who gave him the pies was going to do with the apples? (Answers vary.)
   Why did the lady at the yard sale want the pies? (She hadn't eaten.)
   Why do you think she hadn't eaten? (Answers vary.)
   What did the man give Benny for the baseball card? (a truck)
   How do you think his grandfather felt about getting a new truck? (Answers vary.)
   Did Benny spend any pennies? (No)
   What was the grandfather right about? (You can't buy a truck for pennies.)

6. Use the handwriting sheet or have the children write the following sentences:

   The cars hurried to the cities.
   I carried the jellies made with berries.

LAR Answers

1. S	2. K	3. K
4. K	5. S	6. K
7. K	8. S	9. S
10. S	11. K	12. K

1. ○ pulled ● puppies
2. ● grannies ○ carried
3. ● mommies ○ were
4. ● Daddy ○ copied
5. ● bunnies ○ dense
6. ○ have ● hobbies
7. ● buggies ○ pulled
8. ○ spent ● pennies

SAP Answers

Top

pennies	puppies
cried	bunnics
fried	thirties

Bottom

jellies fried period
families hurried period
babies tried period
worried hobbies period

Lesson 34

Lesson Objectives

1. Students will read a story and answer questions. (L)
2. Students will review spelling words. (S)
3. Students will write a story. (CW)
4. Students will read the story *Benny's Pennies*. (R)
5. Students will copy sentences neatly and correctly. (H)

Materials

LAR
SAP
Benny's Pennies
Writing Skills Workbook page is available

Teaching

1. Read the story and answer the questions on the LAR workbook page.

2. Use the SAP page. **Write the spelling words that match the descriptions.**

3. Students will write a story about a present they would get someone they love. Say: **In the book Benny's Pennies, Benny wanted to get his grandfather a present. He was able to get him a very special present. Maybe you would like to give someone a special gift. Today you will write a story about giving.**

   The following questions may be helpful: **Who is it for? Why did they get it? What would they get? How would they get it? Where would they get the gift? What would the person do after the got it? How would the gift help the person?**

   Maybe it's a gift that doesn't cost anything. Maybe the gift would be doing something special for someone instead of giving a gift. Students may substitute a fictional character for themselves. Students can make a book and write their stories in the book.

4. Read the book *Benny's Pennies* again. Next, have students look at the back of the book and answer the following questions. You may do this orally or have students write answers:

   What words dropped a y and added -ies? (berries, candies, hobbies, jellies, kitties, pennies, puppies, sixties)
   What words dropped y and added ied? (carried, tried)
   What word is a special day of the year? (birthday)
   What word is a synonym of laughed? (giggled)
   What word is a synonym of road? (street)
   What word is the opposite of old? (new)
   What two words begin with the same two letters as whale? (whirred, what)
   What word is something with wheels? (wagon)
   What word is a game? (baseball)

5. Use the handwriting sheet or have the children write the following sentences:

   We tried to pet the bunnies.
   The pennies fell out of my pocket.

LAR Answers

Answers may vary in wording from the following. You may or may not have students answer questions with complete sentences.

1. They made jelly.
2. They got the strawberries in the garden.
3. They made five jars of jelly.
4. Candy bunnies were in the box.
5. (Answers vary)

SAP Answers

fried	families
puppies	babies
cried	hurried
copied	tried
jellies	hobbies
bunnies	thirties
pennies	worried

Lesson 35

Lesson Objectives

1. Students will be tested on phonics concepts. (P)
2. Students will be tested on language concepts. (L)
3. Students will take a spelling test. (S)
4. Students will complete a graphic organizer. (R)
5. Students will read the story they have written. (R)
6. Students will copy a sentence neatly and correctly. (H)

Materials

LAR
Creative writing assignment from Lesson 34
Assessment Lesson 35
Bennies Pennies

Teaching

1. Use part A of the assessment as a phonics test. Have the students fill in the circles next to the words that complete the sentences.

2. Use part B of the assessment page. Students will write a sentence to tell how the groups of words are alike. Key words are given. Not all words are used.

3. Have students number their papers from 1 to 14. Give the following words as dictation.

   Spelling word list: **1. hobbies, 2. puppies, 3. thirties, 4. bunnies, 5. jellies, 6. copied, 7. hurried, 8. tried, 9. babies, 10. cried, 11. pennies, 12. families 13. fried, 14. worried**

4. Use the top of LAR page. **Bennie made several trades in the story. Put the trades in the order they happened. Use the graphic organizer on the workbook page. A list of trades is on the page. You may use your reading book to help find the answers.**

   Bottom of the page: **Answer questions about the story. Fill in the ovals to mark your answers.**

5. Have students read the books or stories that were written during the creative writing section of Lesson 34.

6. Use the handwriting sheet or have the children write the following sentences:

   The pie was made of blackberries.
   He copied the words on the board.

Assessment Answers

1. pennies
2. parties
3. berries
4. hurried
5. stories

(Wording may vary)

1. Things that hop.
2. Things you ride in.
3. Things that are round.
4. Parts of bodies.

LAR Answers

puppies
kitties
apples
pies
card
truck

1. yes ●
2. yes ●
3. ● no
4. yes ●
5. yes ●

Lesson 36

Lesson Objectives

1. Students will review words with the -air sound. (P)
2. Students will review the suffixes -er and -est. (L)
3. Students will review spelling words. (S)
4. Students will copy sentences neatly and correctly. (H)

Materials

LAR pages 35 & 36
SAP

Teaching

1. Review the different spellings of the -air sound found in thefollowing words: air, bear, spare, cherry, carry, their, where. Use LAR workbook page 35. **Solve a crossword puzzle.**

2. Review the suffixes -er and -est. Review the rules for adding suffixes:

   For long vowel words that do not end with a silent e, simply add the suffix: mean, meaner, meanest. This is also true for other vowel digraphs: fair, fairer, fairest.

   For words that end with silent e, drop the silent e and add the suffix: wise, wiser, wisest. This is also true for other vowel digraphs: loose, looser, loosest.

   For one syllable words, if the last two letters in a word are a vowel and consonant, double the consonant and add the suffix: big, bigger, biggest.

   Use the top of LAR workbook page 36. **Fill in the circle next to the word with the correct suffix to complete the sentence.**

   Use the bottom of LAR workbook page 36. **Add suffixes to the words. Add er to the words in the first column. Add est to the words in the second column. Change the roots if needed to add the suffixes.**

3. The spelling list this week consists of words from lessons 1 to 35. Have students read and spell each word in the spelling list: bear, hair, square, very, whale, where, which, whisker, bounce, dance, rinse, princess, puppies, tried, hurried, pennies.

   Use the SAP page. **Alphabetize the two groups of spelling words.**

   On the bottom section, write the four spelling words that rhyme with the words.

4. Use the handwriting sheet or have the children write the following sentences:

   Jerry repaired the airplane.
   I shared the cherries with the bear.

LAR page 35 Answers

												[11]B					
						[4]C	A	R	E	F	U	L				[16]C	
						H						A				A	
[1]D	O	[2]W	N	[3]S	T	A	I	R	[9]S		[12]A	I	R	P	O	R	T
		E		H		I			Q			R				R	
		A		[5]A	I	R			U					[15]P		O	
		R		R					A			[13]H		A		T	
			[6]P	E	A	R			[10]R	E	P	A	I	R		S	
			A						E			I		R			
			I		[8]B	E	A	R	S			R		O			
[7]C	H	E	R	R	Y								[14]S	T	A	R	E

LAR page 36 Answers

1. faster
2. whitest
3. quicker
4. small
5. sweetest

1. smarter	6. reddest
2. greener	7. kindest
3. hotter	8. rarest
4. brighter	9. tallest
5. slower	10. densest

SAP Answers

1. bear	5. hurried
2. bounce	6. pennies
3. dance	7. princess
4 hair	8 puppies

1. rinse	5. whale
2. square	6. where
3. tried	7. which
4. very	8. whisker

tried	whale
very	bounce

Lesson 37

Lesson Objectives

1. Students will review words that begin with the consonant digraph wh-. (P)
2. Students will review categories. (L)
3. Students will review dropping y and adding -ies or -ied. (P)
4. Students will review spelling words. (S)
5. Students will copy sentences neatly and correctly. (H)

Materials

LAR
SAP

Teaching

1. Review the wh digraph. Use the top of the LAR page. Students will fill in the oval next to the word that completes the sentence.

2. Use the bottom of the LAR page. Students will write the wh- word that goes with each group.

3. Use the SAP page, top section: **In each box are three words. Two of them in each box are spelled wrong. Circle the correctly spelled word. These are review spelling words.**

4. Use the SAP page, bottom section: **Proofread the sentences. Circle the misspelled word. Write it correctly on the lines.**

5. Use the handwriting sheet or have the children write the following sentences:

   Which wheel fits the white truck?
   Why can't I whiff the wheat rolls?

LAR Answers

1. Whales
2. wheel
3. whispered
4. What
5. whip

1. whimper
2. white
3. wheat
4. why
5. whittle
6. whack
7. whirl

SAP Answers

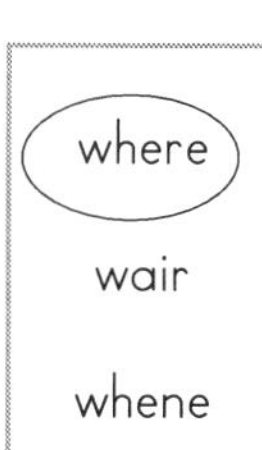

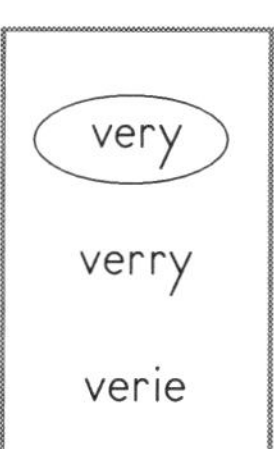

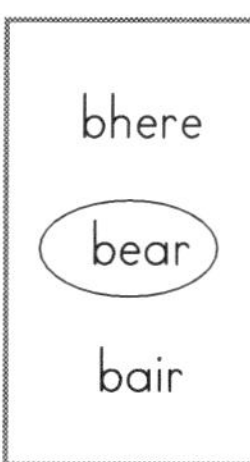

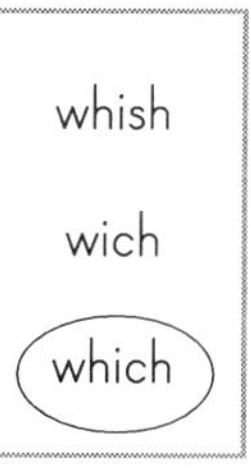

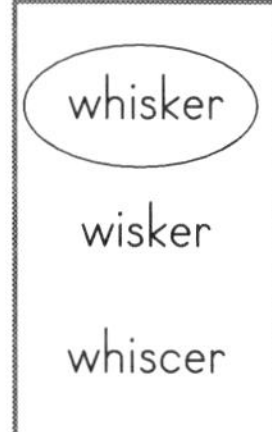

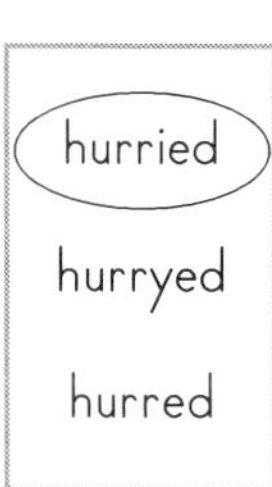

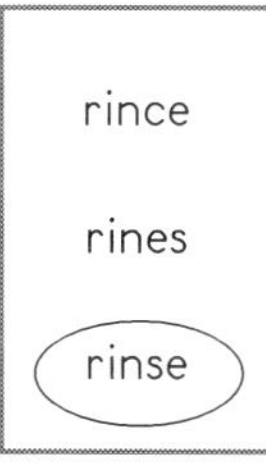

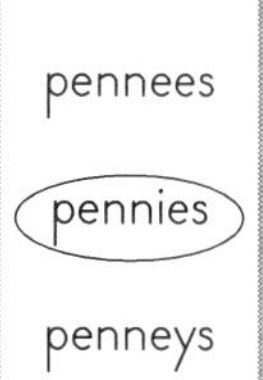

1. princess
2. puppies
3. bounce
4. square
5. whale

Lesson 38

Lesson Objectives

1. Students will review words with the consonant combinations nc and ns. (P)
2. Students will review nouns. (L)
3. Students will review spelling words. (S)
4. Students will copy sentences neatly and correctly. (H)

Materials

LAR
SAP

Review Word List Lessons 26-30

bounce, dance, lance, chance, France, Francis, glance, ounce, pounce, prance, stance, trance, fence, since, sense, tense, mince, rinse, dunce, dense, hence, once, wince, prince, princess

Teaching

1. Review words with nc and ns. Use the top of the LAR workbook page. **Choose the word to complete the sentence. Write the words on the lines at the end of the sentence. A word list is given. Not all words will be used.**

2. Use the bottom of the LAR workbook page. **Fill in the circle next to the word that is used a noun in the sentence.**

3. Use the top of the SAP workbook page. **Fit the spelling words in the grid.**

   Use the bottom of the SAP workbook page. **Write the spelling words that match the descriptions. Write the four spelling words that rhyme with chair. Write the six spelling words that have two syllables.**

   Students will need a piece of paper. Give the students a practice spelling dictation test:

   chance, rinse, princess, puppies, tried, hurried, pennies, bear, hair, square, very, whale, where, which, whisper, bounce

4. Use the handwriting sheet or have the children write the following sentences:

   Is Lance the Prince of France?
   It makes sense to rinse the carrots.

LAR Answers

1. fence
2. pounce
3. bounce
4. rinse
5. dance

1. prize
2. lance
3. grass
4. princess
5. poodle
6. car
7. candy

SAP Answers

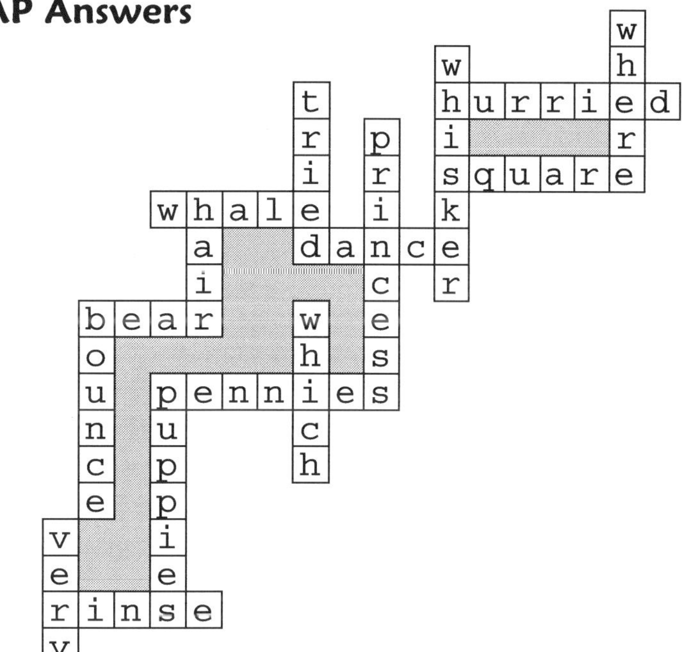

Bottom section
Rhymes with chair. Any order

bear hair square where

Two syllable. Any order

very whisker princess
puppies hurried pennies

Lesson 39

Objectives

1. Students will be tested over phonics concepts
2. Students will review spelling words. (S)

Materials

Test 1, pages 1 and 2
SAP

Teaching

Part 1:

1. Students will write the words that answer the questions.

   Part 2:
   Students will fill in the oval next to the word that completes the sentences.

2. Use the top of the SAP page. **Write the numbers of the spelling words that have the letters to spell the small words.**

   Bottom section: **Write the spelling word that can take the place of the underlined words in each sentence. Choose the word that changes the meaning of the sentence the least.**

Test Answers

Page 1
Part 1

1. whale
2. pennies
3. square
4. lance
5. dance
6. whisper
7. forties
8. parrot
9. bunnies
10. airplane

Page 2
Part 2

1. bunnies
2. prince
3. airplane
4. bear
5. puppies
6. careful
7. wheel
8. pennies
9. white
10. pair

SAP Answers

ear 1,3 we 5,6,8 ski 8
hi 2,7,8,15 rye 4 rise 8,11,12
red 14,15 since 12 ice 12 pies 12,13,16
her 6,8,15 pen 12,16 be 1,9
cane 10 is 8,11,12,13,16 hid 15

1. bear
2. whiskers
3. very
4. square
5. puppies
6. pennies
7. rinse

Lesson 40

Test 1 Objectives

1. Students will be tested over language concepts.
2. Students will take a spelling dictation test.

Materials

* Test 1, pages 3 and 4

Language Test Directions:

Part 3: Students will read the sentences. Students will fill in the oval next to the word that was used as a noun in the sentence.

Part 4: Students will add the suffixes to the root words.

Part 5: Students will number the sets of words in alphabetical order from 1 to 5.

Part 6: Categorize: Write the word that goes with the other two words. The word is like the other two in some way.

Spelling Dictation Test:

Have students number their paper from 1 to 16.

1. puppies, 2. whale, 3. bear, 4. which,
5. dance, 6. whisker, 7. hurried, 8. square,
9. rinse, 10. very, 11. hair, 12. bounce,
13. where, 14. princess, 15. tried, 16. pennies

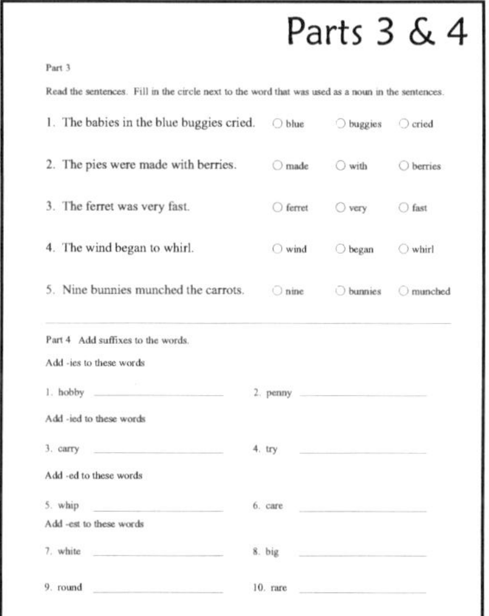

Parts 3 & 4

Part 3

Read the sentences. Fill in the circle next to the word that was used as a noun in the sentences.

1. The babies in the blue buggies cried. ○ blue ○ buggies ○ cried
2. The pies were made with berries. ○ made ○ with ○ berries
3. The ferret was very fast. ○ ferret ○ very ○ fast
4. The wind began to whirl. ○ wind ○ began ○ whirl
5. Nine bunnies munched the carrots. ○ nine ○ bunnies ○ munched

Part 4 Add suffixes to the words.

Add -ies to these words

1. hobby ______ 2. penny ______

Add -ied to these words

3. carry ______ 4. try ______

Add -ed to these words

5. whip ______ 6. care ______

Add -est to these words

7. white ______ 8. big ______

9. round ______ 10. rare ______

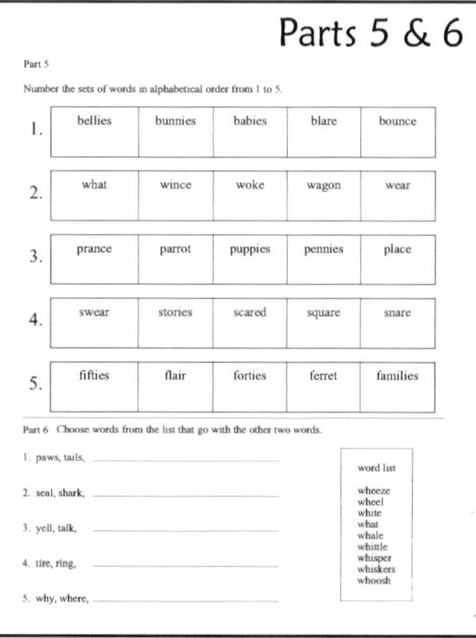

Parts 5 & 6

Part 5

Number the sets of words in alphabetical order from 1 to 5.

1.	bellies	bunnies	babies	blare	bounce
2.	what	wince	woke	wagon	wear
3.	prance	parrot	puppies	pennies	place
4.	swear	stories	scared	square	snare
5.	fifties	flair	forties	ferret	families

Part 6 Choose words from the list that go with the other two words.

1. paws, tails, ______
2. seal, shark, ______
3. yell, talk, ______
4. tire, ring, ______
5. why, where, ______

word list

wheeze
wheel
white
what
whale
whittle
whisper
whiskers
whoosh

Test Answers

Page 3

Part 3

1. buggies
2. berries
3. ferret
4. wind
5. bunnies

Part 4

1. hobbies
2. pennies
3. carried
4. tried
5. whipped
6. cared
7. whitest
8. biggest
9. roundest
10. rarest

Page 4

Part 5

1. 2, 5, 1, 3, 4
2. 3, 4, 5, 1, 2
3. 4, 1, 5, 2, 3
4. 5, 4, 1, 3, 2
5. 3, 4, 5, 2, 1

Part 6

1. whiskers
2. whale
3. whisper
4. wheel
5. what

Lesson 41

Lesson Objectives

1. Students will read words that the oo sound as in moon (ue, ui, oe spellings). (P)
2. Students will add suffixes. (L)
3. Students will spell twelve words correctly. (S)
4. Students will prepare to read the story *Blue Shoe Canoes*. (R)
5. Students will copy sentences neatly and correctly. (H)

Materials

LAR
SAP
Blue Shoe Canoes

Word List: due, hue, Sue, blue, clue, flue, glue, true, fuel, duel, fruit, juice, bruise, cruise, shoe, canoe

Teaching

1. Write the words food and moose. Ask: **Do these words have the same vowel sound?** (yes) **What sound do these words have?** *(long oo)* **What letters spell this sound?** (oo) **Remember oo has other sounds, too. All these words are spelled with oo: book, door, and blood. Not only does oo have other sounds, the oo sound in food and moose is also spelled differently in other words.**

   Write the words blue and fruit, and shoe. **Each of these words have the same vowel sound heard in moose and food. Read the words. What letters spell the sounds? Only shoe and canoe spell the oo sound with -oe.**

   Top of the LAR workbook page: **Fill in the missing word. The picture is a clue. A word list is given. Not all words in the list will be used.**

2. Use the bottom of the LAR page. **Add the given suffix to the words. There is an exception to the rules. The -e can be dropped before adding -ing on words ending with -ue, but it does not have to be dropped.** (bluing, blueing, gluing, glueing)

3. Use the SAP page. Have students read and spell each word. Spelling list: due, canoe, clue, bruise, blue, glue, juice, true, fuel, cruise, cruel, fruit, shoe, pursue, nuisance.

   Top section: **Sort the words by the way the vowel sound is spelled.**

   Bottom section: **Look at the words at the bottom of the page. Some of the words have the same vowel sound as the spelling words spelled in different ways. Circle the words that havethe same vowel sound as the spelling words. Put an x on thewords that have a different vowel sound.**

4. *Blue Shoe Canoes* focuses on words that have the ue, ui, and oe vowel digraphs that make the long *oo* sound as in moon. In addition to those words, the following words may be new to students and will require some instruction: kickball, avenue, idea, love.

The word *kickball:*	Break into two words (kick ball).
The word *avenue:*	Break into syllables, av-e-nue.
The word *idea:*	The i and e are long.
The word *love:*	The o makes a short u sound. The e is silent.

You may also review the words *family* and *chipmunks*.

Introduce the story: Ask a student to read the title of the book. Ask: **Have you ever played in a stream? A girl named Sue played in a stream and something very strange happened to her shoes. Read the story to find out what happened.** Students will silently read as much of the story as they can in the time allowed.

5. Use the handwriting sheet or have the children write the following sentences:

The puppies tore apart the shoes.
Thc car was out of fuel.

LAR Answers

1. glue
2. fruit
3. shoe
4. juice
5. canoe

1. bluest	6. bruised
2. dueling	7. glued
3. gluing or glueing	8. fueled
4. cruising	9. bluer
5. canoed	10. cruised

SAP Answers

ue in any order

due	true
clue	fuel
blue	cruel
glue	pursue

ui in any order

bruise
juicc
cruise
fruit
nuisance

oe in any order

shoe
canoe

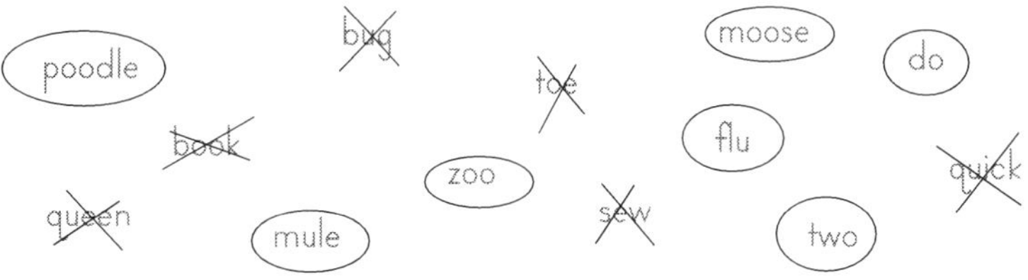

Blue Shoe Canoes

Second Grade Phonics & Reading

Book 8
Lessons 41 to 45

Blue Shoe Canoes

Written and illustrated by
Brian Davis

Sue and her family were on a picnic. They ate fruit and drank juice. Sue's brothers played kickball. Sue wanted to wade in the stream.

"Don't get your blue shoes wet," said her mom.

Sue took off her blue shoes. She was careful.

Sue placed the shoes on the bank of the stream.

The cool water felt good to her feet.

2

3

Blue Shoe Canoes

Two chipmunks were playing on the bank.

"Wait!" squeaked one of the chipmunks. His name was Stue. "Look at that!"

Stue pointed to the blue shoes.

"Blue shoe canoes!" squealed the other chipmunk. His name was Hue.

"Let's go on a cruise," said Stue the chipmunk.

"Yes," agreed Hue the chipmunk. "We can have a blue shoe canoe duel."

4

5

The chipmunks began tugging Sue's blue shoes. Soon, the shoes were next to the stream.

"We can't paddle. Our arms are too short," said Hue. "How can we move the shoes?"

"That's true," said Stue. "These blue shoe canoes will need fuel."

"That's true," said Hue. "Blue shoe canoes do need fuel."

"I have an idea!" squealed Stue. "I need some glue, string, sticks, and fruit."

"I know what you're thinking," squeaked Hue. "We'll be cruising soon."

6

7

Blue Shoe Canoes

Stue ran home to get some glue and string. Hue ran to Sue's picnic. He found some fruit.

Each chipmunk found a stick. They tied the fruit to the string. The chipmunks tied a string to each stick. They glued the sticks to Sue's blue shoes.

"We now have fuel. We can take a blue shoe canoe cruise," said Hue.

"That's true," said Stue. "Who will win the blue shoe canoe duel?"

"We shall see soon," said Hue.

"That's true," said Stue.

8

9

The chipmunks pushed the shoes into the stream. Soon, two turtles came swimming by. They smelled the fruit.

"I love fruit," said the first turtle.

"Yes, the juice tastes good," said the second turtle.

The shells of the turtles pushed the shoes. The blue shoes moved. The fruit on the string moved.

The turtles began to chase the fruit. The blue shoes began to cruise. The chipmunks cruised in the blue shoe canoes.

10

11

Blue Shoe Canoes

The turtles tried and tried to get the fruit.

The chipmunks loved their blue shoe canoe cruise.

Stue's turtle swam faster. He won the blue shoe canoe duel.

The turtles were getting tired. Stue and Hue steered the turtles to shore.

12

"They need their fuel," said Hue.

"That's true," said Stue. "They are due for some fruit."

"I love fruit," said Stue's turtle.

"Yes, the juice tastes good," said Hue's turtle

13

Stue and Hue gave the turtles the fruit.

"Thanks for the cruise," said Stue and Hue.

"Thanks for the fruit," said the first turtle.

"I love the juice," said the second turtle.

The chipmunks tugged Sue's blue shoes. They put them back where they found them. Just then, a blue kickball bounced over Stue and Hue.

14

15

Blue Shoe Canoes

Sue's brothers chased the ball. Sue put on her shoes.

"Who got my blue shoes wet?" asked Sue.

"We don't have a clue," giggled her brothers.

"Who glued sticks to my blue shoes?" cried Sue.

"We don't have a clue," giggled her brothers.

"I'm going to get you!" shouted Sue. She chased her brothers.

Stue and Hue looked at the blue kickball.

"How about a nice cruise down Park Avenue?" asked Stue.

"I know what you're thinking," said Hue. "I'll get a stick."

"Oh, turtles," yelled Stue. "Do you like big blue fruit? It's full of juice."

16

Blue Shoe Canoes

agreed	drank	love	string
asked	due	loved	Stue
avenue	duel	move	Sue
blue	family	next	swimming
bounced	feet	one	tastes
brothers	found	other	too
can't	fruit	over	took
canoes	fuel	paddle	tried
careful	giggled	picnic	true
chased	glue	pointed	tugging
chipmunks	going	shoes	turtles
clue	good	short	two
cool	how	some	very
cried	Hue	soon	wade
cruise	idea	squeaked	water
cruising	juice	squealed	who
don't	kickball	stick	won
down		stream	you're

Lesson 42

Lesson Objectives

1. Students will answer true and false questions. (L)
2. Students will review contractions. (L)
3. Students will review spelling words. (S)
4. Students will read the story *Blue Shoe Canoes*. (R)
5. Students will copy sentences neatly and correctly. (H)

Materials

LAR
SAP
Blue Shoe Canoes

Teaching

1. **I'm going to say some statements. Are they true or false? All dogs are poodles.** (false) **Juice can be made from oranges.** (true) **Blue is a color.** (true)

   Use the top of the the LAR workbook page. **Answer the statements with true or false. Fill in the circles next to the correct answers.**

2. Write the words did not and isn't. **What is a contraction?** (two words put together with some letters left out.) **What punctuation mark is in a contraction?** (apostrophe) **Where do you place the apostrophe?** (in the space where a letter was taken out)

   How would you write a contraction for did not? (didn't) **Now let's do the opposite. Look at the contraction *isn't.* What two words make up the contraction?** (Is not)

   Use the bottom of the LAR page. **Read the sentences. Find the contractions. Write the two words that make up each contraction on the lines after the sentences.**

3. Use the SAP workbook page. **On the top section, fill in the missing vowels in the spelling words. On the bottom section are sentences. Each sentence uses two spelling words. Find the spelling words and write them on the lines.**

4. Review the additional reading vocabulary: kickball, avenue, idea, love.

   Students will read pages 1 to 8 out loud. Next, ask the following questions:

   What game were Sue's brothers playing? (kickball)
   What did the chipmunks call Sue's shoes? (blue shoe canoes)
   Do you think the chipmunks had done this before? (Answers vary.)
   Why or why not?
   What did the chipmunks use as blue shoe canoe fuel? (fruit)
   How did the chipmunks use the glue? (to keep the sticks on the shoes)
   Where did Stue get the string? (from his home)
   What do you think Sue is doing while the chipmunks have her shoes? (Answers vary.)
   What do you think she would do if she caught them? (Answers vary.)

5. Use the handwriting sheet or have the children write the following sentences:

   Sue fell and bruised her knee.
   My library book is now due.

LAR Answers

Top

1. true
2. false
3. true
4. false
5. true
6. false
7. true
8. true
9. false
10. true

Bottom

1. They are
2. she is
3. we will
4. I am
5. can not

SAP Answers

due blue shoe fuel pursue

clue juice true canoe cruel

glue bruise cruise nuisance

1. due fuel
2. cruise canoe
3. fruit juice
4. glue nuisance
5. blue shoe
6. clue true
7. cruel pursue
8. fruit bruise

Lesson 43

Lesson Objectives

1. Students will fill in the missing vowel digraphs. (P)
2. Students will change sentences. (L)
3. Students will alphabetize spelling words. (S & L)
4. Students will read the story *Blue Shoe Canoes*. (R)
5. Students will copy sentences neatly and correctly. (H)

Materials

LAR
SAP
Blue Shoe Canoes
Writing Skills Workbook page is available

Teaching

1. Use the top of the LAR workbook page. **The words are missing letters (oe, ui, ue, or oo). Fill in the missing letters to make words with the long oo sound.**

2. Use the bottom of the LAR workbook page. **Replace the words in black with the long *oo* words in the box.**

3. Use the SAP workbook page. **Decode the spelling words on the top section. On the bottom section, unscramble the sentences. Write the sentences on the lines.**

4. Review the first half of the book *Blue Shoe Canoes*. Next, read the second half of the book. After completing the story ask the students the following questions:

   How did the fruit help fuel the shoes? (The turtles pushed them.)
   What did the chipmunks do with the fruit at the end of the cruise? (They gave it to the turtles.)
   Who won the blue shoe canoe duel? (Stue)
   What did the chipmunks do with the shoes at the end of the cruise? (They put them back where they found them.)
   Who did Sue think got her shoes wet? (her brothers)
   Why didn't she believe them? (Answers vary.)
   Where did the chipmunks want to cruise? (Park Avenue)
   What did the turtles think was a big blue piece of fruit? (a kickball)
   Do you think the chipmunks knew what the ball was? (Answers vary.)

5. Use the handwriting sheet or have the children write the following sentences:

   Are the paddles in the canoe?
   Is the answer true or false?

LAR Answers

1. duel
2. goose
3. canoe
4. blue
5. hue
6. bruise
7. clue
8. moon
9. true
10. fuel or fool

1. glue
2. cruise
3. blue
4. fruit
5. juice

SAP Answers

bruise pursue cruise

fruit juice cruel canoe

fuel blue shoe clue

true nuisance glue due

Did you use glue to fix the shoe?

The box of fruit is in the blue canoe.

The cruise ship needs more fuel.

Lesson 44

Lesson Objectives

1. Students will put a story in order. (L)
2. Students will review spelling words. (S)
3. Students will write a story. (CW)
4. Students will read the story *Blue Shoe Canoes*. (R)
5. Students will copy sentences neatly and correctly. (H)

Materials

LAR
SAP
Blue Shoe Canoes
Writing Skills Workbook page is available

Teaching

1. Use the LAR page. **Read the sentences on the workbook page. Number them from 1 to 7 in the order they happened in the story. You may use the reading book to help you.**

   On the bottom section, fill in the ovals to answer questions about the story.

2. Use the SAP page. **Match the spelling words to the descriptions.**

3. Students will write a story about a picnic. Say: In the book Blue Shoe Canoes, Sue's family was on a picnic. Have you ever gone a picnic and had something unusual happen? (If not, students can imagine going on a picnic). Today you will write a story about a picnic. It doesn't have to be about a picnic you actually went on, but it can be.

   The following questions may be helpful: **What did you (or the characters) eat at the picnic? Where did you go? Who was with you (it could be anyone like a friend, sports star, animal, etc.)? Did you play any games? Was it a special event like the Fourth of July or a birthday party? What are things you like to do on picnics?** Students can make a book and write their stories in the book.

4. Read the book *Blue Shoe Canoes* again. Next, have students look at the back of the book and answer the following questions about the word list.

   What words are contractions? (can't, don't, you're)
   What words are they made up of? (can not, do not, you are)
   What word is something that grows on trees? (fruit)
   What words begin with the same blend as squirrel? (squeaked, squealed)
   What word is the opposite of false? (true)
   What words have homophones on the list? (too, two, one, won)
   What word is a synonym for street? (avenue)
   What words end with the suffix -ing? (cruising, going, swimming, tugging)

5. Use the handwriting sheet or have the children write the following sentences:

   We squeezed the orange juice.
   The bird made a nest in the flue.

Lesson 44

LAR Answers

2	5
7	6
3	1
4	

1. yes **no**
2. **yes** no
3. yes **no**
4. yes **no**
5. **yes** no

SAP Answers

cruise	juice
glue	due
nuisance	fuel
canoe	pursue
cruel	shoe
blue	bruise
fruit	clue
true	

Lesson 45

Lesson Objectives

1. Students will be tested on phonics concepts. (P)
2. Students will be tested on language concepts. (L)
3. Students will take a spelling test. (S)
4. Students will read the story they have written. (R)
5. Students will copy a sentence neatly and correctly. (H)

Materials

Creative writing assignment from lesson 44
Assessment 45

Teaching

1. Use part A of the assessment page as a phonics test. Have thestudents fill in the circles next to the words that complete the sentences.

2. Use part B of the assessment page. Students will answer the statements with true or false. Fill in the circles.

3. Have students number their papers from 1 to 15. Give the following words as dictation.

   Spelling word list:

   1. glue, 2. blue, 3. fuel, 4. juice, 5. Sue, 6. true, 7. clue, 8. canoe,

   9. cruise, 10. bruise, 11. fruit, 12. shoe, 13. pursue, 14. cruel, 15. nuisance

4. Have students take turns reading the books or stories that were written during the creative writing section of Lesson 44.

5. Use the handwriting sheet or have the children write the following sentences:

   We can fix the vase with glue.
   The knights dueled with lances.

Assessment Answers

1. bruised	1. true
2. shoes	2. false
3. fruit	3. true
4. due	4. true
5. clues	5. false

Lesson 46

Lesson Objectives

1. Students will read words with long a spelled with ey, ei, eig, ea and eigh. (P)
2. Students will learn to read the days of the week. (L)
3. Students will spell words correctly. (S)
4. Students will prepare to read the story *Jonathan's Not-So-Great Great Week.* (R)
5. Students will copy sentences neatly and correctly. (H)

Materials

LAR
SAP
Jonathan's Not-So-Great Great Week

Word List: vein, feign, veil, rein, reign, skein, reindeer, eight, weigh, weight, neigh, neighbor, freight, sleigh, whey, they, hey, prey, survey, obey, grey, steak, break, great, Shea, yea

Days of the Week: Sunday, Monday, Tuesday, Wednesday, Thursday, Friday, Saturday

Teaching

1. Write the words rain, way, pray, and brake. **Read the words.** **What vowel sound do they have?** (long a) Next write the words reign, rein, weigh, prey, and break.

   Read the words (the words will most likely be new to them.) **These words are homophones of the first four words. They sound alike but have different meanings and spellings.**

   Which letters in the words reign, rein, weigh, prey and break make the long a sound? Do you hear the g sound in reign? The g is silent. Are there silent letters in any of the other 4 words? (Yes, weigh has a silent g and h.)

   The letters e-y make the same sound as a-y in some words. Write the words key and money. **But what other sound can e-y make?** (long e) **The color gray can be spelled either gray or grey. There are two ways to spell the word.** Gray is the most common spelling, but we will use grey in these lessons (46 to 50) to emphasize the long a sound of -ey.

   The letters e-a make the long a in a few words: steak, break, great. What other sound can ea make? Most of the time it is the long e sound as in treat. It can also make a short e sound as in head (we have not formally introduced this in the curriculum yet).

   LAR workbook page: **Read the words and the meanings. Answer the questions at the bottom of the page.**

2. Students should be able to read all the days of the week from the phonics concepts they have learned with a few exceptions.

   The o in Monday has the short u sound (compare to money). **Wednesday is not pronounced as it is spelled. It may help to remember the spelling by saying it phonetically, Wed-nes-day. The i is long in Friday. All the days of the week end with d-a-y.** Break the other words into syllables. Sun-day, Tues-day, Thurs-day, Sat-ur-day.

3. Use the SAP workbook page. Have students read and spell each spelling word. Spelling list: Sunday, Monday, Tuesday, Wednesday, Thursday, Friday, Saturday, reindeer, weigh, eight, obey, great, feign, neighbor.

   Use the top section of the workbook page. **Alphabetize the words in each box.**

   The days of the week end with the word day. Other words end with the word day. Look at the bottom of the workbook page. Add day to the end of the letters at the bottom of the page to make more words.

4. *Jonathan's Not-So-Great Great Week* focuses on words with long a spelled with ey, ei, eig, ea and eigh. It also emphasizes the days of the week. In addition to those words, the following words may be new to students and will require some instruction: morning, liver.

The word *morning:*	Break into syllables (morn + ing)
The word *liver:*	The i is short even though the form of the word would indicate it is long.

   You may also review the words *Jonathan, Rosie, ounces, idea, friends, downstairs, teacher, front,* and *fries*.

   Introduce the story: Ask a student to read the title of the book. Ask: **Have you ever had a not-so-great week? Have you ever had a great week? What do you think a not-so-great great week is? Read the story to find out what is a not-so-great great week.**

   Students will silently read as much of the story as they can in the time allowed.

5. Use the handwriting sheet or have the children write the following sentences:

   We saw eight reindeer Monday morning.
   The man used reins to steer the sleigh.

LAR Answers

1. neigh
2. steak
3. rein
4. freight
5. prey
6. reign
7. veil
8. feign
9. skein

SAP Answers

1. eight	5. neighbor
2. feign	6. Monday
3. Friday	7. obey
4. great	

1. reindeer	5. Tuesday
2. Saturday	6. Wednesday
3. Sunday	7. weigh
4. Thursday	

Any order

payday birthday holiday weekday someday today

Jonathan's Not-So-Great Great Week

Second Grade Phonics & Reading

Book 9
Lessons 46 to 50

Jonathan's Not-So-Great Great Week

Written and illustrated by
Brian Davis

Sunday

My name is Jonathan. I just had a not-so-great great week. What is a not-so-great great week? Let me tell you about it.

On Sunday morning, I woke up. The sky was grey. It began to snow on the way to church.

I went to my Sunday class. The teacher told us to love our neighbors. I thought that was a great idea.

2

3

Jonathan's Not-So-Great Great Week

We went home after church. My neighbor Sue came out to play. Nothing shows love like a snowball in the face.

I had a great big one. It must have weighed eight ounces. I had been waiting for Sue. This would show lots of love.

Smack! It was a great shot. It smacked Sue in the face.

I didn't know she had eight friends with her.
They showed lots of snowball love.
Sunday was not-so-great.

4

5

Monday

I thought Monday could be better. It started well. I got to be in a play. All the kids would see it Friday.

I was a reindeer. I had to pull a sleigh. It was a great part.

Then, Sue got in the sleigh.
Then, her eight friends got in the sleigh.
They weighed a lot. I was a tired reindeer.

"Maybe you can be a horse," said the teacher.

I said no. I didn't know how to neigh.
Sunday and Monday were not-so-great.

6

7

Jonathan's Not-So-Great Great Week

Tuesday

Tuesday started out great. I learned how to neigh. I told the teacher I could be a horse.

"Great," said the teacher. "There's one horse part left. You will work with Shea."

I didn't get to neigh. I was the back of the horse. Shea got to neigh. Sunday, Monday, and Tuesday were not-so-great.

8

9

Wednesday

Wednesday a beige truck came. It left a box of freight at my house.

"Don't look in the box," Mom told my sister Rosie and me. "It's a gift from your grandmother. We can open it in eight days."

I tried to obey. I shook the box. It weighed about a pound.

"Don't do that," said Mom. "It might break."

I tried to obey. That night I couldn't wait. Rosie and I sneaked downstairs. I opened the box. In it was a grey skirt.

"Yea! I love it! I love it!" shouted Rosie.

"Shhh! You'll wake Dad," I said.

"Too late," said Dad.

I didn't obey. Sunday, Monday, Tuesday, and Wednesday were not-so-great.

10

11

Jonathan's Not-So-Great Great Week

Thursday

Thursday night mom was cooking in the kitchen. I could hear a sizzle.

"This will be great," I thought. "I like a great steak."

Then I found out it was liver. I would rather eat a reindeer. I tried to feign illness. Mom wouldn't give me a break.

I saw my neighbor Sue. I asked if I could eat at her house. She said her mom was fixing curds and whey. I don't even know what that is. I think Sue was teasing.

I didn't eat at the neighbor's house. I ate liver. Sunday, Monday, Tuesday, Wednesday, and Thursday were not-so-great.

12

13

Friday

I had little hope for Friday. I felt it was going to be not-so-great. I was wrong.

The boy named Shea was sick. I got to be the front of the horse. All the kids loved my neighing.

14

At home, another beige truck came. It left freight at our house. The freight weighed eight pounds.

"It's for you, Jonathan," said Mom. "I'll hide the box for now. That should help you obey."

Dad grilled steak for dinner. I still don't know what are curds and whey. At last, Friday was great!

15

Jonathan's Not-So-Great Great Week

Saturday

Saturday the sky was grey again. This time it snowed eight inches. I gave Shea a call.

I said, "Neigh."

He giggled. "That's great," said Shea.

I said, "I'll see you Monday."

Then, I helped my neighbor Sue. We cleared a path in the snow.

"Hey, my mom's cooking steak and fries. Want to eat with us?" asked my neighbor Sue.

My mom said it was OK. I ate steak. It tasted great.

"What kind of steak is this?" I asked my neighbor's mom.

"Reindeer," answered Sue's mom. I think she was teasing.

"At least it's not curds and whey," I said.

Sue's mom giggled. So, Friday and Saturday were great! I hope Sunday will be the start of an all-so-great week.

16

Jonathan's Not-So-Great Great Week

answered
beige
better
break
church
cleared
couldn't
curds
downstairs
eight
feign
Friday
friends

fries
front
giggled
grandmother
great
grey
grilled
idea
illness
Jonathan
liver
love
Monday
morning
neigh

neighbor
night
nothing
obey
ounces
pound
reindeer
Rosie
Saturday
Shea
shook
shows
sizzle
sleigh
smacked

sneaked
snowball
steak
Sue
Sunday
teacher
teasing
thought
Thursday
Tuesday
Wednesday
weighed
what
whey
yea

Lesson 47

Lesson Objectives

1. Students will find homophones for long a words. (P & L)
2. Students will identify nouns and verbs. (L)
3. Students will review spelling words. (S)
4. Students will unscramble the days of the week. (S & L)
5. Students will read *Jonathan's Not-So-Great Great Week.* (R)
6. Students will copy sentences neatly and correctly. (H)

Materials

LAR
SAP
Jonathan's Not-So-Great Great Week

Teaching

1. Review homophones: words that sound alike but have different spellings and meanings. Use the top of the LARworkbook page. The words in black are homophones for the correct word. Fill in the missing words.

2. Review nouns and verbs. **What are nouns?** (people, places, things) **Is the word Wednesday a noun?** (yes) **The names of the days of a week are nouns. They are proper nouns. Proper nouns are names. Name some other nouns.**

   What are verbs? (words that tell what nouns are doing)

   Sentences must have at least one noun and verb. They can have more than one.

   Use the bottom of the LAR workbook page. **Read the sentences. Some of the words have circles above and below them. Notice the letters in the circles. The letter n is on the top row. The letter v is on the bottom row. If a word is a noun in the sentence fill in the n circle. If it is a verb, fill in the v circle.**

3. Use the top of the SAP page. **Fill in the boxes to make spelling words. Fit all the words into the grid. Start with the clue spaces with letters. The number of boxes is also a clue.**

4. Use the bottom of the SAP page. **Unscramble the days of the week and write them on the lines. In the boxes number them in the order they happen in the week from 1 to 7. Sunday is the first day of the week. Saturday is the seventh day of the week.**

5. Review the additional reading vocabulary: morning, liver.

   Students will read pages 1 to 8 out loud. Next, ask the following questions:

   What did Jonathan learn in Sunday school? (to love our neighbors)
   How was Jonathan trying to show love to Sue? (throwing a snowball)
   Do you think Jonathan really thought he was showing love? (Answers vary.)
   Why or why not?
   What part did Jonathan get in the play? (reindeer)
   Why did the teacher ask him if he wanted to be a horse? (The sleigh was too heavy.)
   What happened on Tuesday? (Jonathan had to be the back of a horse.)
   Do you think the Sue in this story is the same one as in Blue Shoe Canoes? (Answers vary.)
   Why or why not?

6. Use the handwriting sheet or have the children write the following sentences:

   We always eat steak on Tuesdays.
   The sky was grey Thursday night.

SAP Answers

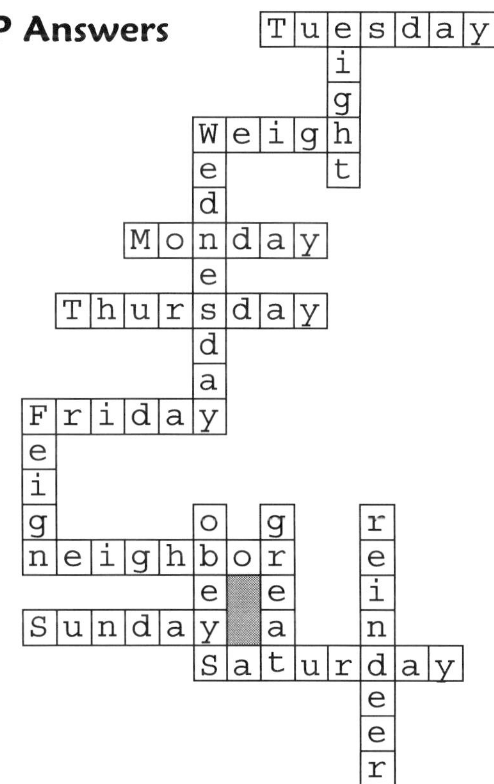

5 Thursday
7 Saturday
2 Monday
4 Wednesday
6 Friday
1 Sunday
3 Tuesday

LAR Answers

1. break
2. sleigh
3. preyed
4. eight
5. weigh

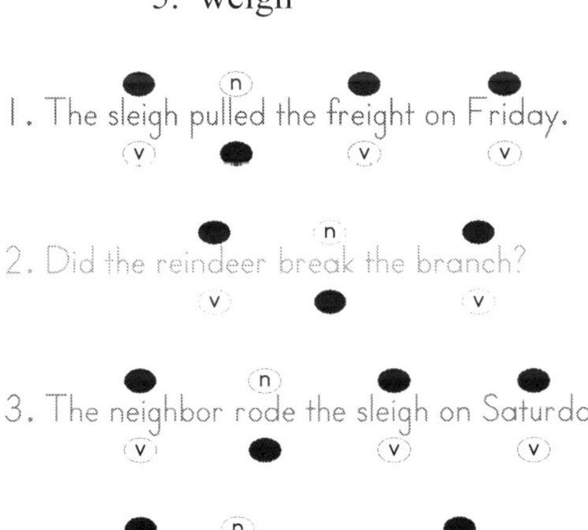

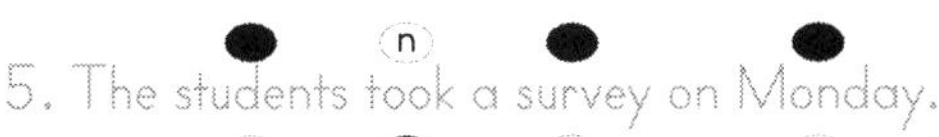

Lesson 48

Lesson Objectives

1. Students will fill in the missing vowel digraphs. (P)
2. Students will change words. (S)
3. Students will write a letter. (CW)
4. Students will read *Jonathan's Not-So-Great Great Week.* (R)
5. Students will copy sentences neatly and correctly. (H)

Materials

LAR
SAP
Jonathan's Not-So-Great Great Week
Writing Skills Workbook page is available

Teaching

1. Use the top of the SAP workbook page. **The words are missing letters. Fill in the missing letters.**

2. Write syllable equations. Fried - ed + day =

   This looks sort of like a word and sort of like math problem. If you see a minus sign, subtract that part of the word. If you see a plus sign add the letters after it. What does this equal? (Friday) Repeat with West - st + igh = Weigh, Money - ey + day = Monday

   Use the bottom of the SAP workbook page. **Add suffixes or syllables to change the words. Plus signs are used to show parts are added. Subtraction signs show parts that are taken away. Write the words on the lines.**

3. Students will write a letter. Use the LAR page. The page models a letter and provides space to write a letter. The student will write a letter from Jonathan in the story. The purpose is for Jonathan to tell a friend about his week.

Describe the parts of the letter. **The salutation is where you write who the letter is to. It usually begins with the word Dear. On the same line you can add the date of the letter.**

The body of the letter is the part you write to the person. It contains the information.

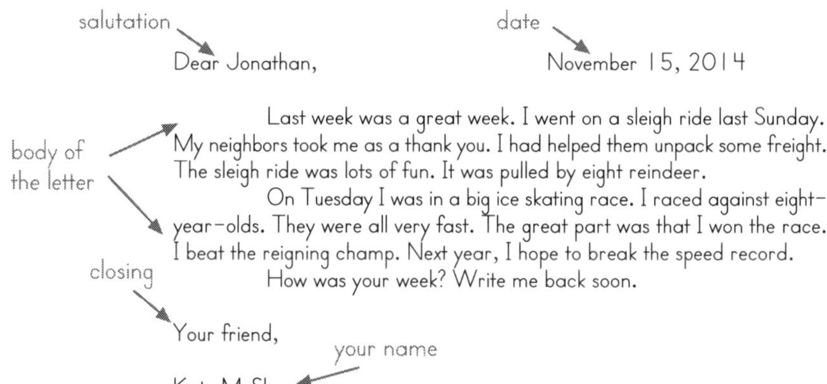
Read the letter from one of Jonathan's friends. The different parts of the letter are labeled.

The closing is a few words before your name. It is a short personal statement. In this letter it was *Your Friend*. It can be other words such as *Love, Yours truly,* or *Sincerely yours*. End the letter by writing your name.

Help Jonathan out by writing a letter back to Kate McShea. Write a letter back. Tell Kate about the week Jonathan had. Tell about some of the things that happened to him. Make the letter sound like it is from Jonathan.

4. Review the first half of the book *Jonathan's Not-So-Great Great Week*. Next, read the second half of the book. After completing the story ask the students the following questions:

   What was in the box on Wednesday? (a skirt)
   Why do you think Rosie got a present? (Answers vary.)
   Why do you think Mom wanted to wait eight days to open the box? (Answers vary.)
   Why do you think Jonathan and Rosie didn't obey? (Answers vary.)
   What does it mean to feign illness? (pretend to be sick)
   What do you think curds and whey is? (Answers vary. People used to get milk straight from cows. Now, milk is taken to a dairy. Milk has different parts. The dairy separates the parts. Parts of milk can get thick. This is the curds. Cheese is made from the curds. The thin watery part is the whey.)
   Do you think Sue's mom was really fixing curds and whey? (Answers vary.)
   What was great about Friday? (Jonathan got to be the front of the horse. He got a package. His dad grilled steak.)
   What happened when Jonathan was nice to Sue? (She invited him to eat with her.)
   What kind of meat did Sue's mom say they were eating? (reindeer)
   Do you think she was teasing? (Answers vary.)

5. Use the handwriting sheet or have the children write the following sentences:

   Shea weighed the freight.
   Little Miss Tuffit ate curds and whey.

SAP Answers

Sunday Monday Tuesday

Wednesday Thursday

Friday Saturday

1. great
2. neighbor
3. eight
4. obey
5. reindeer
6. weigh
7. feign

LAR Answers vary

Lesson 49

Lesson Objectives

1. Students will put a story in order. (L)
2. Students will review spelling words. (S)
3. Students will write a story. (CW)
4. Students will read *Jonathan's Not-So-Great Great Week.* (R)
5. Students will copy sentences neatly and correctly. (H)

Materials

LAR
SAP
Jonathan's Not-So-Great Great Week
Writing Skills Workbook page is available

Teaching

1. **Read the sentences on the LAR workbook page. Write the day of the week that they happened in the story *Jonathan's Not-So-Great Great Week.* Some days of the week are used twice. You may use the reading book to help you.**

2. Use the SAP workbook page. **Look at the top part of the spelling book page. Find the word *sad.* There are six blanks after it. Look at the spelling word list. The words are numbered. Write the numbers for the spelling words that have the letters to spell sad. If a spelling word has the letters s, a, and d anywhere in any order, write that spelling word's number on the blank. There should be a number for every blank after the small words.**

   Bottom section: **A spelling word can be made with the letters in order on each row of letters. Extra letters have been added. Color in the boxes for the letters that do not belong. Each row will spell one spelling word.**

3. Students will write a story about a week. Say: **In the book *Jonathan's Not-So-Great Great Week*, a boy named Jonathan tells about his week. Today you will write a book that takes place over a week. Think of something that happened to you each day in the last week, or you may make something up for each day. Maybe you could write about what you would like to happen instead of what happened.**

   The following questions might be helpful: **What was the best thing that happened? What was the worst thing that happened? Who was with you? What did you do? How could you have changed the situation?** Students can make a book and write their stories in the book.

4. Read the book *Jonathan's Not-So-Great Great Week* again. Next, have students look at the back of the book and answer the following questions about the word list.

   What words are names of people? (Jonathan, Rosie, Shea, Sue)
   What words are people, but not names of people? (friends, grandmother, neighbor, teacher)
   What word is the root word of weighed? (weigh) **Find its homophone in the list.** (whey)
   What two days of the week begin like the word teacher? (Tuesday, Thursday)
   What word has the letters nc together like in the word dance? (ounces)
   What word means to fake something? (feign)
   What words are things that can come from cows? (curds, steak, whey, liver)
   What word is a synonym for tan? (beige)
   What word is something you can ride on in the snow? (sleigh)
   What day of the week comes after the word love? (Monday)

5. Use the handwriting sheet or have the children write the following sentences:

   The kind king reigned over the land.
   Wednesday and Friday were great days.

LAR Answers

1. Tuesday
2. Saturday
3. Friday
4. Wednesday
5. Sunday
6. Thursday
7. Monday
8. Sunday
9. Friday
10. Thursday
11. Saturday

SAP Answers

sad 1,3,4,5,7 hen 14
man 2 sat 3,5,7 hi 9,10, 14
us 1,3,7 if 6,13 the 10
stray 5,7 get 10,12 art 5,7,12
in 8,13,14 be 11,14 wig 9
we 4,9 dine 8 on 2,14
fin 13 boy 11 rat 5,7,12

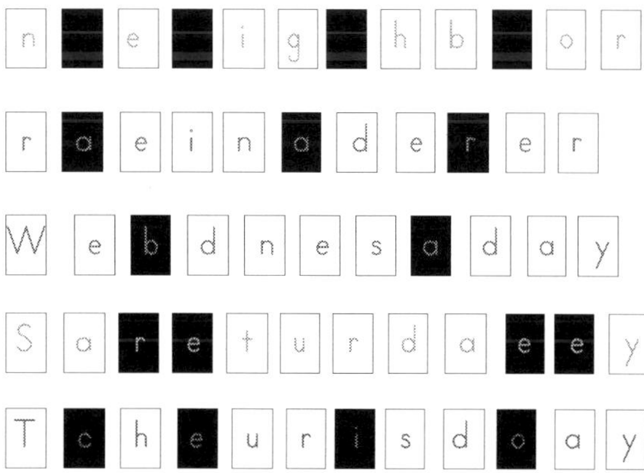

Lesson 50

Lesson Objectives

1. Students will be tested on phonics concepts. (P)
2. Students will be tested on language concepts. (L)
3. Students will take a spelling test. (S)
4. Students will read about reindeer. (R)
5. Students will read the story they written. (R)
6. Students will copy a sentence neatly and correctly. (H)

Materials

LAR
Questions poster
Creative writing assignment from lesson 49
Assessment 50

Teaching

1. Use part A of the assessment as a phonics test. Have the students fill in the circles next to the words that complete the sentences.

2. Use part B of the assessment page. Students will choose the homophones from the list that match the ones next to the lines. Write the answers on the lines.

3. Have students number their paper from 1 to 14. Give the spelling test:

   1. Thursday, 2. reindeer, 3. Monday, 4. obey, 5. feign, 6. Wednesday, 7. Tuesday, 8. great, 9. neighbor, 10. Sunday, 11. weigh, 12. Friday, 13. eight, 14. Saturday

4. Students will read about reindeer on the LAR workbook page. The text is reprinted on the next page as a teacher copy. The workbook page was formatted like a science textbook page to familiarize students with the page design. Point out the section headings and the captions under pictures. Also note the bold print for the word lichens.

   The section headings are useful to quickly find specific information. They often tell the topic for that section.

   Captions explain pictures. Sometimes other words are in bold print like the word lichens. Usually the author will explain the meaning of the word. The bold print highlights it so you will pay more attention to that word, since it is probably a key word or a new vocabulary word.

   After students have read the page, ask true and false questions. You may have students respond verbally or write their answers. Written responses can be T if true, F if false.

   Reindeer antlers fall off. (True)
   Lichens eat reindeer. (False)
   Reindeer like warm places. (False)
   Wild reindeer are called Caribou. (True)
   The word Caribou means snowman. (False)
   Reindeer hooves harden in the winter. (True)
   People milk reindeer. (True)
   Reindeer have three coats of fur. (False)
   Reindeer are great swimmers. (True)
   Reindeer have hollow fur. (True) Continued on the next page.

4. (Continued)

   Use the Question Poster. **Write four questions about reindeer. Use the question words to begin the questions.**

5. Have students take turns reading the books or stories that were written during the creative writing section of lesson 49.

6. Use the handwriting sheet or have the children write the following sentences:

   Our neighbors came over on Saturday.
   The grey horse neighed at me Sunday.

Assessment Answers

1. Wednesday	1. rein
2. preyed	2. whey
3. eight	3. break
4. obey	4. sleigh
5. weighed	5. great

Reindeer

Where reindeer live

Reindeer live in cold, northern places. In the U.S. reindeer can be found in Alaska. They like cold places. There are fewer insects to bother them. They live in places with lots of snow. There are many things about reindeer that help them live in cold places.

Reindeer hooves

They have special hooves. The hooves change in the summer. They become soft to help them walk on spongy ground called **tundra**. Soft hooves help them grip the plants that grow on the ground. Otherwise, they might slip and fall. In the winter the ground freezes and becomes hard. Reindeer hooves harden, too. This helps them cut ruts in ice. It helps them stand and walk.

Food for reindeer

Wild reindeer are called caribou. The word caribou is a French word. It means snow shoveler. Reindeer and caribou can use their hooves like snow shovels. Their food is under the snow. Reindeer hooves can dig for **lichens**, grass, moss, and twigs. Lichens are two kinds of plants that work together to grow. Reindeer moss is a kind of lichen. Because reindeer eat so much of it, the plants are named after them.

Reindeer antlers

A reindeer's antlers also help them dig for food. Both male and female reindeer have antlers. The antlers have upper and lower sets of points. The antlers fall off every year.

Reindeer fur

Their fur coats also help them in the winter. Have you ever worn two coats when it's cold outside? Reindeer wear two coats all the time. The first coat is dense fur. It traps the heat of their bodies. The second coat is made up of hollow hair. Air is trapped inside the hair. This keeps the cold away from their skin. The fur also helps them float. Reindeer are great swimmers. They can even swim in icy water.

Ways reindeer help people

People raise reindeer like ranchers raise cattle. They are very useful animals for people. Reindeer are raised for meat and hides. Even their antlers and bones are used for tools.

Some people use reindeer to pull sleighs. Milk comes from cows. Some people get milk from reindeer, too. They make butter and cheese from reindeer milk. Maybe they could even make reindeer ice cream!

Lesson 51

Lesson Objectives

1. Students will read words with the soft g sound (-dge and -nge). (P)
2. Students will spell words correctly. (S)
3. Students will prepare to read the story *Hedgehog Fudge*. (R)
4. Students will copy sentences neatly and correctly. (H)

Materials

LAR
SAP
Hedgehog Fudge
Writing Skills Workbook page is available

Word List: hedge, ledge, wedge, dredge, pledge, sledge, edge, badge, badger, ridge, fudge, budge, lodge, Madge, hodgepodge, bridge, pudgy, judge, nudge, dodge, sludge, trudge, smudge, hedgehog, smidgen plunge, change, hinge, binge, flange, singe, stingy, lunge

Teaching

1. Write the words bad and bin. Write the letters ge. Say: **Most of the time, g followed by a silent e will make the soft g sound. The soft g sound is the same as the j sound, *j*. Read the first two words.** (bad, bin) Add ge to the end of each. **The e is silent. What sound will the g have?** *(j)*

   Help students blend the words. Have students decode other words from the word list. Tell students that they will be working on words that have dge and nge in them for the next five lessons.

   Top of the LAR page: **Read the words and the meanings. Answer the questions at the bottom of the page.** Note: The word badger has two meanings.

2. Use the SAP page. Have students read and spell each word. Spelling list: ledge, badger, fudge, hinge, smudge, change, plunge, stingy, wedge, sponge, edge, danger, angel, gadget.

   Sort the words by the ng and dg spelling. Write the ng words in the top box. Write the dg spelling words in the bottom box.

   SAP bottom section: **Create more words by adding parts to spelling words. Write the new words on the lines.**

3. *Hedgehog Fudge* focuses on words with long a spelled with -nge and -nce. In addition to those words, the following words may be new to students and will require some instruction: cocoa, course, honey, powdered, refrigerator, sorry, sugar, syrup. The word list and pronunciation guide is printed at the bottom of the LAR page.

The word *cocoa:*	The oa makes the long o sound as in boat.
The word *course:*	The -our- sounds like or. The e is silent.
The word *honey:*	The o makes the short u sound. -ey makes the long e sound.
The word *powdered:*	Point out the suffix -ed. The ow makes the ow sound as in cow.
The word *refrigerator:*	Break into syllables. Re- the e is long, the a is long.
The word *sorry:*	Sounds like sar-ee.
The word *sugar:*	The u has the -oo- sound as in foot.
	The s makes the sh sound with the u, ar makes an -er sound.
The word *syrup:*	syr sounds like sir.

You may also review the words *chipmunks, eight, mind, neighborhood, scurried.*

Introduce the story: Ask a student to read the title of the book. Ask: **A hedgehog is a small animal that has quills like a porcupine. Do you know what fudge is? Do you know how to make it? You will after reading this story.** Students will silently read as much of the story as they can in the time allowed.

Recipe: LAR workbook page 52 (Lesson 55) and a copy master both contain a Hedgehog Fudge recipe. You may make it at anytime during the next five lessons (or not at all). There will be no specific lesson assigned to do this. The recipe requires cooking, so parental or teacher supervision will be necessary. If you do not have access to a candy thermometer, you may determine the soft ball stage of the candy by drooping a small amount into very cold water. It should form a soft ball. The ball should flatten when removed from the water. Margarine may be substituted for butter.

Students will be able to read most of the recipe. They may need help with these words: vanilla, occasionally, remove, medium, tablespoon, teaspoon

4. Use the handwriting sheet or have the children write the following sentences:

Don't stand close to the edge.
Madge singed the pan of fudge.

LAR Answers

1. nudge
2. sludge
3. dodge
4. badger
5. plunge
6. singe
7. hodgepodge
8. badger
9. hedge

SAP Answers

ng words in any order:

hinge
change sponge
plunge danger
stingy angel

dg words in any order:

ledge
badger wedge
fudge edge
smudge gadget

Bottom

1. exchange
2. angelic
3. dangerous
4. knowledge

Hedgehog Fudge

Book 10
Lessons 51 to 55

Hedgehog Fudge

Madge and Pudge were hedgehogs. They loved candy.

"Can we eat some fudge?" they asked their mom.

"No," said Mrs. Hedgehog. "I would need to make it."

She opened the refrigerator. "We are out of milk and butter."

So Madge and Pudge trudged out the door.

2

3

Hedgehog Fudge

"Moo," called the cow.

Pudge nudged Madge. "We can ask the cow for milk."

"And cream to make butter," added Madge.

Madge and Pudge trudged to the barn. The door's hinge squeaked.

"Who's there?" asked the cow.

"It's us, Pudge and Madge," answered Pudge.

"Come in hedgehogs," mooed the cow.

"May we have some milk?" asked Madge.

"And some cream to make butter," added Pudge. "Our mom is making fudge."

"Of course," said the cow. "But don't be stingy with the fudge."

"We won't," said Madge. "We will share it with you."

4

5

Madge and Pudge lugged a pail. It was filled with milk and cream. They took the milk to their mom.

"I am out of more things," said the mother hedgehog.

"What?" asked Madge.

"Just a smidgen of this and a smidgen of that," said Mrs. Hedgehog. "I made a list."

Madge and Pudge took the list.

6

The first thing on the list was honey. They found a hive in a tree trunk. The tree was at the edge of the stream. Pudge had a jar. He plunged the jar into the honey.

"Watch out for bees," shouted Madge.

It was too late. Pudge was dodging bees. He plunged into the stream. Madge grabbed the jar of honey.

"Hey! We'll make you some fudge," Madge said to the bees.

"Mmm Mmm!" hummed the bees.

7

Hedgehog Fudge

"What is all this buzzing in the neighborhood?" asked Bridgett the Badger. "Why Pudge, you are soaking wet. Come on in and dry off. I have a warm fire."

Pudge was quite wet. He was also quite cold.
Bridgett Badger's fire warmed him up.

"Would you like some bug juice?" asked Bridgett Badger.

"No," shivered Pudge.

"How about a cup of cocoa?" asked Bridgett.

"Cocoa!" squealed Madge. "It's on our list."

8

Bridgett Badger gave them some powdered cocoa.

"Now don't be stingy with the fudge," said Bridgett Badger.

"We won't," said Pudge as they left.

9

Next they came to the pecan tree.

"Oh, no!" said Madge. "There is just one pecan left!"

Madge reached for the pecan. A grey squirrel pounced on the pecan.

"My nut, my nut!" squealed the squirrel.

"You stingy squirrel!" yelled Pudge.

Madge nudged Pudge. "Be nice. Don't judge the squirrel. He must not like fudge."

"Fudge?" said the squirrel. "Did you say fudge?
Your mom's great fudge? I change my mind. You can have my pecans."

10

The squirrel scurried up the tree eight times. He gave them all the pecans they needed. The squirrel even gave them peanut butter

11

Hedgehog Fudge

Madge and Pudge crossed a bridge. Two chipmunks were riding turtles.

"Hello Hue," said Madge.

"Hello Stue," said Pudge.

"We are going to make fudge. Can you help us get sugar?" asked Madge.

"We don't like fudge," said Stue.

"Sorry," said Hue.

12

"I love fudge," said a turtle.

"I'd walk eight miles for fudge," said the other turtle.

"Eight miles! I'll get brown sugar," said Stue.

"I'll get white sugar," said Hue.

"We'll get powdered sugar," said a turtle.

13

"Honk, honk!" A goose was drifting under the bridge. "Did some hedgehogs say fudge?"

"Yes," answered Madge.

The goose hopped onto a ledge.

"Let me take a gander at that list," said the goose. "A smidgen of corn syrup. That I have!
I will bring it to your house."

"Yea! We did it," said Pudge.

14

15

Hedgehog Fudge

Pudge and Madge mixed the fudge. Their mom cooked it. Their friends waited for the fudge.

Pudge and Madge were not stingy. The cow ate fudge. The bees buzzed around some fudge. Bridgett Badger said it was the best fudge ever.

"Very nutty, that's the way to make fudge!" said the grey squirrel.

The turtles were trudging after their fudge. Stue and Hue rode on their backs.

"If I were a fudge judge, you would win," honked the goose to Mrs. Hedgehog.

There was one piece left in the pan.

"Oh, no!" said Pudge, "Which one of us will eat it?"

Madge sighed, "I'm not stingy. You can eat it."

Pudge smiled. He started to eat it. Then he saw his mom.

"I'm not stingy," said Pudge.

He took the fudge to Mrs. Hedgehog. She gobbled it up. Madge and Pudge were sad.

"Why are you sad?" asked Mrs. Hedgehog. "I made a pan just for you. It's in the refrigerator."

Pudge and Madge lunged for the fudge. They were two very happy hedgehogs.

16

Hedgehog Fudge

Stir together:

1/2 cup of milk
1/4 cup of cocoa
1/4 cup of brown sugar
1/2 cup of sugar
1/4 cup of honey
1 tablespoon of corn syrup
1 tablespoon of peanut butter

Add:

1 teaspoon of vanilla
1/2 cup of nuts

Stir in:
2 cups of powdered sugar.

Spread the fudge in a pan.
Cool in the refrigerator for 30 minutes.
Cut into bars. Enjoy the fudge!

Cook over medium heat.
Stir until melted.
Keep stirring occasionally.
Cook to soft ball stage
(234° to 240°)

Remove from heat.
Add 2 tablespoons of butter,
but do not stir.
Allow to cool to 120°.

Hedgehog Fudge

badger
bridge
Bridgett
brown
butter
buzzing
candy
change
chipmunks
cocoa
course
cow
cream
crossed
dodging
don't
drifted
edge
eight

friends
fudge
gander
gobbled
goose
great
grey
happy
hedgehog
hey
hinge
honey
honk
Hue
judge
juice
ledge
lunged
Madge
mind

neighborhood
nudged
nutty
opened
other
peanut
pecan
plunged
pounced
powdered
Pudge
refrigerator
scurried
share
shivered
smidgen
some
sorry
squeaked
squealed
squirrel

stingy
stream
Stue
sugar
syrup
they
trudged
turtles
two
under
very
warm
watch
we'll
were
what
white
who's
why
won't
would

Lesson 52

Lesson Objectives

1. Students will review nouns. (L)
2. Students will be proofread sentences. (L)
3. Students will alphabetize the spelling list. (S)
4. Students will read the story *Hedgehog Fudge*. (R)
5. Students will copy sentences neatly and correctly. (H)

Materials

LAR
SAP
Hedgehog Fudge

Teaching

1. Review nouns (people, places, or things). Next, use the top of the LAR workbook page. **Fill in the oval next to the word that was used as a noun in the sentence.**

2. Use the bottom of the LAR workbook page. **Find the mistakes. Sentences may be missing capital letters, periods, apostrophes, or have misspelled words. Write the sentences over again correctly on the lines.**

3. Use the SAP page. Write the words sweet and sixteen. **Look at the two spelling words in the top of the red box. What are the words?** (stingy and wedge) **Below these two words are four more words with circles and squares in front of them. Look at the words. If the word can be made from any of the letters in the two spelling words combined, fill in the yes circle. If not, fill in the no square.**

   Let's practice with the two words I wrote. Can you spell *sweet* with the letters of the two spelling words? You can use the s and t from *stingy* and the w and two e's from *wedge*. The answer is yes. What about the word *sixteen*. (No, there is no x in either word.)

   Bottom section: **Exchange the underlined word in each sentence with the spelling word that changes the meaning of the sentence the least.**

4. Review the additional reading vocabulary: cocoa, course, honey, powdered, refrigerator, sorry, sugar, syrup.

   Students will read pages 1 to 9 out loud. Next, ask the following questions:

   Why couldn't Mrs. Hedgehog make fudge? (She was out of milk and butter.)
   Where did Madge and Pudge get the milk and butter? (from a cow)
   What did Madge promise to give the cow? (fudge)
   How did Pudge get wet? (He plunged into a stream while dodging bees.)
   What kind of juice did Bridgett have? (bug juice)
   What did the hedgehogs get from the badger? (powdered cocoa)
   What did the hedgehogs get from the bees? (honey)
   Do you think the animals had eaten hedgehog fudge before? (Answers vary.)
   Why or why not?

5. Use the handwriting sheet or have the children write the following sentences:

   The judge changed his robe.
   The hedgehog crossed the bridge.

LAR Answers

1. hinge
2. bridge
3. sugar
4. arm
5. hedge

1. Did you change your shoes?
2. The judge liked the fudge.
3. Don't badger me while I'm working.
4. Did the rock plunge off the ledge?

SAP Answers

stingy wedge		
yes	no	
●	□	wing
●	□	dingy
○	■	string
●	□	eggs

badger ledge		
yes	no	
●	□	dad
○	■	great
●	□	blade
○	■	bigger

fudge hinge		
yes	no	
○	■	head
●	□	feed
○	■	fridge
●	□	hug

smudge change		
yes	no	
●	□	dance
●	□	sand
●	□	much
●	□	hands

plunge danger		
yes	no	
●	□	gear
●	□	range
●	□	green
○	■	lamp

sponge gadget		
yes	no	
●	□	ten
●	□	sand
●	□	tagged
○	■	tongue

edge angel		
yes	no	
●	□	legal
○	■	near
○	■	bean
○	■	deep

stingy smudge		
yes	no	
○	■	piggy
●	□	nudge
●	□	misty
○	■	moss

Bottom section

1. fudge
2. sponge
3. gadget
4. smudge
5. plunge
6. badger

Lesson 53

Lesson Objectives

1. Students will solve a crossword puzzle. (P & L)
2. Students will use spelling words in sentences. (S & L)
3. Students will read the story *Hedgehog Fudge*. (R)
4. Students will copy sentences neatly and correctly. (H)

Materials

LAR
SAP
Hedgehog Fudge

Teaching

1. Use the LAR workbook page. Solve the crossword puzzle.

2. Use the SAP workbook page. **Complete the sentences by writing the spelling words. Each pair of sentences needs four words. Choose from the group of five words. Write the word that wasn't used in each group at the bottom of the page.**

3. Review the first half of the book *Hedgehog Fudge*. Next, read the second half of the book. After completing the story ask the students the following questions:

   Who took the pecans? (a squirrel)
   What two things did the squirrel give them? (peanut butter, pecans)
   How was the way Madge talked to the squirrel different from the way Pudge talked to the squirrel? (Answers vary.)
   Who did Madge and Pudge see on the bridge? (Hue, Stue, the turtles, and a goose)
   Why did the chipmunks decide to help? (The fudge would make the turtles walk.)
   What did the goose bring? (corn syrup)
   Why didn't Pudge eat the fudge? (He didn't want to be stingy.)
   Did Pudge and Madge keep their promise to their friends? (yes)
   What was that promise? (They would share the fudge.)
   Did Pudge and Madge get fudge? (yes)

4. Use the handwriting sheet or have the children write the following sentences:

   The man with the badge led the pledge.
   The pudgy badger has sharp claws.

LAR Answers

			1 F	U	2 D	G	E			3 B	U	D	G	E		
					O					A						
			4 H	O	D	G	E	P	O	D	G	E				
		5 B	E		G					G						
		6 E	D	8 G	E					E				15 H	I	16 S
7 B	A	D	G	E	S		12 P		13 B	R	I	D	G	E		T
			E				L							D		I
			9 H	I	N	G	E			14 S	M	I	D	G	E	N
			O				D							E		G
10 S	I	N	G	E			G									Y
					11 S	L	E	D	G	E						

SAP Answers

fudge	ledge
sponge	smudge
badger	danger
change	hinge
wedge	gadget
edge	
angel	

Not used (in order)

stingy plunge danger
(danger was not used in
the third group)

Lesson 54

Lesson Objectives

1. Students will put a story in order. (L)
2. Students will review spelling words. (S & L)
3. Students will write a story. (CW)
4. Students will read the story *Hedgehog Fudge*. (R)
5. Students will copy sentences neatly and correctly. (H)

Materials

LAR
SAP
Hedgehog Fudg
Writing Skills Workbook page is available

Teaching

1. Use the LAR page. **Read the sentences on the top of the workbook page. Number them in order that they happened in the story. You may use your reading book.**

   Use the bottom of the LAR page. **Answer questions about the story. Fill in the ovals to mark your answers.**

2. Use the SAP workbook page. **Write the spelling words that match the descriptions.**

3. Students will write a story about making food. Say: **In the book Hedgehog Fudge, Madge and Pudge made fudge. Today you will write a story about preparing food. Maybe your story will be about a special recipe. Maybe your story will be about a whole meal, like making a Thanksgiving dinner. You can make up your own recipes.**

   The following questions may be helpful: **What is this meal or food for? What are some of your favorite foods? In the story Hedgehog Fudge Bridgett the badger liked bug juice. If the story is about animals instead of people, what foods might they like? Maybe your story happened in another country. What foods do the people there eat?**

4. Read the book *Hedgehog Fudge* again. Next, have students look at the back of the book and answer the following questions about the word list. You may do this orally or have students write answers:

   What word is a box that is cold? (refrigerator)
   What words are spelled with -eigh like in the word weigh? (neighborhood, eight)
   What words have the e sound spelled with e-a? (cream, squeaked, squealed, stream)
   What words end with the long e sound? (candy, honey, nutty, sorry, stingy, very)
   What two days of the week begin like the word teacher? (Tuesday, Thursday)
   What words are contractions? (don't, we'll, who's, won't)
   What words are color words? (brown, grey, white)
   What words are sweet foods? (candy, fudge, honey, sugar, syrup)

5. Use the handwriting sheet or have the children write the following sentences:

   The hinge on the lodge door squeaks.
   Sue added a smidgen of cocoa to the mix.

LAR Answers

Top

7
4
10
1
5
2
8
9
3
6

1. **yes** no
2. yes **no**
3. yes **no**
4. **yes** no
5. **yes** no

SAP Answers

danger	smudge
hinge	edge
sponge	fudge
plunge	angel
stingy	wedge
badger	ledge
change	gadget

Lesson 55

Lesson Objectives

1. Students will be tested on phonics concepts. (P)
2. Students will be tested on language concepts. (L)
3. Students will take a spelling test. (S)
4. Students will read the story they have written. (R)
5. Students will read a recipe. (R)
6. Students will copy a sentence neatly and correctly. (H)

Materials

LAR
Creative writing assignment from lesson 54
Assessment 55
Hedgehog Fudge

Teaching

1. Use part A of the assessment as a phonics test. Have the students fill in the circles next to the words that complete the sentences.

2. Use part B of the assessment page. Alphabetize the words. Students will number the words from one to ten.

3. Have students number their paper from 1 to 14. Give the following words as dictation.

   Spelling word list: **1. fudge, 2. wedge, 3. badger, 4. change, 5. stingy, 6. danger, 7. ledge, 8. angel, 9. edge, 10. hinge, 11. smudge, 12. plunge, 13. sponge, 14. gadget**

4. Have students take turns reading the books or stories that were written during the creative writing section of Lesson 54.

5. Use the LAR page. Have students read the recipe.

   At the bottom of the page is an activity. **Write the kind of animal that gave each item for the recipe. You may use the reading book.**

6. Use the handwriting sheet or have the children write the following sentences:

   We plunged into the sludge.
   The stingy squirrel lunged for the pecan.

Assessment Answers

1. bridges	5	2
2. judge	8	9
3. stingy	3	1
4. hedge	10	6
5. changed	7	4

LAR Answers

1. milk cow
2. cocoa badger
3. honey bees
4. peanut butter squirrel
5. powdered sugar turtle
6. corn syrup goose

Lesson 56

Lesson Objectives

1. Students will read compound words. (P)
2. Students will spell words correctly. (S)
3. Students will prepare to read the story Bobcat Cowboys. (R)
4. Students will copy sentences neatly and correctly. (H)

Materials

LAR
SAP
Bobcat Cowboys
Writing Skills Workbook page is available

Word List: airplane, backpack, baseball, bathroom, bathtub, birthday, bluebird, bobcat, bookcase, campsite, cardboard, chipmunk, cowboy, cupcake, daydream, daytime, doorbell, downstairs, dugout, eyebrow, eyelash, fireman, fireplace, fireworks, flashlight, football, goldfish, grandfather, grandmother, grapefruit, groundhog, haircut, hedgehog, iceberg, icebox, jigsaw, jukebox, knapsack, lifeboat, mailbox, milkman, mushroom, muskrat, network, nightfall, noontime, oatmeal, pickup, popcorn, pushup, rainbow, sailboat, sandbox, sawmill, scarecrow, scoreboard, seacoast, seesaw, shoelace, shoestring, shortstop, snowball, snowflake, spaceship, stagecoach, steamboat, steamship, stickup, strongbox, subway, sundown, sunrise, sunset, sunshine, teaspoon, teenage, thumbnail, toothbrush, toothpaste, towboat, tugboat, woodchuck

Teaching

1. The word list is not complete. You may think of others to add. This week will deal with mainly two-syllable compound words. Some words have already been used in some books such as:

   chipmunk, airplane, hedgehog, grandmother, grandfather, downstairs, snowball, bathroom, upstairs.

   The concept of compound words has not formally been introduced at this point. **Compound words are words made up of complete words.** From the list of words already learned, choose some to introduce the concept of compound words. For example: airplane. **What two words do you see in airplane?** (air and plane)

   LAR workbook page: **Read the words. Separate the compound words into two words. Write the words on the lines.**

2. Use the SAP page. Have students read and spell each word.

   Top section: **Alphabetize the two word lists. Number the words before starting to write.**

   Bottom section: **Make other compound words. Find the spelling words that have a first part that can be combined with the words above the lines to make other compound words.**

3. *Bobcat Cowboys* focuses on compound words. In addition to those words, the following words may be new to students and will require some instruction: Billybob, Bobbybill, Bubba, enter, glove, parade, prairie, sheriff. The list and pronunciation guide is also printed on the LAR workbook page.

The names *Billybob and Bobbybill* are names made up for the story. Separate the "compound names": Billy bob and Bobby bill.
The name *Bubba:* Bub - a
The word *enter:* Divide into syllables en - ter
The word *glove:* Like the word love with a g added to the beginning. The o has a short u sound.
The word *parade:* Break into syllables. Sounds like **pu**-rade
The word *prairie:* Point out the -air combination. -ie makes the long e sound.
The word *sheriff:* Break into syllables. sher-iff. The e has the same sound as the e in the word very.

You may also review the words *reigns, doesn't, table, flew.*

Introduce the story: Ask a student to read the title of the book. Say: **What is a bobcat? A bobcat is a cat that lives in woods. It is bigger than pet cats. As you read this time think about when the story took place. Could it have taken place today or a long time ago.** Students will silently read as much of the story as they can in the time allowed.

4. Use the handwriting sheet or have the children write the following sentences:

You don't need a flashlight in the daytime.
The pickup truck drove to the sawmill.

LAR Answers

1. door bell
2. tug boat
3. cup cake
4. rain bow
5. sand box
6. noon time
7. fire works
8. scare crow
9. night fall
10. tooth paste

SAP Answers

1. bathtub	5. drumstick
2. bobcat	6. fireplace
3. butterfly	7. flashlight
4. cupcake	8. goldfish

1. haircut	4. sailboat
2. mailbox	5. shoestring
3. mushroom	6. toothbrush

bathrobe toothpaste mailman

Bobcat Cowboys

Book 11
Lessons 56 to 60

Bobcat Cowboys

Written and illustrated by
Brian Davis

Otto Muskrat pulled back the reigns. The stagecoach came to a stop. Otto Muskrat shook with fear. The road was blocked. Three bobcat cowboys grinned.

"This is a stickup!" said Billybob Bobcat.

Another Bobcat held a tree limb over his head.

"No it's not, Billybob," said Bubba Bobcat. "This is a stickup."

"Hush up, Bubba," grumbled Billybob Bobcat.

"I'll get the strongbox," said Bobbybill Bobcat.
He pulled the strongbox off the stagecoach.

"Not the goldfish!" groaned Otto Muskrat.

"We love goldfish," grinned Bobbybill Bobcat.
The bobcat cowboys rode off into the sunset.

2

3

Bobcat Cowboys

Grace Groundhog leaned out of the stagecoach. "Who were those mean cats?" asked Grace.

"That was the Bobcat Cowboy Gang," answered Otto Muskrat.

"Oh, my!" sighed Grace. She waved her paper fan.

Walt Woodchuck opened the stagecoach door. "Did they get the strongbox?"

Otto wiped his eyebrows, "I'm afraid so."

"We need to get those goldfish back," said Walt Woodchuck. "Let's go to town."

Otto Muskrat shook the reigns. The stagecoach drove on to Rowdent Gulch.

4

5

It was almost sundown in Rowdent Gulch. The stagecoach rumbled into town. Otto stopped in front of Sheriff Prairie Dog's office. Otto hopped off the stagecoach.

"Sheriff, there was a holdup," yelled Otto Muskrat.

Sheriff Prairie Dog stepped outside. He was eating a cupcake. "Who was it?"

"The Bobcat Cowboy Gang," stammered Otto Muskrat. "They got the strongbox. It was full of goldfish."

The sheriff shuddered, "Those are some mean cats."

"Are you going to get them?" asked Otto.

"No," said the sheriff. "I have a better plan. They will come to us. Go get Babs Bluebird."

Sheriff Prairie Dog started walking to the sawmill.

6

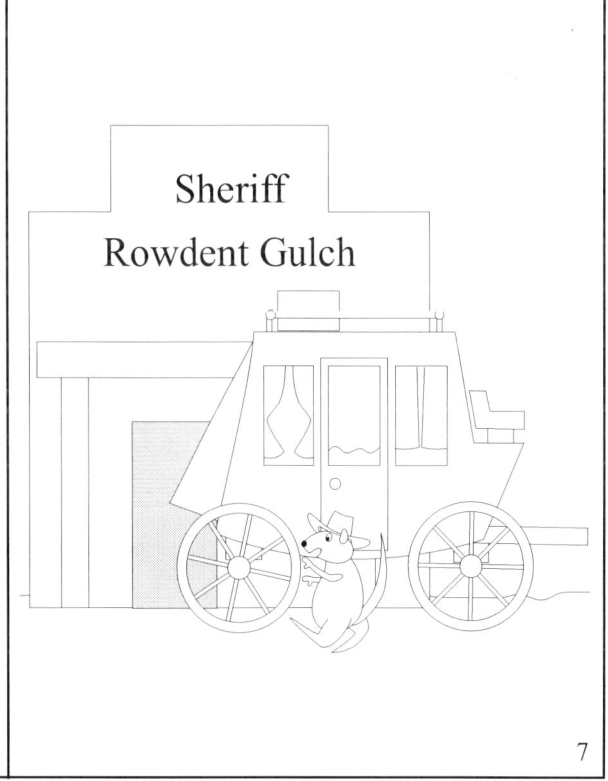

7

Bobcat Cowboys

The bobcats were back at their campsite. They made a big campfire.

"Let's cook some goldfish," said Billybob Bobcat.

"I'll get the strongbox," said Bobbybill Bobcat.

"I'll get my baseball glove," said Bubba Bobcat.

"Baseball glove? Why do we need a baseball glove?" asked Bobbybill Bobcat.

"So I can catch fish," said Bubba.

"Hush up, Bubba," grumbled Billybob Bobcat.

Babs Bluebird flew over the campsite. Babs dropped a paper and left. Billybob picked it up.

"What's it say?" asked Bobbybill Bobcat.

Bubba giggled, "Paper doesn't talk. You have to read it."

8 "Hush up, Bubba," said Billybob Bobcat.

9

Billybob Bobcat began to read the paper.

"It says here that Rowdent Gulch is having a contest. It's a jigsaw puzzle contest. First prize is the biggest goldfish ever. It only costs one strongbox of goldfish to enter."

"Oh! I can win. I'm very smart!" said Bubba Bobcat. Bubba scratched his head. "What's a jigsaw puzzle?"

"Hush up, Bubba," grumbled Billybob Bobcat.

The bobcat cowboys packed up their campsite. The contest began at noontime the next day. They began to ride to Rowdent Gulch.

10

11

Bobcat Cowboys

The town worked all night by the stream. By morning, they were done. An old steamboat looked like the biggest goldfish ever.

"Do you think this will work?" asked a chipmunk. Chip Chipmunk was the steamboat pilot.

Sheriff Prairie Dog patted him on the back. "Yes. We'll see the last of the Bobcat Cowboy Gang."

12

Billybob, Bobbybill, and Bubba Bobcat rode into Rowdent Gulch.

Grace Groundhog was at a table. "May I help you fine bobcats?" asked Grace.

"We're here for the jigsaw puzzle contest," said Billybob Bobcat.

"I thought we were here to steal the big goldfish," said Bubba.

"Hush up, Bubba," grumbled Billybob Bobcat.

"That will be one strongbox full of goldfish please," said Grace.

Bobbybill Bobcat gave her the strongbox. Grace gave them a jigsaw puzzle.

"The contest begins at noontime. Be the first team done with the jigsaw puzzle. You will win the goldfish prize."

13

At noontime the contest began. Now, bobcats are not good at jigsaw puzzles. The bobcats had to win. So, the town had a plan. They would make the bobcats win.

Walt Woodchuck hid behind the bank. He set off some fireworks. Billybob and Bobbybill watched the fireworks. Bubba was still working on the puzzle.

A mouse hopped up to him. "Mr. Bobcat, your shoelace is not tied."

"Thank you mouse," said Bubba.

He bent down to tie his shoelace. Other mice scrambled to put the puzzle together.

Bubba sat up. "Hey! Cowboy boots don't have shoelaces." Then he saw the puzzle. "I won! Our puzzle is done."

The whole town cheered.

"You are good at jigsaw puzzles," said Bobbybill Bobcat.

14

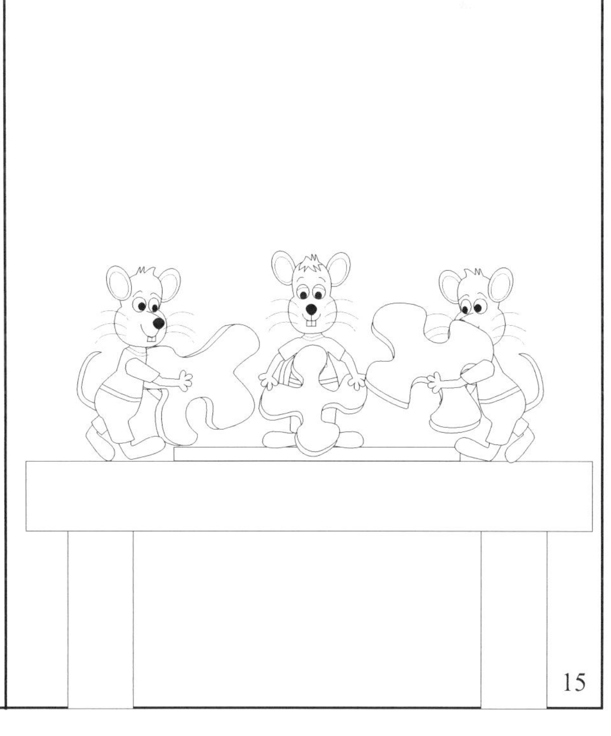

15

Bobcat Cowboys

Sheriff Prairie Dog led a parade. They stopped at the stream.

"There it is!" said the sheriff.

Bubba looked at the goldfish. "Wow!" yelled Bubba.

"It's the biggest goldfish ever," said Billybob.

The bobcats ran to the goldfish steamboat. A door was hidden under a fin. Sheriff Prairie Dog pushed them into the door. He locked the door. The bobcat cowboys were trapped.

Chip Chipmunk steered the steamboat downstream. The bobcats were going to the Dog City jail. The goldfish of Rowdent Gulch were safe.

"I don't think this is a real fish," said Bubba Bobcat.

"Hush up, Bubba," grumbled Billybob Bobcat.

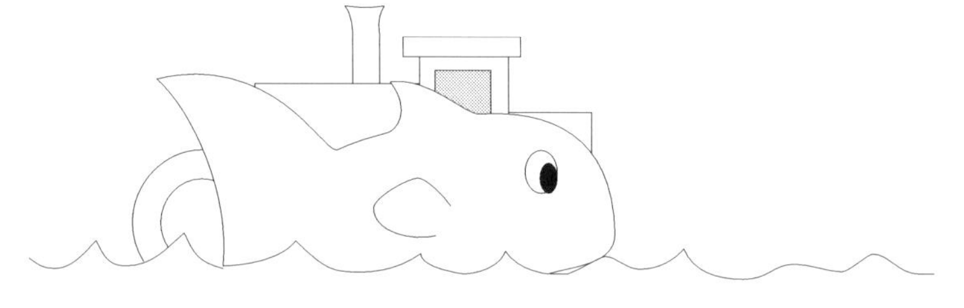

16

Bobcat Cowboys

baseball	enter	Muskrat	shoelace
biggest	ever	noontime	shuddered
Billybob	eyebrows	opened	sighed
bluebird	fireworks	Otto	stagecoach
Bobbybill	flew	outside	stammered
bobcat	Gang	paper	steamboat
Bubba	glove	parade	stickup
campfire	goldfish	pilot	stream
campsite	grinned	Prairie	strongbox
catch	groaned	pulled	sunset
cheered	Groundhog	puzzle	table
chipmunk	grumbled	reigns	team
contest	Gulch	Rowdent	together
cowboys	hidden	rumbled	watched
cupcake	holdup	sawmill	what's
doesn't	jigsaw	scrambled	who
downstream	limb	scratched	window
dropped	morning	Sheriff	Woodchuck

Lesson 57

Lesson Objectives

1. Students will make compound words. (P)
2. Students will identify verbs in sentences. (L)
3. Students will alphabetize the spelling list. (S)
4. Students will read the story *Bobcat Cowboys*. (R)
5. Students will play a compound word game. (R)
6. Students will copy sentences neatly and correctly. (H)

Materials

LAR
SAP
Dog Pound Compound game (gameboard and first sheet)
Playing pieces (die and pawns)
Bobcat Cowboys

Teaching

1. Write the words sun, spoon, shine, and tea. **Make two compound words from the four words.** (teaspoon, sunshine)

   Top of the LAR page: **Make compound words from the word lists on the top of the workbook page. Write the words.**

2. Review the term noun (people, places, things). Next write the sentence: The cowboy chased the horses. **Find the nouns.** (cowboy and horses) **What did the cowboy do to the horses?** (chased). **Words that tell what nouns do are called verbs. Verbs tell what action is taking place.** Use the bottom of the LAR workbook page. **Fill in the oval next to the words used as verbs in the sentences.**

3. Use the SAP workbook page. Top part: **Fit all the spelling words into the grid. This time there is only one clue space, the letter e. It's the fourth letter in a nine letter word.**

   Bottom part: **Complete the sentences with spelling words. Write the words on the lines.**

4. Review the additional reading vocabulary: **Billybob, Bobbybill, Bubba, enter, glove, parade, prairie, sheriff.**

   Students will read pages 1 to 9 out loud. Ask the following questions:

   What are the names of the three bobcats? (Billybob, Bobbybill, Bubba)
   What did the bobcats take from the stagecoach? (a strongbox)
   What is a strongbox? (You may need to tell students. It is a locked box that was kind of a portable safe for hauling valuable things on the stagecoach.)
   What was in the strongbox? (goldfish)
   Where was the stagecoach going? (to Rowdent Gulch) Please note that Rowdent is the name of the town and is a play on words with the word rodent.
   Who was the sheriff of Rowdent Gulch? (Sheriff Prairie Dog)
   What were the bobcats going to do with the goldfish? (cook them)
   Why did Bubba want a baseball glove? (to catch fish)

5. Dog Pound Compound Game. The pieces should be cut apart before playing the first time. The game instructions are on the board. The game may be shortened by rescuing fewer cats. There are two sheets of crates. Only the first sheet will be used in this lesson. The other sheet is for use with the Lesson 146 word list.

6. Use the handwriting sheet or have the children write the following sentences:

   Grandfather made a jigsaw puzzle.
   I played shortstop in baseball.

LAR Answers

Any order:

haircut
grandfather
bathtub
football
spaceship
popcorn
sailboat

1. ● drove ○ stagecoach
2. ○ Billybob ● tied
3. ○ teeth ● brushed
4. ○ thumbnail ● hit
5. ● saw ○ rainbow

SAP Answers

```
                      m
                      a
                      i
                      l
                bathtub
      sailboat  u     o
      h   o  o  t     x
      o   b  o  t d
   fireplace t  e r
   l  s   a  haircut
   a  t   t  b  f m
   s  r      r  l s
   h  i      u  y t
   l  n      s    i
   i  goldfish cupcake
   g              k
mushroom
   t
```

1. goldfish
2. cupcake
3. mailbox
4. shoestring
5. butterfly

Lesson 58

Lesson Objectives

1. Students will complete sentences with compound words (spelling words). (P & S)
2. Students will review verbs. (L)
3. Students will review spelling words. (S)
4. Students will proofread sentences. (S & L)
5. Students will read the story *Bobcat Cowboys*. (R)
6. Students will copy sentences neatly and correctly. (H)

Materials

LAR
SAP
Bobcat Cowboys

Teaching

1. Use the top of the LAR workbook page. **There are mixed-up compound words in each sentence. Fix the compound words. Write them correctly on the lines in the order they are used in the sentence.**

2. Review the term verb (they tell what a noun is doing). Use the bottom of the LAR workbook page. **Choose a verb to complete the sentence. Fill in the circle next to the verb.**

3. Use the top of the SAP page. **Find the spelling words that have the letters to spell the shorter words. The spelling list is numbered. Write the numbers next to the small words if the spelling words have the letters to make that word. There will be a match for every blank set of lines.**

4. Use the bottom of the SAP page. **Proofread the sentences. Circle the misspelled words and write them correctly on the lines. Add a period or question mark at the end of the sentence.**

5. Review the first half of the book *Bobcat Cowboys*. Next, read the second half of the book. After completing the story ask the students the following questions:

   What was the reason the bobcats went to Rowdent Gulch? (a jigsaw puzzle contest)
   What did the town work on all night? (They made a steamboat look like a fish.)
   What did Grace give the bobcats? (a jigsaw puzzle)
   How was Bubba able to solve the puzzle? (The mice put it together.)
   How did the bobcats get into the fish?
   (There was a door under the fin. The sheriff pushed them.)
   Where was Chip taking the bobcats? (to the Dog City jail)
   When do you think this story took place? (Answers vary.)
   What are some things in the story that help you know when it took place?
   (stagecoach, sheriff, cowboys, steamboat)
   Who was your favorite character in the story? (Answers vary.) **Why?**

6. Use the handwriting sheet or have the children write the following sentences:

   I need a toothbrush after eating popcorn.
   The sunlight made the campsite hot.

LAR Answers

1. cowboy, flashlight
2. mushroom, mailbox
3. toothbrush, fireplace
4. goldfish, sailboat
5. cupcake, shoestring

1. ● daydreamed ○ pushup
2. ○ sawmill ● dropped
3. ● stole ○ money
4. ● broke ○ cream
5. ○ stars ● zoomed

SAP Answers

dog 4
lamb 5 sit 7,8,9,12
boa 5,9,10 fail 6,8 sum 2,12
blue 13 rush 1,2 bat 9,10,14
pack 3 shoo 1,2 fig 4,8 leaf 6
hit 7,8,11 ace 3,6 sail 8,9
tub 1,13,14 hog 4,7 cat 10,11

bobcat goldfish period
flashlight sailboat period
butterfly mailbox question mark

Lesson 59

1. Students will put a story in order. (L)
2. Students will review spelling words. (S)
3. Students will write a story. (CW)
4. Students will read the story *Bobcat Cowboys*. (R)
5. Students will copy sentences neatly and correctly. (H)

Materials

LAR
SAP
Bobcat Cowboys
Optional material about the Old West for the creative writing assignment.
Writing Skills Workbook page is available

Teaching

1. Read the sentences on the LAR workbook page. **Number the sentences in the order they happened in the story. You may use your book to check your answers.**

   Bottom section: **Answer the questions about the story by filling in the ovals.**

2. Use the SAP page. **Match the spelling words to the descriptions.**

3. Students will write a story set in the old west. Say: The book Bobcat Cowboys was set in a time when there weren't any cars or televisions. Today you will write a story that happens in the Old West.

   You may want to read some reference materials about the Old West. Talk about the way people traveled, they way they dressed, things they ate, what they did for fun, what kind of jobs they had, what schools were like.

4. Read the book *Bobcat Cowboys* again. Next, have students look at the back of the book and answer the following questions about the word list. You may do this orally or have students write answers:

   What words are animals? (bluebird, bobcat, chipmunk, goldfish, groundhog, muskrat, woodchuck)
   What words are things to ride in? (steamboat, stagecoach)
   What words describe parts of the day? (morning, noontime, sunset)
   What two compound words begin with the same first word? (campfire, campsite)
   What word is love with a letter added? (glove)
   What word is the opposite of smallest? (biggest)
   What is something on your face? (eyebrows)
   What is something that should be tied? (shoelace)

5. Use the handwriting sheet or have the children write the following sentences:

   The steamship had lots of lifeboats.
   We watched the fireworks at sunset.

Lesson 59

LAR Answers

5	4
3	8
10	2
6	7
1	9

1. **yes** no
2. yes **no**
3. **yes** no
4. yes **no**
5. **yes** no

SAP Answers

bathtub	mushroom
bobcat	drumstick
sailboat	toothbrush
shoestring	mailbox
cupcake	butterfly
flashlight	goldfish
fireplace	haircut

Lesson 60

Lesson Objectives

1. Students will be tested on phonics concepts. (P)
2. Students will be tested on language concepts. (L)
3. Students will take a spelling test. (S)
4. Students will read a poem. (L & R)
5. Students will read the story they have written. (R)
6. Students will copy a sentence neatly and correctly. (H)

Materials

LAR
Creative writing assignment from Lesson 59
Assessment 60

Teaching

1. Use part A of the assessment as a phonics test. Have the students fill in the circles next to the words that complete the sentences.

2. Use part B of the assessment page. Fill in the circles next to the words that were used as verbs in the sentences.

3. Have students number their papers from 1 to 14. Give the following words as dictation.

   Spelling word list: **1. mushroom, 2. flashlight, 3. sailboat, 4. goldfish, 5. shoestring, 6. mailbox, 7. toothbrush, 8. cupcake, 9. fireplace, 10. bobcat, 11. butterfly, 12. haircut, 13. bathtub, 14. drumstick**

4. Use the LAR page. Students will read a poem. The poem is reprinted on the next page. Introduce the poem. **Have you ever packed for a trip and couldn't decide what to take? This is a poem about packing for a trip.**

   Have students read the poem. Next, have students find all the compound words in the poem.

5. Have students take turns reading the books or stories that were written during the creative writing section of the previous lesson.

6. Use the handwriting sheet or have the children write the following sentences:

   We ate cupcakes at the birthday party.
   The cardboard box was full of mushrooms.

Assessment Answers

1. baseball
2. fireplace
3. airplane
4. goldfish
5. campsite

1. cooked
2. pounced
3. fell
4. ate
5. pulled

Knapsack
Pack Up

I've been ~~filling up~~ my knapsack
For a short camping trip
It's filled with all I need to pack
But now it's hard to zip

I'll take out my new red flashlight
It's wasting all that space
I won't need it to see at night
I packed ~~a fire~~place

I'll unpack this jug of water
That I brought to drink
For it really will not matter
I brought the kitchen sink

This tent sho~~uld be th~~e next to go
And the icebox too
Since I packed ~~up this~~ cold white snow
To build my own igloo

And there's these heavy cans ~~of food~~
Fresh fruit is best for me
I won't need the canned stuff that's stewed
I brought a grapefruit tree

That's all my knapsack will allow
I couldn't need much more
There's only one small problem now
I can't squeeze though my bedroom door

Lesson 61

Lesson Objectives

1. Students will read words with silent letters. (P)
2. Students will spell words correctly. (S)
3. Students will proofread sentences. (L)
4. Students will prepare to read the story The Kindness of Gnatty. (R)
5. Students will copy sentences neatly and correctly. (H)

Materials

LAR
SAP
The Kindness of Gnatty

Word List: gnarl, gnash, gnat, gnaw, gnu, heir, honor, honest, hour, batch, botch, catch, ditch, Dutch, etch, fetch, hatch, hitch, hutch, itch, latch, match, Mitch, notch, patch, pitch, retch, snatch, snitch, stitch, thatch, witch, castle, hasten, listen, moisten, nestle, thistle, bustle, hustle, rustle, whistle, wrestle

Teaching

1. This week will focus on words beginning with a silent g or h. Also, words that have a silent t before ch or le are featured. Students may remember the word hour. Write the words hour and our. **These words are homophones. They sound alike, but they have different meanings and spellings.**

   There is no rule for when the h is silent, but there aren't too many words. Introduce the words to the students: heir (eir has the air sound), honor, honest, hour. These are the words that begin with silent h that may be in their speaking vocabulary.

   Words that begin with silent g follow a basic rule: If g-n begins a word, the g is silent. Introduce the five words: gnarl, gnash, gnat, gnaw, and gnu.

   Next, write the words patch and castle. Say the words and have students find the silent letter (t). Repeat with other words. There are words with two forms: -tch combinations and -stle combinations.

2. Use the SAP workbook page. Have students read and spell each word. Spelling list: fasten, gnash, hatch, gnaw, honest, hour, catch, ditch, stitch, sign, soften, listen, whistle, kitchen.

   Top part. **Sort the words by the silent letters they contain.** (Note: the h in whistle is not considered silent. Whistle should be written with the silent t words.)

   Bottom section: **Add the suffixes ing and er to the three words at the bottom of the page. Remember the spelling rules for the silent e.**

3. Use the top of the LAR workbook page. **Proofread the sentences. Words may be missing silent letters, words may need to be capitalized, and punctuation may need to be added. Fill in the missing punctuation (apostrophes, question marks, periods). Circle words that need to be capitalized. Write the correct spelling of the words that are spelled incorrectly on the lines.**

4. *The Kindness of Gnatty* focuses on words with silent letters. In addition to those words, the following words may be new to students. The words and pronunciation guides are on the bottom of the LAR workbook page.

The word *anything:*	Compound word, any thing. The y has a long e sound.
The name *Earl:*	Ear- makes the -er sound.
The word *gone:*	Sounds like "gon". The o is short.
The word *kindness:*	The word kind with a prefix -ness.
The word *meow:*	Break into syllables. Me and ow as in cow.
The word *promise:*	The o and i are short.
The word *second:*	The e is short. The o makes a short u sound.
The word *young:*	The ou makes the short u sound.

You may also review the words *couldn't, carried, knights.*

Introduce the story: Ask a student to read the title of the book. Say: **Have you ever heard the name Gnatty before? A character in this book is named Gnatty. See if you can find out why as you read the book. What is kindness? How do you show kindness?**
Students will silently read as much of the story as they can in the time allowed.

5. Use the handwriting sheet or have the children write the following sentences:

Did the frog snatch the gnat?
I played catch for an hour.

LAR Answers

1. (the) lion nawed on the roast.
   gnawed
2. (is) a snake in the dich?
   ditch
3. (is) (mitch) an onest boy?
   honest
4. (i) didn't lisen for the whistle.
   listen
5. (my) mom's dish fell out of the huch.
   hutch
6. (she)'s going to wach (matt's) baseball game.
   watch

SAP Answers

Silent t (any order)
fasten hatch catch ditch
stitch listen whistle kitchen

Silent g (any order)
gnash gnaw sign

Silent h
honest hour

Bottom section
listening whistling fastening
listener whistler fastener

The Kindness of Gnatty

Second Grade Phonics & Reading

Book 12
Lessons 61 to 65

The Kindness of Gnatty

Written and illustrated by
Brian Davis

A long time ago there was a cat. Its name was Scotch. The cat scratched and purred at a door. A man raised the latch.

"What do you want?" gnarled a mean young man.

"Meow," said Scotch.

The man picked the cat up. He gnashed his teeth.

"I don't need a cat. Cats make me itch."

He pitched the cat into a ditch. The ditch was a thistle patch.

2

3

The Kindness of Gnatty

The thistles scratched Scotch. Scotch wrestled with the thistles. His thick fur stuck to the thistles.

"Meow," cried Scotch in pain.

Scotch was stuck for an hour. Something made a rustling sound. It was a poor mouse.

The mouse was called Gnatty. The other mice made fun of him. They said he was as small as a gnat.

"You seem to be stuck," said Gnatty.

"Things are as they seem," meowed Scotch. "A mean young man pitched me. I landed in this thistle patch. The thistles are scratching me.

"Help me please. I will do anything you ask," said the cat.

4

5

Gnatty gave it great thought. It was not safe to help a cat. Gnatty knew that cats catch mice.

"I would like two things," said Gnatty.

The gnarled thistles scratched Scotch. "Just name it," said Scotch.

Gnatty looked Scotch in the eye. "First, don't eat me."

"I agree," said Scotch.

"Second, I want to be king of the mice."

Scotch sighed, "That would be up to King Mitch. I am just a cat."

Gnatty smiled. That was the answer he wanted. "You are an honest cat. You told me the truth. I will help you."

Gnatty gnawed on the thistles. In an hour, Scotch was free.

"The thistles are gone. They will no longer scratch you," said Gnatty.

6

7

The Kindness of Gnatty

Gnatty began to run off. Scotch whistled.

"Stop, Gnatty!" meowed Scotch. "I have a promise to keep. I am a cat of honor."

"You did not eat me," said Gnatty the mouse. "I am glad I am still alive."

"But, I have yet to make you king," said Scotch.

Gnatty giggled, "How can you make me king? I must get back to the hutch. It's my home. I don't need to be king. I don't need a castle."

"I just wanted to help you," said Gnatty. "I know thistles can scratch."

"I am a cat of honor," said Scotch. "Come to the castle in one hour. You will be king of the mice."

8

9

Scotch scratched at a door. A man raised the latch.

"There you are," said the man. "King Mitch has been waiting."

The man carried Scotch to the king.

"What acts of kindness have you seen today?" asked King Mitch.

Scotch told King Mitch about Gnatty.

"He is a mouse like no other," said King Mitch. "I will give him the highest honor."

10

11

The Kindness of Gnatty

A mouse had seen Gnatty help the cat. It snitched to the other mice.

"That cat will catch you," said the other mice. "You should have left him in the thistles."

They teased Gnatty as he walked to the castle. They snatched his hat. The mice pitched it around. Gnatty couldn't reach it.

A mouse pitched it to the ground. Gnatty reached for it. The mice pushed him into the ditch. He landed in the thistles.

"Gnatty, King of the Thistles," teased a mouse.

"King of the Gnats," teased another mouse.

Gnatty hustled to the castle.

12

13

Gnatty squeezed through a notch in the door. He was in the castle.

"My friend Gnatty," greeted Scotch. "King Mitch is waiting for you."

"You know King Mitch?" asked Gnatty.

"I am the Earl of Kindness," said Scotch. "King Mitch is a kind king. We honor acts of kindness."

Scotch took Gnatty to King Mitch. King Mitch made Gnatty king of the mice.

14

15

The Kindness of Gnatty

In a ditch was a thistle patch. In the thistle patch was a mean young man. The king's knights watched the man.

The young man gnashed his teeth. He hated cutting thistles. They scratch.

"I didn't know it was the king's cat," gnarled the man.

Some mean mice were gnawing thistles. "And we didn't think Gnatty could be king," gnarled the mice.

Gnatty and Scotch sat in the castle. They gnawed cake.

16

The Kindness of Gnatty

acts	gnashed	landed	scratched
agree	gnat	latch	second
alive	Gnatty	longer	snatched
answer	gnawed	meow	snitched
anything	gone	Mitch	squeezed
around	highest	notch	teased
carried	honest	other	thistle
castle	honor	patch	thought
catch	hour	pitched	today
couldn't	hutch	promise	truth
cried	itch	purred	waiting
ditch	kindness	reached	what
Earl	king	rustling	whistled
friend	knights	Scotch	wrestled
gnarled	know	scratch	young

Lesson 62

Lesson Objectives

1. Students will learn vocabulary words. (L)
2. Students will review the spelling list. (S)
3. Students will use spelling words in a sentence. (S)
4. Students will read the story *The Kindness of Gnatty.* (R)
5. Students will copy sentences neatly and correctly. (H)

Materials

LAR
SAP
The Kindness of Gnatty

Teaching

1. Use the LAR workbook page. **Read the definitions. Use the definitions to help choose the word that completes the sentences.**

2. Use the top of the SAP page. **Decode the spelling words. Write the words in the boxes.**

3. Use the bottom of the SAP page. **Unscramble the sentences. Write them on the lines.**

4. Students will alphabetize the spelling list. Students will write the list on a separate piece of paper. Students will need to alphabetize some of the words by looking at the second letter.

5. Review the additional reading vocabulary: anything, Earl, gone, kindness, meow, promise, second, young. Students will read pages 1 to 9 out loud. Next, ask the following questions:

   Why didn't the man at the door want a cat? (They make him itch.)
   What was in the ditch? (a thistle patch)
   How did Gnatty get his name? (He was as small as a gnat.)
   Why did Gnatty ask to be king? (He wanted to see if the cat was honest. Only the king could make Gnatty king of the mice. If Scotch said he could make Gnatty king, Gnatty would know the cat was lying, and the cat might lie about not eating him too.)
   After Scotch was free what did Scotch tell Gnatty to do? (come to the castle in one hour)
   Why do you think Gnatty helped Scotch?
   (Answer vary.)

6. Use the handwriting sheet or have the children write the following sentences:

   Mitch whistled for the cat. The gnu ran across the ditch.

LAR Answers

1. hutch
2. snatch
3. gnarl
4. thistle
5. honest
6. notch
7. gnat
8. rustle

SAP Answers

honest stitch fasten
hatch ditch gnash catch
hour gnaw sign soften
listen kitchen whistle

The egg may hatch in an hour.

Did you catch the turtle in the ditch?

Can we listen to the bird whistle?

Lesson 63

Lesson Objectives

1. Students will combine sentences. (L & W)
2. Students will review nouns and verbs. (L)
3. Students will review spelling words. (S)
4. Students will complete sentences. (S & L)
5. Students will read the story *The Kindness of Gnatty*. (R)
6. Students will copy sentences neatly and correctly. (H)

Materials

LAR
SAP
The Kindness of Gnatty
Writing Skills Workbook page is available

Teaching

1. Use the top of the LAR page. **Sometimes when you write, smaller sentences can be combined into a longer sentence. Look at the example on the workbook page. Two sentences were made into one. The words that were used are underlined.**

   The new sentence means the same thing. It just puts more details in one sentence.

   Combine the other sentences. Use the underlined words. Keep the meanings of the sentences the same.

2. Review the term noun (person, place, or thing). Review the term verb (they tell what a noun is doing). Use the bottom of the LAR workbook page. **A word is in bold print. Is it a noun or verb? Fill in the circle next to the word noun or verb at the end of the sentence.**

3. Use the top of the SAP workbook page. **Look at the pairs of spelling words in each box. Which words can be made with the letters from the two spelling words? Answer yes or no by filling in the shapes.**

4. Use the bottom of the SAP page. **Change the underlined words in the sentences. Choose the spelling word that changes the meaning of the sentence the least.**

5. Review the first half of the book *The Kindness of Gnatty*. Next, read the second half of the book. After completing the story ask the students the following questions:

   Did Scotch know the king? (yes)
   What in the story tells you that? (The king was waiting for him.)
   Why did the other mice pick on Gnatty? (He was small and he helped a cat.)
   Who was the cat? (The Earl of Kindness)
   Why do you think King Mitch liked to honor acts of kindness? (Answers vary.)
   What happened to the mean man and mice in the story? (They had to cut thistles.)
   What do you think the mean characters learned? (Answers vary.)
   What country do you think this story took place in? (Answers vary.)
   Who was your favorite character in the story? (Answers vary.) **Why?**

6. Use the handwriting sheet or have the children write the following sentences:

   It was not honest to snatch the cookie.
   The wrestling dogs gnarled at each other.

LAR Answers

The gnat landed on a thistle.
King Mitch lives in a castle.
The warm egg hatched.

1. verb
2. noun
3. noun
4. verb
5. verb

SAP Answers

fasten gnash	yes	no
tag	●	□
not	○	■
neat	●	□
stone	○	■

gnaw honest	yes	no
grow	○	■
west	●	□
than	●	□
wagon	●	□

hour catch	yes	no
church	●	□
than	○	■
crop	○	■
heart	○	■

ditch stitch	yes	no
hid	●	□
chips	○	■
sip	○	■
shin	○	■

hatch sign	yes	no
cats	●	□
than	●	□
hand	○	■
grin	○	■

soften listen	yes	no
fasten	○	■
loft	●	□
nest	●	□
fleet	●	□

gnaw kitchen	yes	no
watch	●	□
wink	●	□
chip	○	■
twig	●	□

fasten whistle	yes	no
steer	○	■
fish	●	□
twist	●	□
whale	●	□

1. gnaw
2. fasten
3. sign
4. catch
5. honest
6. kitchen

Lesson 64

Lesson Objectives

1. Students will put a story in order. (L)
2. Students will review spelling words. (S)
3. Students will write a story. (CW)
4. Students will read the story *The Kindness of Gnatty*. (R)
5. Students will copy sentences neatly and correctly. (H)

Materials

LAR
SAP
The Kindness of Gnatty
Writing Skills Workbook page is available

Teaching

1. Use the LAR workbook page. **Read the sentences on the workbook page. Number them in order that they happened in the story.** Have students do the exercise without looking at the book. After finishing the assignment students may use their books to check or correct their answers.

2. Use the SAP workbook page. **Match the spelling words to the descriptions. Write the words on the lines.**

3. Students will write a story about helping someone (showing kindness). Say: **In the book The Kindness of Gnatty a mouse helped a cat. What is so unusual about a mouse helping as cat? Have you ever been especially kind to someone? Has anyone ever done an especially kind thing for you? Today you will write a story about someone or something that did a kind act. It may be a true story about you, or it may be made up like the story The Kindness of Gnatty.**

   The following questions may be helpful: **When did it happen? Where did it happen? How did the characters feel about it? What happened to the helper after helping?**

4. Read the book *The Kindness of Gnatty* again. Next, have students look at the back of the book and answer the following questions about the word list.

   What word means to chew? (gnaw)
   What words that do not begin with g or h, begin with silent letters? (knights, wrestled)
   What word is a contraction? (couldn't)
   What word is a compound word? (anything)
   What word is the opposite of old? (young)
   What word is opposite of lowest? (highest)
   What word is something found on a door? (latch)
   What is a kings house? (castle)

5. Use the handwriting sheet or have the children write the following sentences:

   The egg hatched an hour ago.
   James is an heir of Tom's.

LAR Answers

2
9
4
10
6
1
8
3
5
7

1. **yes** no
2. **yes** no
3. yes **no**
4. **yes** no
5. yes **no**

SAP Answers

whistle	gnash
hour	ditch
stitch	sign
fasten	gnaw
catch	soften
hatch	listen
honest	kitchen

Lesson 65

Lesson Objectives

1. Students will be tested on phonics concepts. (P)
2. Students will be tested on language concepts. (L)
3. Students will take a spelling test. (S)
4. Students will complete a cloze activity. (R)
5. Students will read the story they have written. (R)
6. Students will copy a sentence neatly and correctly. (H)

Materials

LAR
Creative writing assignment from Lesson 64
Assessment 65

Teaching

1. Use part A of the assessment as a phonics test. Have the students fill in the circles next to the words that complete the sentences.

2. Use part B of the assessment page. Read the sentences. A word is in bold print. It will be a noun or a verb. Fill in the circles next to the word noun or verb to describe the word in bold print.

3. Have students number their papers from 1 to 14. Give the following words as dictation.

   Spelling word list: **1. honest, 2. catch, 3. listen, 4. kitchen, 5. hour, 6. gnaw, 7. stitch, 8. gnash, 9. whistle, 10. ditch, 11. fasten, 12. sign, 13. hatch, 14. soften**

4. Use the LAR page. **Read the story. Words are missing. Use the word list in the box to complete the sentence, but before you begin writing, read the whole story. This will help you decide where the words should go.** The story is reprinted on the next page with the answers.

5. Have students take turns reading the books or stories that were written during the creative writing section of the previous lesson.

6. Use the handwriting sheet or have the children write the following sentences:

   The boy didn't listen to his mom.
   The mouse gnawed on the thistle.

Assessment Answers

Top	Bottom
1. gnarl	1. verb
2. hutch	2. verb
3. thistles	3. noun
4. honest	4. noun
5. fetch	5. verb

Read the story. Complete the sentences with words from the list.

honor	rustling	watch	snatcher	patch	hours	nestled
latch	whistle	listen	gnawed	catch	thistles	snatch

I like to be outside for hours. I like to listen to the birds in trees. They whistle happy songs.

I take care of my own carrot patch. Tiny seeds were planted. It's fun to watch them grow.

I have to keep weeds out. One of the worst are thistles. They have sharp points like needles. I wear gloves to snatch them from my carrot patch.

One day I found some of my carrots had been gnawed on. I made a cage with a latch. I wanted to catch the carrot snatcher. The next day I could hear a rustling in the cage. I had caught a rabbit.

My neighbor saw the rabbit. "She has a nest under my shed," said my neighbor. "Her children are nestled there waiting for her."

I didn't know the rabbit had children. I wouldn't want my parents trapped in a cage. I let the rabbit go. I pulled up a carrot and put it by my neighbor's shed.

"It would be an honor to help you feed your children," I said to the rabbit.

Lesson 66

Lesson Objectives

1. Students will read words that end with the long o sound (ow and oe spellings). (P)
2. Students will spell words correctly. (S)
3. Students will learn vocabulary words. (L)
4. Students will prepare to read the story *Jonathan and Rosie.* (R)
5. Students will copy sentences neatly and correctly. (H)

Materials

LAR
SAP
Jonathan and Rosie

Word List: arrow, bellow, below, borrow, elbow, fallow, fellow, follow, hollow, marrow, mellow, narrow, pillow, shadow, sorrow, sparrow, tomorrow, wallow, willow, window, yellow, doe, foe, goes, hoe, Joe, toe, woe

Teaching

1. Review the words; row, low, and snow. Have students read the words. Ask students how many syllables the words have. (one) Ask what sound the -ow makes in these words. (long o) Say: **Today we will learn some words that have more than one syllable that end with -ow.** Write the words follow, window, and yellow. Have students try to read the words. Students should know the word yellow.

   Words with double r's in the middle have different vowel sounds. If an a precedes the r's, the ar has the "air" sound as in hair and bear. These include the words narrow and sparrow. If an o precedes the r's, they have the -ar sound as in star. These words include borrow, sorrow, and tomorrow.

   Write the words shoe and canoe. Have students read the words. Say: **Some other words end with the long o sound. The vowel sound is spelled the same was as in the words shoe and canoe, but the letters make the long o instead.** Write the words toe, hoe, Joe.

2. Use the SAP page. Have students read and spell each spelling word. Spelling list: sparrow, follow, doe, below, window, hoe, goes, shadow, borrow, rowboat, owner, toenail, mower, poem.

   Top section: **Sort the words by the way the long o sound is spelled. Write the ow words in the top box. Write the oe words in the bottom box.**

   Bottom section: **Add the suffixes to the words. Look at the first word. Hoe + ing. Normally the silent e would be dropped. This time it is not. If the e were dropped, you would have an o and i together which looks like the vowel digraph oi as in oil. It would look like it should read *hoing*, which is a nonsense word.**

3. Use the LAR workbook page. Read the definitions. Use them to decide which words to use to complete the sentences.

4. *Jonathan and Rosie* focuses on compound words. In addition to those words, the following word may be new to students and will require some instruction: movie

   The word *movie:* Sounds like moovee. It has the oo sound as in moo and -ie has the long e.
   You may also review the words *gnashed, neighbor, outside, Saturday*

   Introduce the story: Ask a student to read the title of the book. Say: **Have you read a book about Jonathan before?** *Jonathan's Not-So-Great Great Week.* **What happened in that story?** (Answers vary.) **What is the name of this story?** (Jonathan and Rosie) **Who is Rosie?** (Jonathan's Sister) **In this story, Jonathan has a problem with his little sister. Read the story to find out what is the problem.**

   Students will silently read as much of the story as they can in the time allowed.

5. Use the handwriting sheet or have the children write the sentences:

   Did Joe borrow the pillow?
   My elbow was out the window.

LAR Answers

1. foe
2. sorrow
3. doe
4. wallow
5. elbow
6. bellow
7. hollow
8. fellow

SAP Answers

ow words (any order)
sparrow follow below window shadow
borrow rowboat mower owner

oe words (any order)
doe hoe goes toenail poem

Bottom section
hoeing borrowed shadowing
following follower hoed

Jonathan and Rosie

My name is Jonathan. This story is not just about me. It's also about my little sister. Her name is Rosie.

Saturday started like any other day. I was sound asleep. I snuggled with my yellow pillow.

Then it started. It was right below my window.

2

3

Jonathan and Rosie

"Give me that hoe!" bellowed Rosie.

"No!" bellowed Joe.

Joe is our neighbor. He is Rosie's best friend.

"You almost hit my toe," said Rosie. She gnashed her teeth. "You are not being a nice fellow."

"You're not being a nice fellow, too!" answered Joe.

"I'm not a fellow at all!" yelled Rosie.

I pulled my yellow pillow over my ears.

4

5

Joe ran home. Rosie sat under my window. She started crying.

"Woe is me. Woe is me," Rosie kept moaning.

I couldn't sleep. I went to the window.

"Woe is me?" I said to Rosie. "Where did you hear that?"

"In a movie," said Rosie. "I am wallowing in sorrow."

"It looks like you are wallowing in dirt," I said.

Rosie and Joe had hoed the dirt. They had dug under my window.

"We were sowing flower seeds," said Rosie. "Joe almost hoed my toe. He wasn't careful with the hoe.
He wasn't being a nice fellow."

"I know," I said. "Maybe he will be nice tomorrow."

"Oh no," said Rosie. "Joe is no longer my friend."

6

7

Jonathan and Rosie

I got dressed. I had many things planned. Rosie was outside my bedroom door.

"I'm going to follow you," she said.

"Why?" I asked.

"You are my best friend," said Rosie.

"Woe is me," I thought. I was wallowing in sorrow.

"I forgot something in my room," I said to Rosie.

I closed the door. I climbed out the window.

8

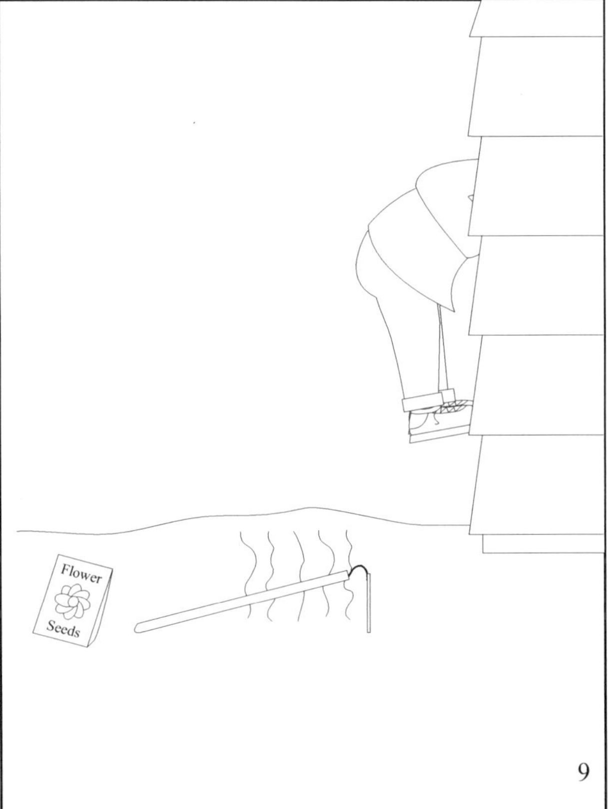

9

"I'm following you," said Rosie.

She was already outside. Rosie was standing by my window.

"How did you get here so fast?" I asked.

"I am your shadow," said Rosie. "Let's sow the flower seeds. I'll use the hoe. I won't hit your toe."

"Woe is me," I thought.

"The seeds will need water. I'll go borrow a bucket," I said. "Keep hoeing."

I ran away.

10

11

Jonathan and Rosie

I hid under a willow tree. It was my best quiet spot. It was by a pond. I once saw a deer there. I think it was a doe.

"Tweet, tweet," said Rosie. "I am a sparrow."

She was swinging on a branch.

"How did you find me?" I asked.

"I am your shadow," said Rosie. "I followed you."

"Woe is me," I thought. "Would you get us some yellow apples?" I asked.

I had to find a place to hide.

12

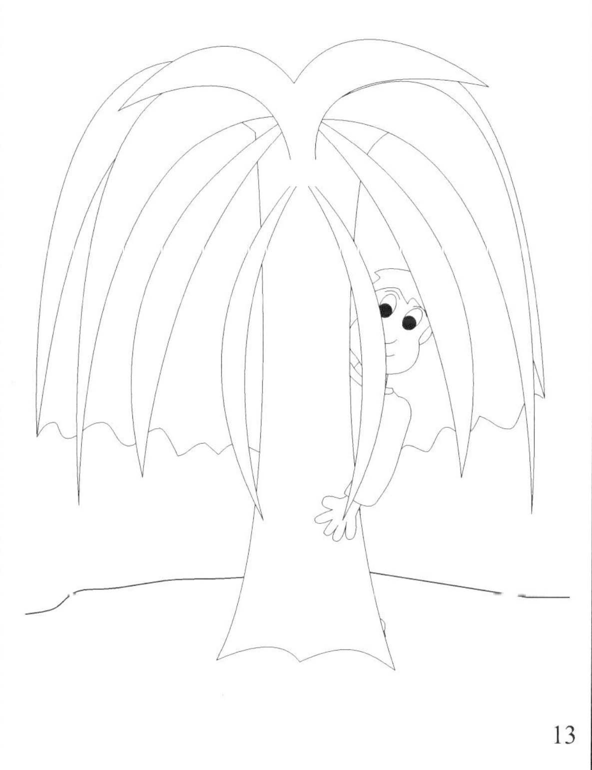

13

I had been making a tree house. I borrowed dad's hammer. I ran to another tree. I climbed a ladder.

"This is your shadow. I am following you," said Rosie.

I looked out the tree house window. Rosie was at the bottom of the ladder. Rosie climbed the ladder. She had two yellow apples.

"Thanks," I said. "Woe is me," I thought.

I picked up the hammer. I hit the nail. The tree house was narrow. I almost hit Rosie's toe.

"You almost hit my toe!" bellowed Rosie. "Give me the hammer."

I said no.

"You're not a nice fellow," said Rosie.

"I am your best friend," I said.

"No you're not," Rosie gnashed her teeth. "Joe is."

14

15

Jonathan and Rosie

Rosie left.

"Good," I thought. After an hour, I felt alone. "Woe is me," I thought.

I went to the willow tree. Rosie didn't follow me. I didn't see a doe. All I saw was a sparrow.

I went to my room. I snuggled on my yellow pillow. Soon, Rosie was outside my window.

"You can use the hoe," said Joe.

"Thank you," said Rosie. "You are a nice fellow."

"You are a nice fellow too," said Joe. "Am I your best friend?" asked Joe.

"Yes," said Rosie.

"Woe is me," I thought. I was wallowing in sorrow.

Then Rosie said, "But, Jonathan is my best friend tomorrow. I am his shadow."

That made me smile.

16

Jonathan and Rosie

about	fellow	narrow	story
almost	flowers	neighbor	thought
also	follow	outside	toe
another	forgot	over	tomorrow
answered	gnashed	pillow	tweet
apples	hammer	quiet	under
bedroom	hoe	Rosie	wallowing
bellowed	hoed	Saturday	water
below	hour	shadow	why
borrowed	Joe	sister	willow
careful	Jonathan	snuggled	window
climbed	know	something	woe
closed	ladder	sorrow	won’t
couldn’t	moaning	sowing	yellow
doe	movie	sparrow	you’re

Lesson 67

Lesson Objectives

1. Students will divide words into syllables. (L)
2. Students will use the correct form of plurals. (L)
3. Students will review spelling words.(S)
4. Students will write questions. (L)
5. Students will read the story *Jonathan and Rosie*. (R)
6. Students will copy sentences neatly and correctly. (H)

Materials

LAR
SAP
Jonathan and Rosie

Teaching

1. Review rules on dividing syllables. Words that have double-medial consonants are divided between the consonants. Clap to words with more than one syllable.

   Use the top of the LAR workbook page. **Read the words. Divide the words into syllables. Draw lines between the syllables.**

2. Use the bottom of the LAR workbook page to discuss plurals. **Nouns and verbs must agree. Plural nouns need plural verbs in a sentence. Remember, plural means more than one. Singular means a single one. What is the most common way to make nouns into plurals?** (add s) **It works the opposite way for verbs. Adding an *s* to a verb make the verb singular.**

   Look at the example in the workbook: one dog, two dogs. To make dog plural, an s was added. You do the opposite for lots of verbs. If you want to make a verb singular, add an s.

   The dog walks. (singular noun and verb)
   The dogs walk. (plural noun and verb)

   Complete the sentences using forms of words that agree.

3. Use the top of the SAP workbook page. **Fit all the spelling words into the grid. Start with the three clue spaces.**

4. Use the bottom of the SAP workbook page. **Read the two sentences. Move a word in each sentence to turn it into a question. Don't forget to add a question mark.**

5. Review the word movie. Students will read pages 1 to 8 out loud. Next, ask the following questions:

   What did Rosie want Joe to give her? (a hoe)
   Why? (Because he almost hit her toe)
   How do you think Rosie and Joe could have acted better? (Answers vary.)
   What was Rosie going to plant? (flower seeds)
   What was Rosie moaning? (woe is me)
   What did Jonathan do to help his sister? (Answer vary.)
   What did Jonathan do when Rosie said she was going to follow him? (climbed out the window)
   Why do you think he did that? (Answers vary.)

6. Use the handwriting sheet or have the children write the following sentences:

   We followed the doe into the woods.
   I left the hoe under a willow tree.

LAR Answers

yel|low   pil|low

wal|low

nar|row   to|mor|row

Either order of sentences:

The sparrow whistles.
The sparrows whistle.

The does follow the shallow stream.
The doe follows the shallow stream.

SAP Answers

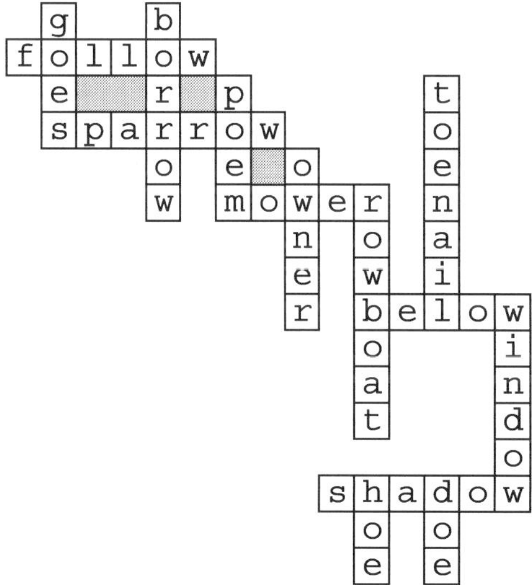

1. Can we borrow the rowboat from its owner?
2. Did the sparrow hide in a shadow below the window?

Lesson 68

Lesson Objectives

1. Students will match words with the same vowel sounds. (P)
2. Students will use words that tell where things are (prepositions). (L)
3. Students will review spelling words. (S)
4. Students will read the story *Jonathan and Rosie*. (R)
5. Students will copy sentences neatly and correctly. (H)

Materials

LAR
SAP
Jonathan and Rosie
A box and an object that will fit in the box.
Writing Skills Workbook page is available

Teaching

1. Use the top of the LAR workbook page. **There are two columns or words. In each word letters are circled. Draw lines to the words in the other column with circled letters with the same sound.**

2. Put the object in the box. **Where is the object?** (in the box) Put the object on top of the box. **Where is the object?** (on the box) **The words *in* and *on* tell where things are. What are other words that tell where things are?** (under, over, beside, etc.)

   Use the bottom of the LAR workbook page. **Read the sentences. Circle the word in each sentence that tells where things are. Write a sentence using a word that tells where to find something.**

3. Use the SAP workbook page. Top section: **What spelling words can make the short words? Write their numbers on the lines. There will be a number for every set of lines.**

   Bottom section: **Look at the longer words. The words contain spelling words. Find the spelling words in the longer words and write them on the lines.**

4. Review the first half of the book Jonathan and Rosie. Next, read the second half of the book. After completing the story ask the students the following questions:

   What did Rosie say she was? (Jonathan's shadow)
   Where was the first place Jonathan hid? (under a willow tree)
   Why do you think Jonathan asked Rosie to get some apples? (so he could run away)
   What was Jonathan building? (a tree house)
   What almost happened to Rosie in the tree house? (Jonathan almost hit her toe.)
   Why do you think Jonathan was sad? (Answers vary.)
   What did Rosie say that made Jonathan feel better?
   (He would be her best friend tomorrow)
   Why do you think it made him feel better? (Answers vary.)

5. Use the handwriting sheet or have the children write the following sentences:

   The shoe was too narrow for my toe.
   The shadow was below my feet.

LAR Answers

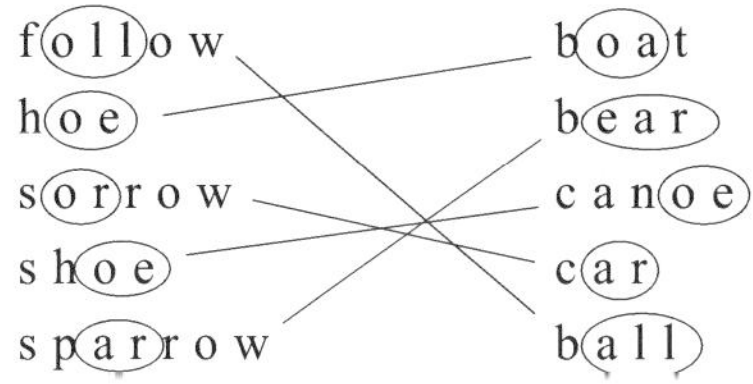

1. under
2. below
3. inside
4. outside
5. over

SAP Answers

row 1,9,10,11,13 mop 14
bow 4,9,10 me 11,14 won 5,13
go 7, he 6, wash 8, ode 3, line 12
low 2,4 oat 10,12 in 5,12 note 12
owe 4,11,13 do 3,5,8 rob 9,10
bat 10 sow 1,8 so 1,7 8

hoe goes
below window mower
shadow owner doe

Lesson 69

Lesson Objectives

1. Students will put a story in order. (L)
2. Students will review spelling words. (S)
3. Students will write a story. (CW)
4. Students will read the story *Jonathan and Rosie*. (R)
5. Students will copy sentences neatly and correctly. (H)

Materials

LAR
SAP
Jonathan and Rosie
Writing Skills Workbook page is available

Teaching

1. Use the LAR page. **Read the sentences on the workbook page. Number them in order that they happened in the story.** Have students do the exercise without looking at the book. After finishing the assignment students may use their books to check or correct their answers.

   Bottom section: **Fill in ovals to answer questions about the story.**

2. Use the SAP page. **Match the spelling words to the descriptions.**

3. Students will write a story about siblings. Say: **The book Jonathan and Rosie is about a brother and sister. Today you will write a story about siblings. Sibling is a word that means brother or sister. You will write a story about you and your brother(s) or sister(s). If you don't have a brother or sister, you can make one up, or you can write about someone else's brother or sister, or you can make up the whole story.**

   The following questions may be helpful: **What does your sibling do that you like? dislike? How do they make you feel? How do you make them feel? How have you helped each other?**

4. Read the book *Jonathan and Rosie* again. Next, have students look at the back of the book and answer the following questions about the word list. You may do this orally or have students write answers:

   What word means to have yelled loudly? (bellowed)
   What word is a kind of tree? (willow)
   What words are days? (Saturday, tomorrow)
   What words are parts of a house? (bedroom, window)
   What words tell where things are? (below, outside, over, under)
   What words are contractions? (couldn't, won't, you're)
   What words are they made up of? (could not, will not, you are)
   What word is the opposite of loud? (quiet)

5. Use the handwriting sheet or have the children write the following sentences:

   That sparrow goes into the hollow log.
   Was that the fellow that bellowed?

LAR Answers

4
8
1
5
2
10
7
3
6
9

 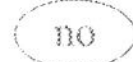

SAP Answers

rowboat	sparrow
hoe	window
toenail	mower
below	goes
shadow	doe
owner	poem
follow	borrow

Lesson 70

Lesson Objectives

1. Students will be tested on phonics concepts. (P)
2. Students will be tested on language concepts. (L)
3. Students will take a spelling test. (S)
4. Students will read about sparrows. (R)
5. Students will read the story they have written. (R)
6. Students will copy a sentence neatly and correctly. (H)

Materials

LAR
Question Poster
Creative writing assignment from Lesson 69
Assessment 70

Teaching

1. Use part A of the assessment as a phonics test. Have the students fill in the circles next to the words that complete the sentences.

2. Use part B of the assessment page. Read the words. Divide them into syllables. Draw lines between syllables.

3. Have students number their papers from 1 to 14. Give the following words as dictation.

   Spelling word list: **1. window, 2. doe, 3. shadow, 4. sparrow, 5. rowboat, 6. hoe, 7. follow, 8. borrow, 9. goes, 10. below, 11. poem, 12. mower, 13. owner, 14. toenail**

4. Use the LAR workbook page. **Look at the workbook page. What does the dark print tell you?** (The names of different kinds of sparrows.) **How do the captions help?** (They match the pictures to the descriptions.)

   Read about sparrows. Then I will ask you some questions. Allow students time to read the page. Ask the following questions. Students may refer back to the article for the answers. The text from the LAR page is reprinted on the next page.

   What kind of sparrow...

   is no longer living? (Dusky Seaside)
   picks its spot at the bird feeder? (Golden Crowned)
   learns songs from the sounds around them? (White Crowned)
   would rather run from you than fly? (Savannah)
   will pretend to have a broken wing? (Fox)
   changes its head markings? (Chipping)

   The author stated that the fox sparrow had an unusual eating habit. What reasons did the author give to support the idea that the eating habit was unusual?

   Use the Question Poster. **Write four questions about sparrows. Use the question words to begin the questions.**

   Pick one sparrow and do more research. What additional information did you find?

5. Have students take turns reading the books or stories that were written during the creative writing section of the previous lesson.

6. Use the handwriting sheet or have the children write the following sentences:

   It may snow tomorrow.
   We felt great sorrow and woe.

Text from LAR page

Many kinds of birds are called sparrows. They are alike in many ways. Here are some facts about different kinds of sparrows. Look at the pictures. How are they all alike? How are they different? Have you seen a sparrow? Maybe now you can discover what kinds of sparrows you see.

The **Savannah Sparrow** returns home to the place they hatched every year. If you see a Savannah Sparrow, they would rather run from you than fly.

The **Golden-Crowned Sparrow** has a yellow streak on its head. They make nests in the ground. If you have a bird feeder they will pick their own spot to eat. No other bird will use that spot.

The **Fox Sparrow** has an unusual eating habit. They are very noisy eaters. They scratch the ground with both feet at once. This uncovers seeds and insects. They are much larger than most sparrows. If they feel you are attacking their nests, they will pretend to have a broken wing. They want you to follow them away from the nest.

The **Dusky Seaside Sparrow** has a very sad story. You will never see one alive. The last one died in 1987. It spent the last eight years of its life at Walt Disney World Resort.

The **Chipping Sparrow** changes its head markings in the fall and winter. They build very thin nests. You can see light through them.

The **White-Crowned Sparrow** learns to sing sounds from what they hear around them. White-Crowned Sparrows from different areas learn different songs.

Assessment Answers

1. yellow
2. borrow
3. foe
4. toe
5. narrow

s p a r | r o w   f e l | l o w

s o r | r o w

h o l | l o w   t o | m o r | r o w

Lesson 71

Lesson Objectives

1. Students will read words with the long e sound spelled with -ie-. (P)
2. Students will spell words correctly. (S)
3. Students will learn vocabulary words. (L)
4. Students will prepare to read the story *Connie the Caterpillar.* (R)
5. Students will copy sentences neatly and correctly. (H)
6. Students will read a book of their choosing. (R)

Materials

LAR
SAP
Connie the Caterpillar
Additional book to read
Writing Skills Workbook page is available

Word List: brief, chief, Connie, Debbie, field, fierce, grief, grieved, Jackie, niece, piece, pier, pierce, shield, siege, spiel, thief, tier, Vinnie, wield, yield

Teaching

1. Write the words Steve, need, seat, and funny. Say: **What vowel sound do each of these words have in common?** (long e)

   What are the ways the long e was spelled? (Steve-silent e at the end, need-ee, seat-ea, funny-y) **Today you will learn a new way to spell long e.**

   Write the letters ie.

   Have students review the rule that if two vowels go walking, the first one does the talking. Then tell them that these words break the rule. The second vowel, e, does the talking. Choose words from the list and have students read them. Note: some words will not be in the child's speaking vocabulary, but these are useful for applying the phonics rule.

2. Use the SAP page. Have students read and spell each word. Spelling list: thief, piece, chief, fiesta, shield, field, brief, grief, niece, yield, siege, fierce.

   Next, students will alphabetize the words in each box.

   At the bottom of the page, add suffixes to the words. Add ly to the first set and ing to the second set.

3. Use the top of the LAR page. **Read the definitions. Use the definitions to help choose the words to complete the sentences.**

4. Connie the Caterpillar focuses on compound words. In addition to those words, the following word may be new to students and will require some instruction: butterflies, caterpillar, cocoon, suddenly, watched. The following words and pronunciation guide is on the bottom of the LAR workbook page.

   The word *butterflies:* Separate the compound word: butter flies. Flies had the long i sound.
   The word *caterpillar:* Separate into syllables: cat-er-pil-lar
   The word *cocoon:* The first o has the schwa sound like the a in about.
   The word *suddenly:* Sudden + ly the y makes the long e sound.
   The word *watched:* The a has the short o sound. The t is silent.

   Introduce the story: Ask a student to read the title of the book. Say: **What is the name of this story?** *Connie the Caterpillar* **What is a caterpillar? Have you ever seen one? What happens to caterpillars? In this story, a girl finds a caterpillar. Read to find out what happens to it.**

   Students will silently read as much of the story as they can in the time allowed.

5. Use the handwriting sheet or have the children write the following sentences:

   Jackie has the shield.
   We picked the corn in the field.

6. Students will prepare a book report on a book of their choosing in lesson 75. Give students the opportunity to find and read a book before lesson 75.

LAR Answers

1. thief
2. field
3. pierce
4. yield
5. brief
6. fierce
7. grieved
8. siege

SAP Answers

1. brief
2. chief
3. field
4. fierce
5. fiesta
6. grief

---

1. niece
2. piece
3. shield
4. siege
5. thief
6. yield

chiefly fiercely briefly

shielding yielding sieging

Connie the Caterpillar

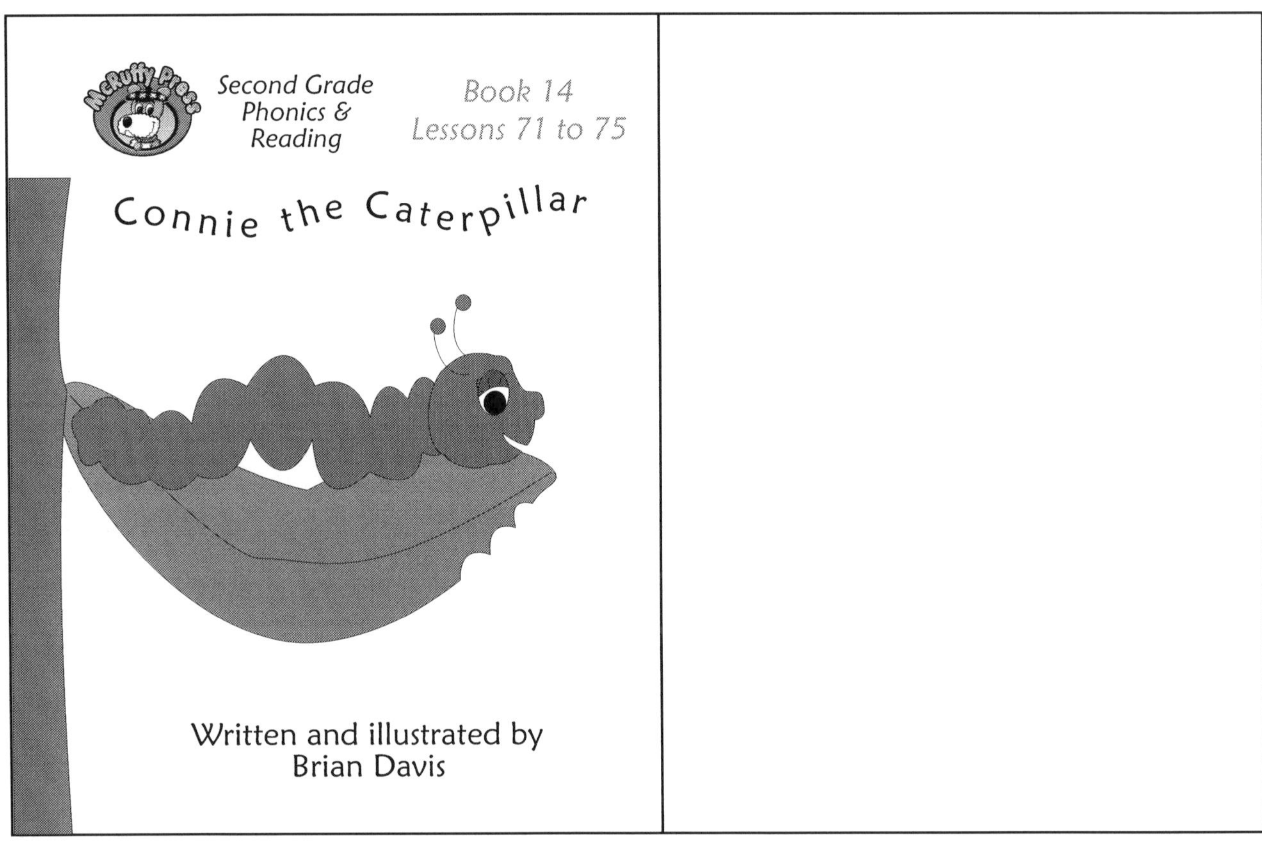

Connie the caterpillar lived in a field. She gnawed on a leaf. Suddenly, a fierce wind swept the field.

The leaf sailed into the breeze. Connie was flying.

"Help!" screamed Connie.

Suddenly, the leaf stopped.

"Lunch time!" said a fierce voice.

"Who said that?" asked Connie.

"My name is Vinnie. I am a spider. And, your name is lunch."

"No, I'm Connie," said Connie.

The leaf stuck to the web.

"I don't want to be lunch," grieved Connie.

2

3

Connie the Caterpillar

"A caterpillar!" said a girl.

The girl's name was Debbie. She held a jar.

The jar pierced the web.

"Lunch thief! Lunch thief!" Vinnie let out his fiercest scream.

Debbie didn't hear the spider.

"I like fuzzy caterpillars," said Debbie.

Debbie put a piece of leaf in a jar. She walked across the field. Debbie took Connie the caterpillar home.

Connie was glad to be safe. The caterpillar would miss the field. At least she had a piece of leaf.

4

5

Debbie liked her new friend. "I will call you Chief," said Debbie.

She let Connie crawl around her room. Connie nibbled a leaf. Debbie and Connie played for hours.

Debbie put Connie back into the jar. She turned out the lights.

"Good night Chief," said Debbie.

6

7

Connie the Caterpillar

Vinnie was running across the field.

"Stop lunch thief!" shouted Vinnie.

The spider ran for two days. The spider came to the edge of the field.

"I will get my caterpillar. I hope the thief hasn't eaten it. I will lay siege to the house," said Vinnie in a fierce voice.

Vinnie slipped in a window. Vinnie saw Debbie.

"The caterpillar thief is sleeping," thought Vinnie.

He scurried to the jar. Connie was asleep. Vinnie started to grab Connie. The jar shielded Connie.

Vinnie tried to pierce the jar.

"Ouch!" cried Vinnie.

The jar was hard. Vinnie was grieved. He hid in a notch in the desk.

Vinnie had a fierce smile. "I will wait."

8

9

Vinnie waited for morning. Debbie and Connie were playing.

"I'll be right back, Chief," said Debbie.

She left the room for a brief time. Connie munched a piece of leaf.

"The lunch thief is gone," said a fierce voice.

Vinnie crawled out of the notch. Connie ran from the fierce spider. She crawled to the jar.

"That will not shield you," said Vinnie.

The lid was not on the jar.

10

11

Connie the Caterpillar

Debbie came back into the room.

"A spider!" screamed Debbie.

She picked up a piece of paper. Vinnie stopped chasing Connie. He saw the paper. He was filled with grief.

"Don't squish me lunch thief," pleaded Vinnie.

Connie also saw the paper. She too was filled with grief. Connie ran to Vinnie.

Debbie didn't want to hit Connie. She stopped.

"I'll be right back," Debbie said to Connie.

Debbie grabbed the jar. She scooped up Vinnie. Debbie carried the spider to the field.

12

13

Vinnie went back to his web. Connie and Debbie played bug games. Then one day, Connie did not play.

She had something to do. Connie made a cocoon. Debbie missed playing with Connie.

One day, the cocoon began to shake. Debbie watched.

"Wake up, Chief," said Debbie. "It's spring."

Connie broke out of the cocoon. She was no longer a caterpillar. She was a butterfly.

Debbie carried the jar to the field. It grieved her to let Connie go.

"Butterflies should fly," her mom had told her.

Debbie opened the jar. Connie flew into the sky.

"Good-bye Chief," said Debbie.

14

15

Connie the Caterpillar

Connie liked having wings. She swooped and dove. Connie fluttered in the breeze. Suddenly she stopped. Her wings couldn't flutter.

"It's lunch time," said a fierce voice.

Vinnie scurried to Connie.

"Vin...Vinnie," stuttered Connie.

Vinnie looked at Connie.

"Is that you Connie?" asked Vinnie.

"Yes," said Connie.

Vinnie scurried off. He came back with a leaf. He snipped the web. Vinnie handed Connie the leaf.

"It's lunch time," said Vinnie. "Let's eat."

The two of them gnawed a piece of leaf.

16

Connie the Caterpillar

across
around
asleep
breeze
brief
butterflies
butterfly
carried
caterpillar
chasing
Chief
cocoon
Connie
crawl
Debbie
didn't

eaten
field
fierce
fiercest
flew
fluttered
flying
fuzzy
gnawed
gone
grief
grieved
hours
house
leaf
least
lights

morning
munched
new
nibbled
notch
opened
paper
piece
pierce
pierced
scooped
scream
screamed
scurried
shield
shielded

siege
sleeping
snipped
something
spider
spring
squish
stuttered
suddenly
swooped
thief
Vinnie
voice
waited
watched
window

Lesson 72

Lesson Objectives

1. Students will add -er and -est to words that end with y. (L)
2. Students will review spelling words. (S)
3. Students will use spelling words in sentences. (S)
4. Students will read the story *Connie the Caterpillar.* (R)
5. Students will copy sentences neatly and correctly. (H)

Materials

LAR
SAP
Connie the Caterpillar

Teaching

1. Write the words carry and hurry. Ask students to change them to carried and hurries. Ask how the words changed. (Dropped the y added i and then the suffix.) The rule is also true for other suffixes beginning with e. Have students add -er and -est to funny and messy.

   Use the LAR workbook page. **Read the words. Drop the y, add i, and the suffixes -er and est. Next, compare the parts of clothing using the suffixes er and est.**

   Write three sentences comparing three things using a root word and the suffixes er and est.

2. Use the top of the SAP page. **Write the spelling word that is a part of each of the longer words.**

3. Use the bottom of the SAP page. **Read the sentences. Change the underlined word to a spelling word. Choose the word that changes the meaning of the sentence the least.**

4. Review the words butterflies, caterpillar, cocoon, suddenly, watched. Students will read pages 1 to 8 of *Connie the Caterpillar* out loud. Next, ask the following questions:

   Where did the leaf land? (a spider web)
   How did Connie get out of the web? (Debbie put her in a jar.)
   What did Vinnie call Debbie? (Lunch thief!)
   Why do you think Debbie didn't hear Vinnie? (Answers vary.)
   Where did Debbie take Connie? (to her room)
   What did Debbie call Connie? (Chief)
   What did Vinnie do? (He chased Debbie.)
   Why couldn't Vinnie get Connie? (She was in a jar.)

5. Use the handwriting sheet or have the children write the following sentences:

   Debbie painted the funniest clown.
   That piece of candy is stickier than honey.

Lesson 72

LAR Answers

dirtier, dirtiest
grumpier, grumpiest
lumpier, lumpiest
prettier, prettiest
yummier, yummiest

dirty
dirtier
dirtiest

SAP Answers

brief shield
yield siege field
piece niece chief

1. fierce
2. chief
3. niece
4. fiesta
5. piece
6. thief

Lesson 73

Lesson Objectives

1. Students will use words that end with -ier and -iest in sentences. (L)
2. Students will identify nouns and verbs. (L)
3. Students will recognize the correct spelling of spelling words. (S)
4. Students will read the story *Connie the Caterpillar*. (R)
5. Students will copy sentences neatly and correctly. (H)

Materials

LAR
SAP
Connie the Caterpillar
Writing Skills Workbook page is available

Teaching

1. Review adding -er and -est to words that end with y. Use the top of the LAR workbook page. **Add the suffix to the word above the lines. Write the word on the lines.**

2. Use the bottom of the LAR workbook page. Review nouns and verbs. **Every sentence must have a noun and a verb. Some sentences can have more than one noun and verb. Read the sentences on the bottom of the workbook page. There are circles above and below nouns and verbs. Fill in the n circle if the word is a noun. Fill in the v circle if the word is a verb.**

3. Use the SAP page. **Read the sentences. Words are spelling incorrectly. Circle them and write them correctly under the sentences.**

4. Review the first half of the book *Connie the Caterpillar.* Next, read the second half of the book. After completing the story ask the students the following questions:

   Why couldn't the jar save Connie the next morning? (The lid was off.)
   Why do you think Debbie was going to squish Vinnie? (Answers vary.)
   What did Connie do to save Vinnie? (She ran to Vinnie)
   What did Debbie do to Vinnie? (She took him to the field.)
   What did Connie make? (A cocoon)
   How do you think Debbie felt when Connie made the cocoon? (Answers vary.)
   What did Connie turn into? (a butterfly)
   Why did Debbie let Connie go? (Answers vary-her mother told her to.)
   Was Vinnie grateful to Connie? (yes) **How do you know?** (He didn't eat her.)

5. Use the handwriting sheet or have the children write the following sentences:

   The fierce lion is the scariest cat.
   Winnie's niece is named Connie.

LAR Answers

1. funniest
2. bumpiest
3. weedier
4. messier
5. shiniest

1. Did the yellow bird fly to catch the sparrow?

2. The doe ran when it saw its shadow

3. The fellow will replace the window tomorrow.

4. We leaned the hoe on the trunk of the willow.

5. Joe rested his sore toe on the pillow.

SAP Answers

1. fierce chief shield
2. niece piece fiesta
3. thief brief field
4. siege yield grief

Lesson 74

Lesson Objectives

1. Students will put a story in order. (L)
2. Students will review spelling words. (S)
3. Students will write a story. (CW)
4. Students will read the story *Connie the Caterpillar.* (R)
5. Students will copy sentences neatly and correctly. (H)

Materials

LAR
SAP
Connie the Caterpillar
Optional material about insects and spiders.

Teaching

1. Use the LAR workbook page. **Read the sentences on the workbook page. Number them in order that they happened in the story.** Have students do the exercise without looking at the book. After finishing the assignment students may use their books to check or correct their answers.

   Bottom section: **Answer the questions. Fill in the ovals to mark your answers.**

2. Use the SAP workbook page. **Match the spelling words to the descriptions. Write your answers on the lines.**

3. Students will write a story about insects.

   Say: **The book *Connie the Caterpillar* is about a spider and a caterpillar. Today you will write a story about insects. Maybe it can be an insect that you found or it can be just about insects. It can be a book that tells about insects or a story.**

4. Read the book *Connie the Caterpillar* again. Next, have students look at the back of the book and answer the following questions about the word list. You may do this orally or have students write answers:

   What word means someone who steals things? (thief)
   What word means to attack something? (siege)
   What word means to poke a hole in something? (pierce)
   What words are bugs? (butterflies butterfly, caterpillar, spider)
   What word is a synonym of furry? (fuzzy)
   What is a place where food grows? (field)
   What word is a part of the day? (morning)
   What word is a season? (spring)
   What word is the opposite of closed? (opened)
   What word is the opposite of whisper? (scream)

5. Use the handwriting sheet or have the children write the following sentences:

   We played for a brief time.
   The arrow pierced the tree.

Lesson 74

LAR Answers

10
5
2
7
9
3
8
1
6
4

1. yes **no**

2. **yes** no

3. yes **no**

4. **yes** no

5. **yes** no

SAP Answers

niece	shield
brief	yield
field	siege
piece	chief
grief	thief
fiesta	fierce

Lesson 75

Lesson Objectives

1. Students will be tested on phonics concepts. (P)
2. Students will be tested on language concepts. (L)
3. Students will take a spelling test. (S)
4. Students will read the story they have written. (R)
5. Students will write a book report. (R)
6. Students will copy a sentence neatly and correctly. (H)

Materials

LAR
Creative writing assignment from Lesson 74
Assessment 75

Teaching

1. Use part A of the assessment as a phonics test. Have the students fill in the circles next to the words that complete the sentences.

2. Use part B of the assessment page. Read the words. Add the suffixes -er and -est. Write the words on the lines.

3. Have students number their papers from 1 to 12. Give the following words as dictation.

   Spelling word list: **1. piece, 2. brief, 3. grief, 4. yield, 5. chief, 6. shield, 7. siege, 8. field, 9. thief, 10. niece, 11. fierce, 12. fiesta**

4. Have students take turns reading the books or stories that were written during the creative writing section of the previous lesson.

5. Students will use the LAR page to write a book report. The form is copied on the next page. Help students read through the form.

6. Use the handwriting sheet or have the children write the following sentences:

   The grieving puppy was happier today.
   Did a thief take the gold?

Assessment Answers

1. thief
2. shield
3. piece
4. field
5. grieved

1. rainier, rainiest
2. chunkier, chunkiest
3. fluffier, fluffiest
4. sunnier, sunniest
5. sleepier, sleepiest

Choose a book that you read and liked to write a report. You can't use the books that are a part of the reading curriculum. Use this form and answer the questions. Tell your report to someone. Tell them things that will get them interested in the book, but don't give away the ending!

Book Report

Title

Author

Illustrator

Setting: Where did it happen? When did it happen?

Who was your favorite character in the book? Name the character. Describe the character. Tell why you like that character.

What did you like best about the book?

Who might enjoy this book? Why would other people like to read it?

Lesson 76

Lessons 76 to 78 will review phonics and language concepts taught in Lessons 41 to 75. There will be no reading book or creative writing assignment given. Students may read books from previous weeks or have students try reading library books. **Lessons 79 and 80** will be set aside for the second unit test.

Lesson Objectives

1. Students will review words spelled with ue and ui, long a words spelled with e, long o words spelled with ow and oe. (P)
2. Students will review the days of the week. (L)
3. Students will review spelling words. (S)
4. Students will copy sentences neatly and correctly. (H)

Materials

LAR
SAP

Teaching

1. Review the different spellings of the sounds. For example **"How do you spell the *oo* sound in blue and fruit? How do you spell the long a in came? How do you spell long o in show and in toe?"** etc. Next, do the crossword puzzle. Use the LAR workbook page.

2. Review the days of the week. Have students write the days in order on a piece of paper.

3. Use the SAP page. Have students say and spell each word. Spelling list: glue, fruit, great, neighbor, change, stingy, toothbrush, flashlight, gnaw, catch, whistle, sparrow, tomorrow, piece, field.

   Top section: **Alphabetize each group of words.**

   Bottom section: **Write the spelling words that rhyme with the four words.**

4. Use the handwriting sheet or have the children write the following sentences:
   The yellow fruit juice tastes great. Is the doe out my window a reindeer?

Review Word List

From Lesson 41: due, hue, Sue, blue, clue, flue, glue, true, fuel, duel, fruit, juice, bruise, cruise

From Lesson 46: vein, feign, veil, rein, reign, skein, reindeer, eight, weigh, weight, neigh, neighbor, freight, sleigh, whey, they, hey, prey, survey, obey, grey, steak, break, great, Shea, yea

Days of the week: Sunday, Monday, Tuesday, Wednesday, Thursday, Friday, Saturday

From Lesson 66: bellow, below, borrow, fellow, follow, hollow, mellow, narrow, pillow, shadow, sorrow, sparrow, tomorrow, wallow, willow, window, yellow
doe, foe, goes, hoe, Joe, toe, woe

LAR Answers

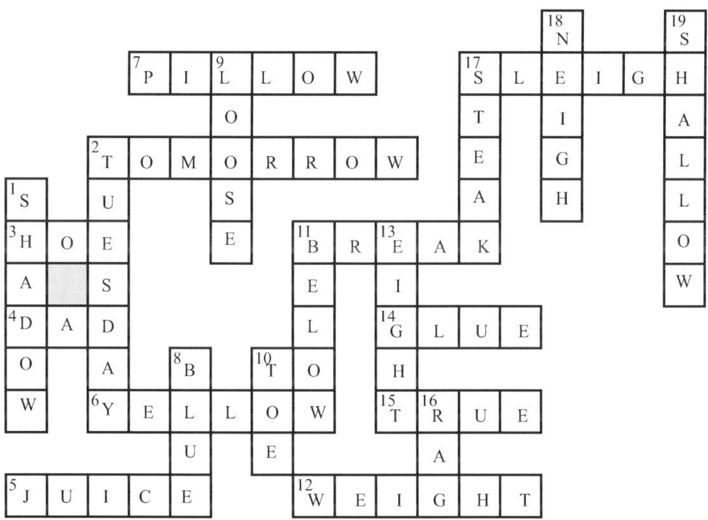

SAP Answers

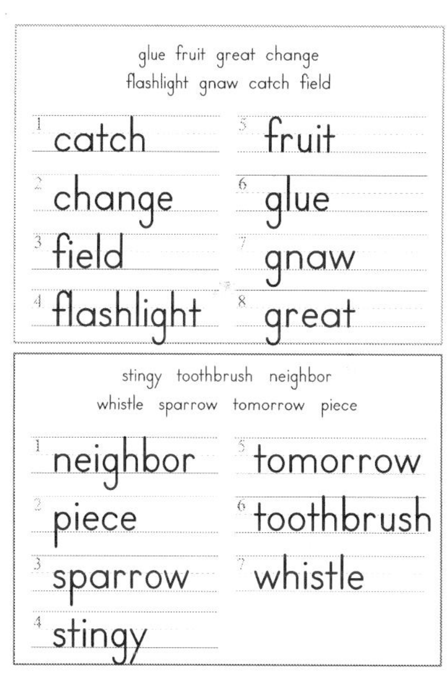

shoe glue saw gnaw
boot fruit hatch catch

Lesson 77

Lesson Objectives

1. Students will review -dge and -nge words, words with silent letters (g, h, and t), and long e words spelled with ie. (P)
2. Students will review nouns and verbs. (L)
3. Students will review spelling words. (S)
4. Students will copy sentences neatly and correctly. (H)

Materials

LAR
SAP

Teaching

1. Review the word groups. Next use the LAR workbook page.

   Top part **Read the sentences. Some words are missing letters. Fill in the missing letters.** (reviews Lesson 51 words)

   Middle part: **Read the words. Circle the silent letters.** (reviews Lesson 61 words)

2. Review the terms noun (person, place, or thing) and verb (tells what a noun is doing).

   Use the bottom part of the LAR workbook page. **A word is in bold print. Fill in the circle to tell how it was used** (noun or verb). The sentences will feature words from Lesson 71.

3. Use the SAP workbook page. **Fill in the grid to complete with the spelling words. On the second part, write the words that fit the description.**

4. Use the handwriting sheet or have the children write the following sentences:

   The badger gnawed on a piece of wood.
   Debbie listened to Madge for an hour.

Review Word List

From Lesson 51: hedge, ledge, wedge, dredge, pledge, sledge, edge, badge, badger, ridge, fudge, budge, lodge, Madge, hodge, podge, bridge, pudgy, judge, nudge, dodge, sludge, trudge, smudge, plunge, change, hinge, binge, flange, singe, stingy, lunge

From Lesson 61: gnarl, gnash, gnat, gnaw, gnu, heir, honor, honest, hour, batch, botch, catch, ditch, Dutch, etch, fetch, hatch, hitch, hutch, itch, latch, match, Mitch, notch, patch, pitch, retch, snatch, snitch, stitch, thatch, castle, hasten, listen, moisten, nestle, thistle, witch, bustle, hustle, rustle, whistle, wrestle

From Lesson 71: brief, chief, Connie, Debbie, field, fierce, grief, grieved, Jackie, niece, piece, pier, pierce, shield, siege, spiel, thief, tier, Vinnie, wield, yield

LAR Answers

1. hinge
2. stingy fudge
3. changed, pledge
4. hedgehog, budge
5. badger, plunged, bridge

gnat honor watch castle hour

whistle listen gnaw pitch catch

1. noun
2. verb
3. verb
4. noun
5. verb

SAP Answers

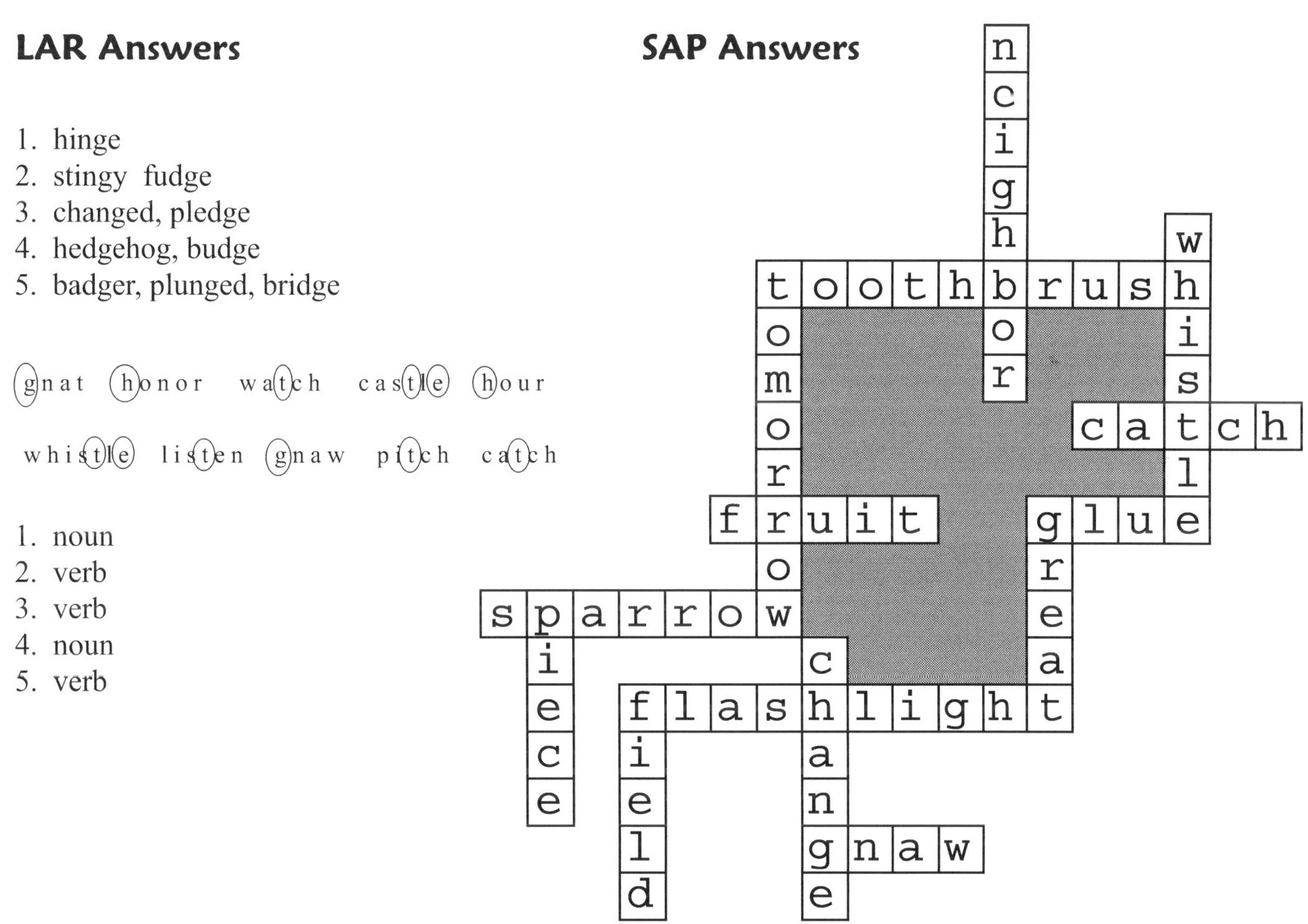

Any order per section

Silent g: neighbor, flashlight, gnaw

Silent t: catch, whistle

Digraphs: change, toothbrush

Lesson 78

Lesson Objectives

1. Students will review compound words. (P)
2. Students will review dividing words into syllables. (L)
3. Students will review spelling words. (S)
4. Students will copy sentences neatly and correctly. (H)

Materials

LAR
SAP

Teaching

1. Use the top of the LAR workbook page. Choose words from each column to make compound words.

2. Use the bottom of the LAR workbook page. Draw lines between the syllables in the words.

3. Use the SAP page. **Read the sentences. Change the underlined word with the spelling word that changes the sentences the least.**

   On the second part, unscramble the spelling words.

4. Use the handwriting sheet or have the children write the following sentences:

   The baseball rolled into the dugout.
   We ate cupcakes at the campsite.

Lesson 78

Review Word List

From Lesson 56: airplane, backpack, baseball, bathtub, bobcat, bookcase, campsite, cardboard, chipmunk, cowboy, cupcake, daydream, daytime, doorbell, dugout, eyebrow, eyelash, fireman, fireplace, fireworks, flashlight, football, goldfish, grapefruit, groundhog, haircut, iceberg, icebox, jigsaw, jukebox, knapsack, lifeboat, mailbox, milkman, mushroom, muskrat, network, nightfall, noontime, oatmeal, pickup, popcorn, pushup, rainbow, sailboat, sandbox, sawmill, scarecrow, scoreboard, seacoast, seesaw, shoelace, shoestring, shortstop, snowflake, spaceship, stagecoach, steamboat, steamship, stickup, strongbox, subway, sundown, sunrise, sunset, sunshine, teaspoon, teenage, thumbnail, toothbrush, toothpaste, towboat, tugboat, woodchuck

LAR Answers

Any Order:

airplane
rainbow
sundown
iceberg
nightfall
bobcat
bathtub
sailboat
cupcake
stagecoach

SAP Answers

1. change
2. fruit
3. pieces
4. glue
5. great
6. flashlight
7. stingy

sparrow	whistle
tomorrow	gnaw
toothbrush	field
neighbor	catch

camp|site pil|low tooth|brush

hedge|hog Tues|day hol|low ice|box

fel|low eye|lash bel|low life|boat

Lesson 79 Test 2

Test 2 Objectives

1. Students will be tested over phonics concepts.
2. Students will review spelling words.
3. Students will copy sentences neatly and correctly. (H)

Materials

Test 2, pages 1 and 2
SAP

Test Directions:

1. **Phonics Test:**

   Part 1: Students will write the words that answer the questions.

   Part 2: Students will fill in the oval next to the word that completes the sentences.

2. **Spelling:** Use the SAP page: **Match the spelling words to the descriptions.**
3. Use the handwriting sheet or have the children write the following sentences:

   The neighbor loaned us a flashlight.
   I will buy a new toothbrush tomorrow.

Lesson 80

Test 2 Objectives

1. Students will be tested over language concepts.
2. Students will take a spelling dictation test.
3. Students will copy sentences neatly and correctly. (H)

Materials

Test 2, pages 3 and 4

Test Directions:

1. **Language Test:**

   Part 3: Students will read the sentences. A word is in bold print. Is it a noun or verb? Fill in the circle that tells how the word in bold print is used.

   Part 4: Students will read the sentences. Each sentence contains two mixed-up compound words. Write the words correctly on the lines in the correct order they occur in the sentence.

   Part 5: Students will read the words and divide them into syllables. Draw lines.

   Part 6: Write the days of the week in their correct order.

2. **Spelling Dictation Test:** Have students number their papers from 1 to 15.

   1. flashlight, 2. pieces, 3. fruit, 4. catch, 5. whistle, 6. change, 7. stingy, 8. neighbor, 9. sparrow, 10. gnaw, 11. toothbrush, 12. great, 13. tomorrow, 14. glue, 15. field

3. Use the handwriting sheet or have the children write the following sentences:

   Will the sparrow peck at the fruit?
   The stingy dog gnawed on the bone.

Test 2 Answers

Page 1
Part 1

1. juice
2. moisten
3. narrow
4. gnarl
5. honest
6. bridge
7. castle
8. shield
9. hinge
10. field

Part 1

Part 1

Read the questions. Write the word that answers it on the lines. A word list is given. Not all words will be used.

1. What is something you drink? ______
2. What means to make wet? ______
3. What word means not wide? ______
4. What word means to growl? ______
5. What are you if you tell the truth? ______
6. What is something cars drive over? ______
7. What is a queen's house? ______
8. What is a piece of metal a knight carries? ______
9. What holds up a door? ______
10. What is a place to play baseball? ______

word list: bridge gnarl reign moisten honor blue shield woe field smudge cruise pierce castle juice latch hinge honest narrow

Page 2
Part 2

1. hour
2. fudge
3. window
4. thief
5. weigh
6. gnawed
7. steak
8. plunged
9. obey
10. ditch

Part 2

Part 2

Read the sentences. Fill in the circle next to the word that completes the sentence correctly.

1. Did you wait an ____ for a bus? ○ eight ○ hour ○ itch
2. We cooked the _____ on the stove. ○ fudge ○ wallow ○ flue
3. The breeze came in the ______. ○ gnu ○ window ○ sludge
4. A man with a badge stopped the _____. ○ woe ○ fetch ○ thief
5. How much does that box ______? ○ whey ○ [illegible] ○ weigh
6. The mouse _____ the wire. ○ gnawed ○ lodge ○ spiels
7. Did dad grill the _____? ○ nudge ○ steak ○ true
8. The swimmers _____ into the pool. ○ due ○ retch ○ plunged
9. Did you _____ your mother? ○ obey ○ gnat ○ tier
10. The truck was stuck in the ____. ○ vein ○ ditch ○ brief

Page 3
Part 3

1. noun
2. verb
3. noun
4. verb
5. verb

Parts 3 & 4

Part 3

Read the sentences. A word is in bold print. Fill in the circle next to the word that tells how it was used in the sentence.

1. A thistle pierced my **toe**. ○ noun ○ verb
2. Did Mitch **catch** a fish? ○ noun ○ verb
3. I snatched the yellow **pillow**. ○ noun ○ verb
4. The sparrow **followed** us. ○ noun ○ verb
5. Joe **listened** to Sue. ○ noun ○ verb

Part 4

Each sentence contains two compound words. The words are mixed up.
Write the words the correct way on the lines.

1. The boyboat rode the steamcow.
2. I saw the sunflakes at risesnow.
3. The bobchuck chashed the woodcat.
4. The basestop pitched the shortball.
5. I left the flashcamp at the sitelight.

Parts 5 & 6

Part 5

Divide the words into syllables. Draw lines.

s p a r r o w   r e i n d e e r

t o m o r r o w

w i n d o w   s u n s h i n e

Part 6 Write the days of the week in order.

Part 4

1. cowboy, steamboat
2. snowflakes, sunrise
3. bobcat, woodchuck
4. shortstop, baseball
5. flashlight, campsite

Part 5

s p a r | r o w   r e i n | d e e r

t o | m o r | r o w

w i n | d o w   s u n | s h i n e

SAP page Answers

field
neighbor
toothbrush
pieces
gnaw
whistle
stingy
great
tomorrow
flashlight
glue
sparrow
catch
fruit
change

Made in the USA
Monee, IL
08 June 2023

35180412R00153